Success in Newsletter Publis

A Practical Guic

By Frederick D. Goss

 **naa** *published by*
The Newsletter Ass

ISBN 0 9610

ACKNOWLEDGEMENTS

This book would not have been possible without the contributions of many members of the Newsletter Association of America and their willingness to share experience and expertise. Many are cited within the text of thebook, and many others have contributed to my own education in newsletter publishing.

Specific thanks are necessary to Tamra Dicken and Mary Margaret Evans of the NAA staff, Richard M. Hagan, Executive Editor of Capitol Publications, who reviewed and critiqued the manuscript, and Penny Fletcher who, doing her best with my punctuation, typing and passion for interlinear comments, edited and typed the entire book.

While newsletter publishing is certainly not a science, this book attempts to synthesize the conventional wisdom gained by the literally hundreds of successful publishers. Responsibility for errors and misinterpretations, however, is entirely mine.

F.D.G.

Graphics and Design by J. Nick Davis, Sans Serif Graphics, Ltd., Alexandria, VA.

Success in Newsletter Publishing...A Practical Guide is the first book published by the Newsletter Association of America. Before putting quill to parchment some 206 years ago, Thomas Jefferson wrote that "a decent respect for the common good opinion of mankind" compelled him to explain the reasons behind the drafting of the Declaration of Independence. Our purpose in this book is simple to explain. We want to provide a service to those interested in becoming newsletter publishers, to provide a practical guide to success in an often misunderstood business. Self-interest, as usual, is not far from the surface. The larger the number of successful newsletter publishers in the industry, the better for NAA as the industry association. And if, by producing this book, we discourage a few would-be publishers by pointing out some of the many pitfalls on the road to success, if we clear their rose-colored glasses to the extent that they understand newsletter publishing is not a "get rich quick in your spare time without knowing how to write or edit" business, then we have done the industry another service by eliminating some of the types of people who have, in the past, given newsletter publishing a black eye.

Newsletter publishing is one of the fastest growing segments of the information industry. It is so fluid, and ease of entry is so great, that no one knows how many commercial (subscription) published-for-profit newsletters are currently being produced. NAA estimates at least 2500-3000, including both those published (as the industry cliche runs) "from the kitchen table," and those done by organizations of the size and scope of the Newsletter Publishing Center at McGraw-Hill.

Newsletter publishing isn't an easy way to make a fast buck or a fool-proof tax shelter. It is different from other kinds of publishing in many ways. This book will provide you a practical, how-to approach to newsletter publishing. It covers business management, promotion, editorial style, renewal strategies, fulfillment of subscriptions, sources of additional income and many other areas. We have devoted a chapter to each of these subjects, and most chapters also contain a number of additional articles reprinted from the NAA biweekly newsletter *Hotline*. Because of the willingness of newsletter publishers and industry consultants to share their experiences and insights with their peers, the *Hotline* frequently contains invaluable information and practical how-to suggestions from successful publishers that isn't available from any other source. In the chapter texts we try to give, in most cases, the "conventional wisdom" in a subject area. For example, the key chapter on promotion focuses on the "norms" of successful newsletter direct mail promotion—where do I get names?, should I include a sample newsletter?, how much should my package cost? etc. The *Hotline* articles following give specific examples of concrete promotional ideas—concepts and approaches developed and used by successful publishers.

We wish you every success in your endeavors. We hope to welcome you in the near future as an active member of the Newsletter Association of America.

Table of Contents

CHAPTER I
Introduction

One of the difficult aspects in writing the definitive treatise on how to begin a newsletter business is not being able to define precisely what a newsletter is. If pressed, NAA normally says that a newsletter is a specialized information publication which is supported by subscription sales and doesn't contain advertising. A few newsletters do contain advertising, either within the body of the editorial product or as supplemental inserts. A few are also available on newsstands. Ray Henry, publisher at Plus Publications (and president of NAA in 1980) once said, "It's usually printed on paper, distributed to clients and you usually charge a high price. But not always and it doesn't always go to clients."

Others, asked to define "newsletter," emphasize "timeliness" and the concise nature of the news and information conveyed. Each of these points has its drawbacks as a characteristic of newsletters. Most are fairly brief, compared to magazines, but some successful newsletters go to considerable lengths—perhaps 60 pages or more in some issues—because they serve as the "publication of record" in their field. Similarly, while all publishers strive to provide current information, in a world where current events are flashed by satellite to television screens worldwide on a real-time basis, a weekly, bi-weekly or even monthly publication can hardly be described as "timely" in a comparison to the state of the art in the information industry.

Successful newsletters convey specialized information to narrow markets. There are exceptions to every rule of course, but what creates a market place for a newsletter is a need for a volume of specialized information that is not available from any other single source. These markets can usually only be identified and marketed by direct mail. The expense of gaining subscribers in that way (and in producing quality editorial product) often requires a high subscription price. Why will a subscriber pay more for a year's subscription to a ten page bi-weekly than for a 5 year subscription to *Time?* Because he needs news about the subject and understands that every issue of the newsletter will contain more on the subject than *Time* will over a five year period.

The public's increasing demand for specialized information has made the growth of newsletters in the information industry phenomenal. In addition to the 2500-3000; commercial newsletters, there are probably 10,000 more published by trade and professional associations, (and countless thousands of corporate, internal publications—not even to think about the proliferation of newsletters from every cooperative pre-school, church youth group and condo-housing association in existence.)

What is the Oldest Newsletter?

Statements like this are always subject to qualification, but the *Whaley-Eaton Letter* published in Washington in 1918 appears to have been the first modern non-investment type newsletter. The *Kiplinger Letter,* first published in 1923, appears to be the oldest continually published newsletter. A number of other newsletters, including *The Value Line* published in New York and *Telecommunications Report* in Washington, are nearing their half century mark, but the great growth in newsletters has been in the past 20 years or even just in the past decade.

An examination of the information available on the industry at present indicates that about three quarters of all newsletters currently being published are less than 10 years old and certainly well over 80% have been founded since 1960. This is only a part of the increasing tendency towards specialization in the publishing industry. That same period has seen the demise of *Life, Look, Colliers* and (maybe) *Harpers* and other familiar general interest magazines, while dirt track motorcycle enthusiasts, cross-country skiers and others appear to have their choice of a constant proliferation of magazines aimed at their special interest and bursting with advertisements.

Can I be an Overnight Success in the Newsletter Business?

The newsletter industry is prospering. Today it's a more than two-billion-dollar annual revenue industry. A number of individuals have started literally from scratch and built very successful publishing firms in the newsletter industry. One of the attractions of the newsletter business is the relative ease of entry; compared to most types of business only a small capital investment is required. One of the purposes of this book, however, is to say, tactfully, it isn't as easy as it looks. The newsletter industry has been blighted by the appearance of too many get-rich-quick articles and manuals. "How to Make a Fortune in Your Spare Time as a Newsletter Publisher Without Knowing Nothing."

What are the Odds on Success and How Much Should I Expect to Invest?

Basically, that's what is wrong with get-rich-quick publications. They don't tell you these salient but prickly facts:

● It takes more time than you think. If Henry Kissinger wanted to publish a newsletter on world affairs, he could very probably dictate copy in a couple of hours each week and his opinions would very likely be quite salable. Most other editors have to do quite a bit more reportorial legwork to come up with solid news copy for a newsletter.

● Direct mail promotion is very chancy. It's true that if you spend $14,000 to mail 40,000 promotional pieces, and get a one percent response to your offering of a $150 newsletter, you have just taken in $60,000. You could also send out those 40,000 pieces and get 3 orders. It has happened.

● Newsletter publishing is a complex business. In this book we will try to give you some guidelines on how to go about being a good reporter, editor, promotional copy writer, production manager, bookkeeper, fulfillment specialist and more, because, if you hope to start a successful newsletter from scratch, you need to be able to handle all of these tasks simultaneously.

Figures on success vary. Some have said that 90% of all new newsletter ventures fail. Thst is probably too pessimistic, but quite possiblely more than half do. Established publishers succeed with about 2 of 3 or perhaps 3 of 4 of their new starts, but they have more expertise and, often, the financial ability to wait several years to see black ink on the ledger. Successful publishers say you should expect to invest at least $20,000 to $30,000 in launching a new newsletter. You can scratch by with less. An income/expense statement is included in the chapter on Accounting and Financial Operations for an imaginary new start. Obviously, if you intend to do all the work yourself, all you need to spend is the money to send out the first promotion. If it succeeds, you start publishing the newsletters using the cash flow from incoming orders and continuing this process throughout the year as succeeding promotions also generate business and cash. This sort of shoestring venture is also responsible for considerable portion of the high failure rate—the editor/publisher gets tired of working his/her butt off for no immediate response. Or, you may have built the beginnings of a subscription list, but your venture capital for new promotions is exhausted. (More later on the fallacy of being too poor to promote.)

What is NAA?

The Newsletter Association of America is a non-profit trade association of newsletter publishers founded in 1977. Howard Hudson, publisher of the *Newsletter on Newsletters,* began having conferences for newsletter publishers soon after he purchased the *NL/NL* in 1968, the first was held in New York in 1973. Several years later, a group of the principal participants in these conferences decided to organize NAA as a successor organization to the existing local newsletter groups in Washington and New York. (These groups became the first local chapters of NAA.) From 16 founding members, NAA has grown to an organization representing more than 700 publishers, who collectively produce some 1,700 newsletters. For these publishers the Association provides a number of services:

● the NAA annual international conference and seminars devoted to nuts-and-bolts aspects of newsletter publishing

● local chapter activities

● legislative efforts—representing publisher interests before Congress and federal and state regulatory bodies

● group insurance for publishers and their employees

● a bi-weekly Washington newsletter, *The Hotline,* and the *NAA Guidebook to Newsletter Publishing,* a serial textbook covering a broad range of topics of interest to newsletter publishers

● industry studies and surveys. NAA compiles and disseminates information on topics of concern to publishers including studies of promotional and renewal practices and results, salaries and compensation, financial operations and more.

● postal affairs. NAA maintains liaison with the U.S. Postal Service on matters of concern to newsletter publishers.

(For further information on these and other NAA activities contact the association at NAA, Colorado Building #603, Washington, D.C. 20005, 202-347-5220.)

CHAPTER II
How to Select a Subject
for a Newsletter

People interested in getting into the newsletter business generally approach the question of selecting a topic for their first newsletter in one of two ways.

1. Most commonly, prospective publishers have been in a position to gain information they feel could be marketed as a newsletter—as in "I've spent the last five years as an AP reporter covering the Environmental Protection Agency, I know as much as anyone about what's going on there, what's likely to happen next, etc.—why couldn't I write a newsletter?"

2. Less commonly, an entrepreneur may identify newsletter publishing as a potentially attractive venture and set about looking for a subject area.

In the first instance, what the potential publisher is most concerned with is "what newsletters are already being published about EPA?" NAA has information on newsletters published by members, but perhaps the best single source of information is the *Newsletter Clearinghouse Directory* published by Howard Penn Hudson. The directory is available in some libraries, or direct from Newsletter Clearinghouse (44 W. Market Street, Rhinebeck, New York 12572). When you are checking potential competition don't forget trade associations. Gale Research publishes a directory of associations. Investigate which are serving the industry or market you are interested in and what they are publishing. Similarly, trade magazines service a number of interest areas. The American Business Press in New York may be able to give you information on what is being published by subject areas.

Some Additional Points to Consider

It isn't necessarily bad that someone is already publishing a newsletter in the subject area you are considering. "If I have an idea and find it appears to be a virgin territory" one publisher told NAA, "it may be there isn't a market, because I don't think I'm smart enough to think of something which never occurred to anyone else." A successful newsletter in the subject you are considering could mean there is still a market for another letter that takes a different approach. For example, you could offer:

1. Different frequency or price. If the competition is a $500 weekly, a $165 bimonthly might be quite popular.

2. Different slant on news. If one newsletter covers an industry, could another be slanted to concentrate only on Washington news affecting the industry?

3. Different format. Including periodic special reports or a reference file could make your product distinct from the competition.

You might steer away from crowded subject areas, and you might also be well advised not to try to jump on the hottest topic in town. For several years "energy" was a buzz word and new energy-oriented newsletters sprung up at a pace of about two a month. As this is written, the hottest subject area is genetic engineering. NAA is aware of at least five publications launched in the past few months. A neophyte publisher would not be well advised to attempt this area. Very probably not all of these newsletters will succeed, although to the extent that a certain number of people in every field will buy everything, all may get off the ground. In the long term, the ones published by larger, more experienced firms with greater resources for promotion may well have an insuperable advantage.

Evaluating a Newsletter Subject Idea

Example #1: There has been a tremendous amount of news about the telephone industry in recent years, starting with some still controversial Federal Communications Commission decisions, several years of highly visible congressional debate and a Justice Department anti-trust action. Shouldn't there be a market for a Washington-based telephone industry newsletter?

Investigation will show that *Telecommunications Report* has been publishing weekly in Washington for 45 years. In 1980 Phillips Publishing launched *Telephone News* as a bi-weekly, and Television Digest launched *Communications Daily*. Several other publishers also have products that address one or another segment of the communications industry.

There are four significant industry associations, all of which have newsletters and one a monthly magazine. In addition, there are three well-established trade magazines—a weekly and two bi-weeklies.

In this field it is hard to see a market opportunity for another publication.

Example #2: A sport that appears to be growing considerably in popularity, from both a participant and spectator viewpoint, is figure skating and yet, it appears, no publication currently serves the interests of figure skating freaks (Peggy Fleming Groupies). While there are at least a dozen skiing publications, there are none, magazine or newsletter, available for ice skating fans. (The U.S. Figure Skating Association publishes a membership magazine from Colorado Springs, but considering both editorial quality and timeliness, in itself it shouldn't discourage competition.)

Yet there certainly appears to be a market; more than 100,000 people attended a series of post-Olympic skating exhibitions following Lake Placid, and over 18,000 bought out the Capital Centre in Washington, D.C. in December 1980 and again in December 1981 for the first Professional Figure Skating Championships.

This situation raises a number of questions the would-be newsletter publisher has to ask:

● Is it a market you can reach?—It is obvious there are a lot of people interested in ice skating; but how do you reach them with a promotion? Are there any lists? Would you have to build your own list through space ads in magazines you hope would be read by your potential market (and how much would that cost?)? If you had been publishing, you might have arranged to be on hand in Washington to pass out brochures to the fans attending that performance. Is that the only way to go?

● Is there enough news? Important national and international competitions are held in January through March. What would you cover the rest of the year? Coaching trends? New techniques? News of people in the business?

● Where do you find someone with the expertise to write a publication aimed at aficionados—people who can recognize the difference between a double toe loop and a triple salkow? Should you contract Dick Button as a contributing editor? Can you afford it?

● Can you get the news? Recently major competitions were held simultaneously in San Diego and Innsbruck, Austria. Your newsletter would need to cover both. Similarly, a lot of news in skating occurs in the Soviet Union. How will you get it? Some of your most devoted readers, the 11 year prospects and their mothers or coaches, would certainly like to know what international coaches like Carlo Fassi are doing, but will he tell you?

These two examples, taken together, are typical of the problems faced by beginning publishers. The two situations profiled appear to present opportunities for different types of newsletters (perhaps a $150 bi-weekly in telecommunications and a $24 monthly in figure skating), but in the one instance while it isn't difficult to anticipate how you would gather and report the news and reach the market, it does appear doubtful whether you have a really good opportunity in an area already blanketed with specialized publications. On the other hand, the skating field looks wide-open, but so are the problems—getting the news and reaching a potential market in an economically viable way.

The Future: Narrow or Broad Market NL's?

Ken Kovaly, publisher at *Technical Insights,* predicts the rosiest future for specialized information publishers is in the area of narrow-market high-price newsletters.

● Costs less to launch.

● Higher price should equal greater profits, more cash flow and a higher reserve you can bank in the money fund.

● Less competition. While, he notes, theirs is currently one of eight biotechnology letters and "they probably won't all make it," they have positioned themselves in a sub-narrow area on genetics.

● Less susceptible to recession because the high-price information buyer really needs the information.

● This type of newsletter can more readily give you entree to the international business which Kovaly finds to be a strong business "and they pay cash up-front."

● Although lists may be hard to find, you can pinpoint your audience for marketing efficiency.

● These types of publications traditionally show the highest renewal rates.

● Having identified high-ticket information buyers as your subscribers, the potential is high for collateral products, special reports, etc.

● With the mass market newsletter, success can kill you. Trying to cope with 20,000 subscribers, fulfillment problems, etc.

Ken Kovaly, Technical Insights, Inc., Box 1304, 2337 LeMoine Avenue, Fort Lee, NJ 07024 (201) 944-6204.

A Short List of Ten Points to Consider in Evaluating a Concept for a Newsletter

1. You must be able to anticipate subscription revenues to support the operation in a profitable manner (without $$ from advertising, newsstand or other single copy sales).

2. You must envision covering editorial objectives in 10 pages or less per issue with an editorial content lending itself to a tight, closely written style.

3. Your subscription price must be realistic in terms of existing competition and your costs in gathering materials.

4. You must set a price that generates sufficient revenues in realistic anticipation of probable market penetration for your newsletter.

5. Determine your frequency both by timeliness and amount of information available—usually more frequent publication (even in a smaller format—four page vs. eight) is desirable.

6. Do everything possible to design a format to save on paper, postage and production costs without sacrificing value to the reader.

7. Choose the delivery method which is most economical without hurting the value or image of the product.

8. Be prepared, at least in a planning stage, to consider the potential impact of electronic communications technology on the product as you currently envision it.

9. Make certain the editor is actively involved in marketing planning and is responsible for the financial operation and success of the newsletter.

10. Plan to have as small a staff as possible at all times.

CHAPTER III
A Short Course in Newsletter Design

Good layout and design are very much in the eye of the beholder. All this chapter is intended to do is describe some features common to successful newsletters. Perhaps it is easier to start out by describing features which are not common to design of commercial newsletters. Non-profit associations and corporate house organs often are designed more like mini-magazines, going to two and three column typeset formats, with headlines in various typefaces, pictures, captions, continuing stories, etc. As a general rule, you don't see this type of layout and design in commercial newsletters.

Points for Basic Newsletter Design:
1. Use an 8½ x 11 size—it's cheapest.
2. Get a professional to design an attractive masthead you can pre-print.
3. Use a paper color other than white.
4. The masthead should include your ISSN number (see page 136), your trademark registration for the title (if applied for or received) and your volume and issue number and date. Some publishers put some of these materials elsewhere to avoid cluttering their mastheads. This is a design consideration.
5. Most newsletters use full page width stories. Studies suggest that narrow columns, two 20-pica columns with center gutter, give improved readability. Only a minority of newsletters are designed this way, usually those published by large firms with in-house word processing or typesetting equipment that can justify the right-hand margins (most full page width newsletters use ragged-right columns). Although use of type-set copy is increasing, many successful newsletters still use typewriter copy.
6. Use hole punched paper if you hope your readers will be saving every precious issue (or if you mean to suggest they should). Conversely, some feel that not hole punching is a subliminal way of indicating this news is "so hot" it will be out-of-date by next issue (so there is no point in your filing it).
7. Many publishers still use typewriter copy headlines—although typeset headlines can add to appearance of a typewriter-copy newsletter. Headlines should probably be one line and use upper and lower case (not all caps or capitalizing every word). If you run longer stories, subheads may be a useful way to break up the columns and provide reference points for the reader. Classically, newsletter journalism consisted of short stories, short paragraphs and short sentences. Not every subject lends itself to this treatment, however, so if your personal editorial style doesn't fit the mold it certainly doesn't mean you can't be successful with your newsletter.
8. Most newsletter publishers pre-print at the bottom of page one the necessary information on copyright, publisher's name and address, editor's name, frequency and price. Others prefer to put this somewhere inside the newsletter so it doesn't clutter up the appearance of page one.
9. Many newsletters include on page one an index such as a table of contents or "highlights in this issue."
10. Publishers producing typewriter copy newsletters can vary the appearance by using all caps or underlines of key elements within a story, or rules or boxes to set

off particularly important stories. This can be overdone and leads to a choppy appearance where every other sentence is emphasized.

11. Select your paper and envelope stock with an eye to appearance, price and postage. A combination of 40 lb. (offset) paper and a 24 lb. (offset) envelope will permit you to go to 8 or 10 pages (4-5 sheets printed on both sides) and remain under one ounce for postage purposes. The opacity of paper at this weight is not outstanding. Publishers using an 11 x 17 folded format often use a heavier paper for four-page newsletters.

Beginning publishers are often concerned about such questions as "How often should I publish the newsletter? How long should it be?" The answer to all of these questions is "It depends." We can certainly tell you, however, a bit about what the norms are. Newsletters aimed at corporate or business audiences tend to be published at least twice a month. Monthlies are seldom aimed at these audiences. They are outnumbered by weeklies (there are a few daily newsletters, but only a relative handful of the some 2,500-3,000 newsletters currently published).

Consumer-oriented newsletters tend to be published less often; monthly may well be the most common frequency, although some are bi-weekly.

While it is normally the depth and specificity of information published in a newsletter that leads to its success, rather than the timeliness—in the sense of rapid delivery of information—one school of thought does hold that frequency is important and that a publisher would be better off to promote a 4 page weekly than an 8 page bi-weekly. McGraw-Hill publishes *Oilgram Price Report* daily. People interested in oil price changes from all over the world need this information every day. Capitol Publications publishes *Education of the Handicapped* bi-weekly because its audience needs the information, which is so specialized as to not be readily available from other sources, but news developments are not so fast as to demand more frequent publication.

Newsletters aimed at corporate audiences tend to be a bit longer. A greater number of these are eight to ten pages long while most consumer newsletters are four pages. (These are simply "medians.") Of course, some successful newsletters, as we've mentioned, run 40 or more pages and some corporate newsletters are only 4 pages.

Design Your Newsletter for Maximum Readability

"Remember, the majority of your readers are visually impaired," says Ed Grunewald, "they wear glasses, and they tend to read newsletters in places like commuter trains which are the visual quality equivalent of caves."

Grunewald emphasizes that the suggestions he makes for designing a newsletter product with enhanced readability are not his opinions, but the results of studies made by universities and researchers.

 • Maintain a high contrast between type and paper. ("Obviously, good old black-on-white is best.")

 • Don't use glazed or shiny paper. Color tints are also risky.

• Use a serif type for body copy, preferably something in the times roman family.

• Typewriter type is still very common for newsletters, but it finishes down the list of reader preferences.

• Avoid italics almost completely. Don't overuse underlining.

• Avoid mixing type faces.

• For a single column page format. 30 picas is about maximum. For a two column format 16 to 18 picas per column.

• Readers like ragged right format. Use it to avoid hyphenation. At the least, don't give the reader both a justified right column and hyphenation.

• The smaller the typeface used, the more leading is necessary for readability. As a general rule, be hesitant about using anything smaller than 9 point.

• Don't expect too much of second color. It's all right in a masthead. Remember, for example, if you use red or green, nearly 10 percent of men are color-blind and see both those as grey.

• Don't use jump run-overs. Studies show you lose 30 to 50 percent of readers when you continue a story.

• Avoid 'furniture' items like rules and boxes. The only people who benefit from those are printers.

Ed Grunewald, Consultant, 3 Eatons Neck Road, Northport, New York 11768

Ragged Right vs. Justified Column

Ragged right for readability? Grunewald recommends it over a justified column, but adds the purpose of ragged right is to avoid hyphenations.

A couple more comments on the same question:

A Cahners Publishing Company study shows that poor readers find ragged right columns easier than justified, but that good readers are unaffected by a justified column. The Cahners report also states that bar charts are superior to line graphs for comprehension, black-on-white copy is read nearly 12% faster than the reverse, upper/lower case copy is read more than 13% faster than all caps.

Gerre Jones, editor of *Professional Marketing Report,* feels the whole thing is simply a matter of preference. "Editors and layout people who use ragged right (usually for typewriter-produced publications) are staunch defenders of the format, while users of justified columns have a deep-rooted preference for the neater, more familiar justified right column setting."

Is the 8½ x 11 Typewriter Format Still Acceptable for Newsletters?

The answer is yes. Preparing camera-ready copy for your printer in a typewriter format is the classic newsletter style. This format has two great tangible advantages: it saves time and it saves money. Going out-of-house to a typesetter will add about 50% to your total production costs and is bound to add a couple days to the production time when proof reading and corrections are added. NAA has observed a trend towards

The following five samples provide a quick overview of newsletter layout and design feature common among subscription newsletters.

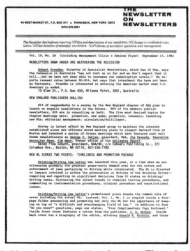

#1 *Newsletter on Newsletters*. The classic "newsletter style" typewriter copy with a pre-printed masthead (this one is black on lite brown), headlines are all caps. ISSN number on "flag," subscription information appears on page 4.

#2 *The Pet Animal Health Letter*. Here we have a word-processor-produced newsletter, again with a preprinted masthead (in this case red on gray) with bold face headlines. Front page includes a table of contents (masthead and subscription information is on page four). NOTE: this newsletter numbers its pages consecutively throughout the year which is unusual.

#3 *CCAN Construction Computer Applications Newsletter*. A new style produced entirely on their in-house mini-computer (with preprinted masthead, red on ivory). This front page includes two column format (ragged right) table of contents for issue and complete masthead information at bottom of page.

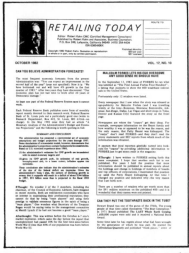

#4 *Retailing Today,* a personal vehicle newsletter, word-processor copy, two column with justified margins. In this instance, the "flag" at top on page one includes complete information on publication including pix of editor... this one is black on white.

#5 *Revenue Sharing Bulletin.* Typeset copy, three-column justified margins. Almost a newspaper format, it uses preprinted mastheads, green on ivory. In this publication, complete subscription information appears inside on bottom of page 2. The other four publications are hole-punched, this one only indicates with circles where the reader can put his own holes....

Having looked at literally hundreds of newsletters, it's fair to comment that the great majority are designed in one of these (or very similar) formats.... Anything different in size, format or graphics would certainly be out of the usual.

typeset newsletters, but mostly in corporate newsletters published by the larger firms that can afford in-house typesetting facilities. These are fairly big ticket items that a beginning publisher is probably not going to have available. (In theory it shouldn't take any longer for a production typist to use a typesetting machine than a typewriter once you've reached the stage at which you can afford it). A greater number of consumer newsletters are typeset because, for monthlies, the element of time is not so vital. An intangible asset of the typewriter style is the supposed "air of immediacy" it lends, the concept that copy was snatched red-hot from the reporter's typewriter and rushed into print. You see, in *U. S. News & World Report,* among others, typewriter-copy inserted "newsletter pages" within the magazine format for just this purpose.

We also see a greater number of newsletters published in an 11 x 17 format, folded to a four page self-contained issue. This requires a larger press and is probably a bit more expensive to print, but it does permit an attractive 4 or 8 page newsletter. It locks you into the format, however. When you are using single sheets it is no real trouble to print 10 instead of 8 pages if news warrants for a particular issue.

If you want to dress up the typewriter copy a little, headline machines available for about $600 will allow you "typeset" headlines. You can also have your printer pre-print a number of stock headlines for departments you know you will be featuring regularly, e.g., "News from the Postal Service," "Publications of Interest." Simply insert them at those sections when you prepare the copy for the printer. One publisher told NAA, "I hope to gross over $2,000,000 this year, and my newsletters are all typewriter-copy with headlines in all upper case underlined." You don't have to be fancy to be successful.

Most publishers invest a little money in designing an attractive flag or masthead for the first page (red on ivory paper, or dark blue on light green, or what have you). These, used in combination with some headlines if you want them, can produce a very professional appearing newsletter for a minimum of production costs, allowing you to continue to use typewriter copy for the text. Similarly, it doesn't cost very much to modify the masthead design for reproduction on your envelopes. That cost, spread over the couple of hundred thousand envelopes you may use in a year for both circulation and promotion, is miniscule.

Newsletters give a more professional appearance when they come in an envelope. You can design a newsletter as a self-mailer and eliminate envelope costs entirely, but it doesn't give the same impression when it reaches the subscriber. This is only opinion, of course, but almost no commercial newsletter publisher NAA knows uses self-mailers for delivery of their newsletter. (Self-mailers are sometimes used for promotional brochures.)

The most common sizes are 8½ x 11 or folded 11 x 17 just because they're standard. You do see some newsletters in different sizes, but they are unusual and more expensive to produce. Almost all the odd-size newsletters NAA sees are produced outside the U.S. If you want a different size, for some reason of design or intended impact on the reader, remember that you will be paying extra to your printer to order that type of stock or to cut standard stock to the size you have specified.

Designing the Typewriter Copy Newsletter

Despite continuing advances in word-processing and typesetting equipment, a considerable percentage of newsletters continue to use "typewriter type."

Here are six suggestions from Jan White, Author of *"On Graphics: Tips for Editors"* (Lawrence Ragan Communications), for using the typewriter to dress up the apperance of the 'typewriter copy newsletter.'

● *Space*—Do not separate paragraphs within a story by a full line of space. Use a deep indent to signal the start of a fresh paragraph. If you are afraid of too much massiveness, deepen the indent to half a line in length. Reserve spacing for separating stories.

● *Headlines*—Three ways to make them more visible:

THIS IS A HEADLINE   Here is where you start the text of the article,
TYPED IN ALL CAPITALS

THIS IS THE
FIRST LINE
OF A NICE LONG
HEADLINE THAT
READS INTO THE TEXT, THUS Here starts the text of the story

THIS IS A CLEVER HEADLINE THAT IS SUSPENDED FROM THE MAST

Here is the start of the text. . . .

● *Sideheads or subheads*—You can use the same type of indenting talked about above. Underline the space. Type the subhead there. Keep it short. End with a colon.
    Subhead words: First word begins two spaces after the colon.

● *Pagination*—Often not handled well in typewriter copy newsletters. Here's one suggestion: Space down three spaces from the page top. Type an underscore across the page and type the page number directly beneath the underscore, flush left. Allow two lines of space and then begin text.

02

FIRST STORY BEGINS HERE . . .
● *Lists*—On a typewriter you have only numerals, space and horizontal rules to use, rather than the plethora of choices typeset offers. Don't let numbers stand alone. Beef them up with underlines.

Begin the first word at the seventh character.
Repeat the pattern precisely for each item.

You can also use characters like the lower case "o" as emphasis indications or bullets.
o Precede each item in your list with a lower case "o".
o Indent or type flush left depending on taste.

o Double space between entries.

o This method is ideal for items with more than one line and multi-sentence lists.

** *Initials*—You can use beginning initials any number of ways. Here are some ideas:

T his is an initial cap hanging at the left, outside the left-hand margin, whose
. . .

Another way to do the same sort of thing is this one. This is nearly irrestible on a page.

If you purchase some presstype or transfer type and have a little patience, you can do any number of things to dress-up layouts.

A typewritten newsletter's "magic" is the illusory quality of a "personal" communication—the inside stuff, the latest scuttlebut. This illusion is destroyed by introduction of formal typesetting. Why are you making the reader plow through typewriter copy, which is far from the easiest to read anyway? You can effectively use typeset copy for mastheads and other features, *often in combination with a second color which has obviously been preprinted.*

- Set headlines to fill all or most of a column.
- Use standard column widths. Vary with wider or narrower columns only for a specific purpose.
- Set headlines in caps and lower case—it's easier to read than all caps.
- The current style is to set first lines of text flush left and indent all other paragraphs.
- Use headlines and subheads to break up copy and separate stories. You don't need rules or other separating devices.
- If you choose a sans serif type, remember it is harder to proofread (l's and t's, etc., tend to look alike).
- Stick to one idea per sentence.
- Editing excess verbiage, even articles such as "the," can cut story length by 10%.
- Conduct a readership survey to find out what your readers want. ("How to Conduct a Readership Survey" is available from Anderson Press for $6.50.)
- Consider having an expert critique your publication periodicaly. (The Anderson Press can also do this.)

The Anderson Press, P.O. Box 774, Madison Square Station, New York, N.Y. 10010.

How to Spot Typos Before Printing
After the newsletter has been printed and mailed, it's amazingly easy to spot typos. Anyone can do it and frequently does. Here, however, are suggestions to aide in proofreading efforts before the issue goes to press:

- *Use Different People*—The person who wrote and/or typed an article usually is not a good proofreader.
- *Familiarity Breeds Contempt*—The same person looking over the copy again and again at different stages of production will miss new errors.
- *Mistakes Tend to Cluster*—If you find a typo, look very carefully for others nearby.
- *Be Careful of Changes in Typeface*—If you change to all caps, or italics, or boldface, or underlined typewritten copy, it's easy to miss errors.
- *Sequences Often Go Awry*—Be careful of duplications of page numbers or lettering of items in sequence in lists or outlines.

- *Watch Out for "Call-Outs"*—References such as 'see table below,' 'as indicated in chart elsewhere on this page' can easily get separated from material in question.
- *Look for Complete Sets*—Anything which takes two. Brackets, parentheses, quotations, marks and sometimes dashes.
- *Numbers and Totals*—Recheck all numbers. Use your hand calculator to retotal all column figures. Watch for misplaced decimal points. The simplest math can go wrong.
- *Be Particularly Careful of Copy Which Discusses Errors*—Grammar, spelling, punctuation. If you are ever going to miss an error it will be here.

13 Tips for Effective Newsletter Design

Some considerations for effective design of a newsletter from Robert L. Baker's newsletter, *Impact:*

- Ten-point type and the single column layout are still the most popul;ar. Be especially wary of smaller type if you have many older readers.
- Try starting each new article with two or three words in all caps or boldface to draw readers' attention.
- "Underlining for emphasis is as common as freckles and about as helpful." Be similarly sparing with italics and boldface.
- Be generous with white space—make your page look inviting, not formidable.
- Emphasize short, pithy, bold headlines. Use a typeface four to eight points larger than the body type.
- Keep line length at 20 picas or less.
- Use a second color, perhaps for headlines. If budget considerations prevent this, you can preprint a year's supply of nameplates.
- Follow the trend to short narrow columns and ragged-right lines.
- Define and visually separate editorial items with columns or rules.
- Don't waste valuable front page space with your masthead.
- Choose only a few typefaces and establish a head schedule.
- Maintain adequate margins (at least one-half inch).
- Break-up grayness of large blocks of copy with subheads.

11 More Ideas to Improve Your Newsletter

"How to Produce the Perfect Publication"...Here are 11 suggestions from the publication of the same name by Walter Anderson, publisher of the *Editors Newsletter:*

- Use a second color only if it improves readability.
- Don't, as a rule, use color in headlines.
- Make sure your spacing is uniform between headlines and the first lines of articles.
- Don't leave a space between paragraphs. It creates a loose look.

What Every NL Publisher Should Know About Printers (Or Doing It Yourself)

The business of newsletter publishing is delivering information, many like to say, not pieces of printed paper in envelopes. And, while the dawn of the electronic publishing age is here, the business of publishing a newsletter today (1982), most publishers admit, still involves purchasing a great number of pieces of printed paper, not to mention envelopes, letterheads, ordercards, brochures, etc., etc. Since one of the largest expenses of newsletter publishing is printing, it behooves the publisher to learn as much as necessary about the printing business.

Doing your own printing. Unless you are (a) printing a daily newsletter or (b) already have the equipment and the skills necessary, most conventional opinion is that newsletter publishers are well advised not to attempt to get into the printing business.

While operating a basic multi-lith press is not technically complex (anyone who can change a sparkplug on a Triumph can certainly learn to do it), it tends to take more time and be more difficult than you expected. Second, if you decide to hire a part-time printer, you invariably get someone who is moonlighting from another job and reliability tends to be a problem. Then the printer, not the publisher or editor, appears to become the most important person in the operation.

The following breakdown is provided by Newsletter Services, Inc. in Washington, D.C. The figures are circa 1980, but the points made are still quite valid. If you spend $75,000 annually on printing, you might be able to save by converting to in-house.

The advantages to an in-house printing operation:

● Timing. No one's job ever comes ahead of yours. You control deadlines absolutely.

● Quality. With the obvious personal attention you give your own work.

● Avoid Disasters. With things in-house, you spot trouble before it develops. Hopefully the things which can't happen (but sometimes do), like printing newsletter "A" on "B" mastheads, are spotted and stopped.

● Putter with printing. Many newsletter people like to putter with printing— you save additionally if you run the press yourself. This means putting on the apron and actually running the machine.

● Incentive to expand. Having that expensive equipment sit idle is a great incentive to expand. It has helped Newsletter Services, for example, go from three newsletters to nine.

The pitfalls and drawbacks to in-house printing:

● Running the printing operation is time-consuming. You have to serve as supervisor and manager, or hire a supervisor, which is expensive.

● As an inexperienced printer, you'll make costly mistakes, particularly in buying equipment.

● Reliability. If, in your printing operation, you have one of everything your whole operation halts if one piece of equipment breaks down on Friday afternoon.

● Good help is hard to find. The rule of thumb is that it takes four "hires" to get the right person in every print shop operation. This is especially true if you are looking for part-time moonlighters.

● Cost. The prices here are approximate—you can spend less. If you buy plates and negatives, you don't need a darkroom, but you give up some of the control you opened a printing operation to achieve. You can insert by hand for small runs. You can spend $2,500 for a small collating machine which will prove to be more trouble than it's worth (or up to $18,000 or $20,000 for a large one). You could use a hydraulic three-hole punch, but you could also decide that your readers can hole punch themselves if they feel like it.

● One final caveat. Buying used equipment is merely asking for trouble.

Here is a cost estimate for a basic in-house printing operation:

AB Dick or Multi-lith
11 x 17" 2-color press	$18,000
Small Camera & Plate Burner	5,000
Darkroom Equipment	3,000 *(you can spend $16,000 on automatic negative maker)*
Folder	4,000
Inserter	5,000
Binder	2,000
Miscellaneous Tables, Cabinets, etc.	2,000
Total approximate Cost	$40,000 to $45,000

Then there are your out-of-pocket capital expenses. The following breakdown is for annual operating costs:

Fixed Costs (no matter how much you print)
Depreciation of Equipment	$ 8,000-9,000 (5-year straight line)
Rent (500 sq. ft. at @ $12 per ft.)	6,000
Income foregone on capital investment	4,000
Approximate Total	$18,000

Variable Costs (expressed as a percentage of your present printing bills)
Labor	35-50%
Paper and Ink	15-20% (full-time print shops can get below these costs, but the type of operation you will run will not)
Supplies	3-5%
Maintenance	2-3%
Addressing	7.5%
Insurance/Deliveries	1%
Total	65-80% of your present printing bills

From that you can deduce the $75,000 break-even figure. If your current bills are $75,000, following the formula your variable cost in-house might be $56,000 plus the

$18,000 fixed cost. If you're willing to do the work yourself, you can save considerably more even at this level.

To really save money you need to be doing about $200,000 to $250,000 in printing and that brings new problems. You can't print a quarter million dollars of business on one multi-lith; you'll have to have additional equipment and a full-time supervisor and decide, among other things, if you want to be in the printing business (versus the publishing business).

If you've decided not to take printing in-house at the present time, you still have basically two options for buying printing: (1) developing a more or less exclusive relationship with a printer and relying on them for your work or (2) bidding every job around among a half dozen printers and always using the low bid.

Each style has its advantages. If you are going to seek bids for most jobs you need to realize several things. Not every printer can do all jobs equally well. One printer, for example, may be good for regular issues of your newsletter, but not really equipped to run large quantities of 2 or three-color brochures.

Develop a form and learn to specify jobs exactly. If the printer who gave you the low bid didn't realize the 'third color was a bleed on two sides' or 'the order card was perforated and the letter folds to number 10' until he gets the job in hand, the price advantage may evaporate. To do this right, you have to be able to specify ink and paper stock, etc.

Advantage. As a general rule, you can save money.

Disadvantage. (1) Time. It takes longer to assemble a promotion mailing if three different printers are doing the letter, order card and envelope. (2) Quality. For obvious reasons. (3) Reputation. Printers in every city appear to have a marvelous grapevine. Developing a reputation for being a pain in the rear or one who 'nickels and dimes you to death on every job' may not help your firm in the longer run. (4) Special Services—or lack thereof. As a rule the regular customer gets the special service when he needs it.

How to Develop a Relationship with a Printer
How to Pick a Printer

● *What type of equipment do they have and how much?* To get a better view of what scale of operation you are dealing with and whether they have the capacity to do the work you'll need.

● *What turnaround time do they offer?* Get the printer to tell you when he has to have the work to finish it on your schedule. It's important to learn if they're an integrated shop. Do they offer composition and mailing, or will those services have to be handled by someone else—at a cost of additional time.

● *Do they print newsletters now?* Ask to see all of them. It will tell you a lot about the type of work they do.

● *Price.* Put this last because it isn't always the most important consideration in view of the other factors above. (Ask for a bid for a full year—if they can count on your job coming in every Wednesday p.m. and build a schedule around it, you'll often get a better price and better service.)

How to work with the printer after you've selected:

● *Always give written instructions.* If you don't have purchase orders, type out directions clearly—it avoids confusion about who said what to whom.

● *Learn the printing process.* If you don't know anything about the various steps from copy through mailing, you're pretty much at the printer's mercy.

● *Be realistic about deadlines.* If you haven't cried "Wolf!" once too often, your printer will break his neck for you when you really need help.

● *Talk over your requirements.* Some types of paper, for example, have been short. If the printer knows you're planning a 100,000 brochure mailing, he can shop around and have the necessary material on hand at job time.

● *Get a blue-line on big jobs.* It protects both sides when, on a large project like a promotion brochure, you check over a blue-line proof before it goes on the press.

● *If you use graphic designers, make sure they communicate with the printer.* This avoids a situation where the designer didn't know that your regular printer can't handle bleeds before he put them on all four sides of the brochure cover.

"Despite the impression you probably have, printing is a high capital, low profit, low return on investment business," comments Larry Blumenfield of Plymouth Printing, a Washington firm with extensive experience with newsletter publishers. Blumenfield gives the following suggestions on selecting and working with printers:

● *Decide what you want to accomplish.* Different jobs and different printers involve considerations like, (1) speed, (2) economy, (3) reliability, and (4) high quality ("something we all like to promise to deliver, although I'm never sure how precisely to define it").

● Then: *Discuss this with your printer.* He needs to know what you want and what is most important to you.

● *Don't make price THAT significant a consideration.* (Obviously Blumenfield's suggestions are most applicable to developing and maintaining an on-going relationship with a single printer—conversely, the publisher can bid out every single job among half dozen printers and always go with the low bid.)

● *Evaluate management attitude.* All printers have pretty much the same equipment and, within a labor market, probably pretty much the same level of skilled personnel. What makes the difference is the willingness of the printer to accept your requirements as theirs.

● *Think long term.* At Plymouth Printing, by plan, they conduct business so that they are a profitable account for each of their suppliers. When the occasion arises in which they need special service, they claim they generally get it.

● *Some truisms about the printer-publisher business relationship:*
   — Printers are human. When pressed they often promise more than they know they can deliver.
   — Almost every printing firm is supported by three to five dominant accounts. If your job gets in the way of that bulldozer, it can be flattened.
   — Who put the "lie" in reliable? Probably the printers. Printers have a stable of excuses you wouldn't believe. "The job is on the truck," "It won't dry so we can fold it," etc., etc. *but...*

— If you don't get what you expected, look carefully at who failed. "In our experience," says Blumenfield, "without intending to brag, more customers miss deadlines with us than we do with them."

— One of the things printers do best is follow instructions. One of the things they do worst is attempt to follow inadequate instructions while getting the rush job out on time.

CHAPTER IV
New Technologies in
Newsletter Journalism

Journalism is not generally considered to be a high-technology business, but in recent years a certain amount of excitement has been generated about new equipment for use both in the publishing office and for delivery of information. In this chapter we'll discuss some of the pros and cons of word processing equipment and electronic delivery of newsletter information.

A word processor is a glorified typewriter. There are a number of models on the market. Those most suitable for newsletter use have a display screen which will show at least a good chunk of the page—30 lines or so. Editors who use them quickly become proficient at making corrections and editing on the machine which can then print out the final version in camera-ready copy form.

You can also get word processors which produce a tape or disk compatible with typesetting systems. It can convert your typed copy into typeset (either on your own type setter or using the equipment of a typesetting house). This, again, is probably beyond the financial resources of the smaller publishers. As indicated earlier, while typewriter copy is still quite common in newsletter copy, there is a growing trend toward typeset copy. Even a used typesetting machine suitable for newsletter publishing use is probably a $10,000 item.

A word processing system can also store whole issues on floppy disks or cassette tapes, and you can rewrite stories by inserting a couple of paragraphs on new developments without retyping the whole piece. Some word processors also can maintain list information and produce labels for mailing and also for accounting, record keeping and billing.

The drawbacks. They're expensive. The models described probably would go for $8,000-10,000 (or several hundred a month to lease). While they are great for editing and preparing copy, testimony from NAA members indicates they aren't really satisfactory for list maintenance or accounting. (Models of the type described don't have the capacity. They can produce your list of 3,000 labels, but will take literally the whole day to do so, keeping the machine from any other uses.)

We would recommend that the beginning publishers purchase a reconditioned selectric typewriter (the self-correcting models are certainly nice) and have a local computer service bureau maintain his list. They will put yoursubscribers on file for 20 to 30 cents each and print out labels as you need them for 2 or 2½ cents. Handle your invoices by hand. This type of set-up is quite feasible for an operation with 500-1500 subscribers. Later on, as your operation grows, you'll have the time and cash flow to think more carefully about purchasing word processing equipment, in-house small computers, etc. Part of this decision rests on personal preference. Some publishers are interested in learning about computers, software, programs, etc. For them, a mini-computer or dedicated word processor is probably the right choice from the beginning. Others quite simply are not. For them, at least initially, a selectric and a service bureau may be the best answer.

The Electronic Wizardry in Our Future

A lot of what is being written about the coming of the electronic revolution to the publishing industry sounds like something out of "Captain Billy's Whiz Bang." Soon the U.S. will be a "wired nation." No one will ever have to leave home; home terminals will assist you to order groceries, balance your checkbook, turn on and off the garden sprinkler and with a CRT with print-out capacity the subscriber will be able to preview an incredible smorgasbord of information and select what meets his needs and interests and have it displayed on his home screen or printed out for permanent reference.

Technology for all of the above is here today. The question is how soon is how much of it going to be of practical interest to the newsletter publisher? Today McGraw-Hill is sending several of its information services by Telex, and some of its major price services are on computer. They don't even think of those as newsletters, they have told NAA, although the type of information is similar to what goes into their printed letters. Some publishers have contracted to put their information into one of several large data banks now offering a tremendous amount of information to subscribers.

Every publisher thinking about "electronic publishing" applications to his operation has to answer several hard questions:

1. Is the hardware in place? The investment you have to make so you can transmit information is not insurmountable, but do your subscribers and potential subscribers have the hardware in their offices or homes? Not every home has a computer, although when you remember how recently digital display watches cost $500, you can see the day may well be coming.

2. How do I price? It's simple now. Your newsletter costs $150 a year for twenty-four eight page issues. While you don't assume your reader necessarily pores over every single word in every issue, you trust that, 192 pages later, the subscriber will have found enough of benefit to renew—you have only to motivate him to make a buying decision once a year. If he can call up a display of the headlines from the current issue on his screen and pick only the one or two he wants to read—how do you set a price?

3. "How do I make him remember me?" Can you picture your subscriber looking at his watch and saying, "I see it's 10:30 Tuesday, I better check and see what the *WIN Letter* has in this issue." That's why a lot of publishers are interested in systems that will deliver material without waiting for the subscriber to ask for it.

The most important thing to do is to develop the proper mind-set to investigate the opportunities. The first time I saw an advertisement for a television screen with print out capacity, I suddenly knew how a buggy-whip manufacturer felt when he saw the first Ford chug around the corner and past his factory. Newsletter publishing is an information industry—successful publishers are not marketing printed pieces of paper to be delivered in envelopes, they are selling specialized information. At present, and very probably for the near-term future, printed newsletters handled by the U.S. Postal Service will continue to be the most practical delivery system for the majority of publishers—more and more may find, however, that one of the electronic transmission options now being developed becomes viable for some users.

How to Determine Which Word Processing Equipment is Right for You

Martin Simpson, publisher of the *Office Products Analyst,* outlines considerations which, he believes, will cause continued rapid growth in use of word processing equipment by newsletter publishers and, interestingly, the reasons responsible for the hesitance of smaller publishers to move quickly into this area.

Why then .do publishers hesitate in converting or upgrading to more sophisticated word processing operations?

1. *The Fear of Becoming a Dead Pioneer.* Everyone knows how fast technology is moving in this area. Simpson recommends considering only equipment which has been on the market long enough to be technically debugged. Further, he suggests, lease or rental may be a good idea, although more expensive in the short term, to insure that you have the right product for your firm.

2. *Fear of New-Fangled Gizmos.* There is some training required. Publishers are well advised to allow those who will be using the equipment to participate as fully as possible in selection decisions.

3. *Fear of an Administrative Hornet's Nest.* Simpson believes this can be alleviated by the participatory approach. Your people won't tend to "fight the system" if they've been allowed to help develop it.

4. *Too Busy to Stop and Think Syndrome.* No one should be so busy they can't spare the time to plan to work more efficiently.

5. *Fear of Hidden Costs.* There *are* "hidden costs" associated with word processing costs in training as well as maintenance contracts and the obsolescence factor if you decide to buy. These can be planned for. (If you select the right equipment for your applications, it really doesn't matter that much if something still snazzier comes out a year later.)

6. *Fear of Software Bugs, Systems Failures and Buzz Word Gobbeldygook.* Intelligent planning, Simpson says, can enable you to select equipment that is right for your firm, equipment of which you understand the operations and capabilities.

Martin Simpson Company, 115 Broadway, New York, New York 10006, 212-349-7450.

Electronic Publishing is Here Today

"Electronic publishing is already a reality and is poised to rapidly spread to every sector of the information industry."

"What is electronic publishing? The definition is evolving rapidly. Obviously there must be a computer in the mix somewhere, though it need not necessarily belong to the publisher. Basically, it is disseminating an information product, with the aid of the computer, via an electronic medium to a distant receiving unit.

"What does it mean to my newsletter operation? Am I suggesting that there is a way for you to participate in the successor to the industrial revolution? That is exactly what I'm suggesting . . . many of you are in a position to play the game."

"First you need to understand a bit about the players. There are already nearly 500 on-line data bases world wide. These data bases are accessible for the most part over phone lines by anyone with a computer terminal or a communicating word processor.

"The major factor in full text data bases is *Mead Data Central* which, with its combined Lexis and Nexis services, currently has 18 billion characters on-line. Nexis now offers full texts of the Washington Post, Newsweek, U.S. News and World Report, the AP newswire, Reuters, the Economist, Dun's Review, Congressional Quarterly and the UPI newswire.

"What does all this mean to you? My advice is get involved in some way now so that your level of awareness is raised to the point where you can recognize a real opportunity when it comes along.

"Mead is now actively seeking licenses from newsletter publishers in the U.S. and abroad. Specifically, Mead is interested in newsletters with strong archival or research value. Examples include newsletters covering major American or international industries, branches or government, functional or professional specialties. Mead will write a non-exclusive contract, bear all the costs of converting archival material to machine-readable form and pay you 20-25% for the newsletter as royalty. You need only be able to provide your current issues in machine-readable form.

"*Bibliographic Retrieval Service,* has announced what it's calling an electronic newsletter service. For a flat $200 a month, plus a minimal connect charge, you can put your newsletter on-line and update it daily if you wish. BRS requires no minimum commitment. Your subscribers would be able to call up a menu of headlines and print out whatever they wanted. You could charge for it any way you wanted. BRS currently serves nearly 2,000 librarians which could represent a target audience for a new on-line newsletter.

"*VNU,* a Dutch publisher is seeking rights to U.S. newsletters to put on its private viewdata network.

"What can you do with electronic mail? All you need is a terminal—or a home computer or a word processor. That can be as little as a few thousand dollars worth of equipment. With it you can communicate electronically on a pay-as-you-go basis with any subscriber who has similar equipment.

For further information:
- Mead Central, Mel Beiser, 200 Park Avenue, New York, N.Y. 10017
- BRS, Corporation Park Building, #702, Scotia, N.Y. 12302
- VNU Data International, Jay Curry, De Boelelaan 14, 1083 HJ Amsterdam, The Netherlands, Telex 10366
- GTE Telenet, 8330 Old Courthouse Road, Vienna, Va. (703/827-9200)

Getting Into Electronic Publishing

"How can I get involved in electronic publishing?" The answer is simple, according to Mel Beiser of Mead Data Central. "Look into your bathroom mirror in the morning and say, 'Yesterday I was a newsletter publisher, today I'm a data base producer (or narrowcaster, or defined market software producer)." People who were your readers or subscribers just as suddenly become "end-users."

The first experience of newsletter publishers in electronic publishing came about rather simply, according to Beiser, former Executive Editor of McGraw-Hill's *Platt's Oilgram.* McGraw-Hill had problems with timeliness of delivery; therefore, they abstracted some key features from several of their newsletters calling them "newswires" and delivered them domestically by Western Union's TWX or internationally by Telex. They used systems for delivery that were already in place, thus requiring no further investment in hardware.

Today Mead Data Central has established a system called Nexis. Already available to Nexis subscribers are Associated Press and United Press materials, the *Washington Post, Newsweek, U.S. News* and *Congressional Quarterly.* Soon all 31 McGraw-Hill magazines and the newsletters published by Latin American Reports will be added and publications of several other newsletter publishers.

How Does Nexis Work? Nexis is an on-line information system which makes available full texts of previously published materials. They install their custom terminal in the end-user's office, and he pays a price (established by Nexis) to access the materials. Nexis realizes that by developing a system which requires its own custom terminal, they are, essentially, opting out of the consumer market.

The Terms of the Agreement. Nexis normally signs five-year licensing agreements. The copyright remains with the publisher and Nexis will display it on every page of material. Within reason the data base producer (that's you remember) can also request certain deletions or embargoes on the material which is made available through the Nexis system.

The data base producer also gets, complimentary, a terminal in his office and three hours a month usage.

Nexis pays the producer a royalty, normally beginning at 20% of Nexis fees, and escalating, over time, to 25%.

The fee on which this royalty is calculated is base on several elements:

1. connect time (approximately $1.50 a minute)/

2. search time (varies, depending on extensiveness of material; if the end-user requests "all materials referencing Ronald Reagan" this will be expensive);

3. print-out charges for whatever number of pages the end-user wishes.

The key question every newletter publisher has is "How will this royaltiy, this 20% or 25%, compare with what I'm now charging for a subscription?" That question is not really a relevant one. The Nexis price arrangement is structured to permit a user to access key bits of information from a number of sources which interest him. It will not be economical to utilize Nexis to obtain print-outs of entire issues of a specific publication on a regular basis. It will cost much more than taking a subscription.

Electronic Publishing: State of the Art

"To get successfully into electronic publishing, most newsletters will need to offer something besides on-line delivery of print products." David Gump, associate publisher at Pasha Publications, comments that creation of new services like instantaneous delivery of bulletin-type information or selective search for key topics are the keys to success for most publishers, except those relatively few who produce extremely time-sensitive information, such as pricing, for which customers will pay a premium just to receive it quickly.

At present, Gump's research shows four valid options for newsletter publishers considering electronic delivery.

1. *Go on-line solo with a time-sharing service.* You get the computer resources at the lowest cost, can sell service for whatever you choose and *keep all the profit.* Drawbacks: you get no assistance with marketing or massaging customers—getting their equipment coordinated with the system, etc.

2. *Go on-line with a time sharing service which already has* a customer base that is likely to be interested in your *products.*

3. *NewsNet*—They will be spending heavily for promotion and provide customers with a terminal (on a lease basis). Publishers will get a percentage royalty—your trade-off is taking less yourself than you could get solo to have NewsNet take on the marketing and equipment headaches.

4. *Source*—Biggest plus appears to be they have 20,000 customers hooked up now. Royalty arrangements are less generous than NewsNet. They don't provide equipment to customers and their promises on marketing help are limited.

In all cases, the publisher may establish an up-front subscription fee like a print product.

Pasha is making their products available on the Nexis system, but that is really an archival service—not desirable or intended to facilitate regular delivery of information. Pasha is on a contract basis, "Although," Gump comments, "it may be beyond mortal man to understand fully the Nexis royalty contract arrangements."

Television Digest's Move to Electronic Delivery

"We are completely confident we can deliver our information product to a centralized network for distribution," says Jonathan Miller of *Television Digest.* "We're not at all confident there is an enormous amount of money to be made."

"It is certainly technically feasible. All of the systems we tested have worked." The first key to moving to electronic delivery is being equipped to produce your information product in a satisfactory format. At *Television Digest* this is a Wang OIS-140 centralized word processing.

Systems they've studied: Prestel operates on the philosophy that publishers should pay them for the privilege of being on the system. "Our feeling at *Television Digest* is directly opposite."

General Electronic Information Services Company (GEISCO). Very interesting. All the other services work on the taxi meter concept, you pay for the time you spend on the system. They propose that the publishers can offer discrete information items and establish prices for them.

NewsNet. Seems, on the whole, the most satisfactory present choice, especially their level of knowledge of the newsletter business.

"We don't know what use of our products people will want to make electronically. Do they want to print out hard copy or selectively query? You have to be confident you have a valuable product."

David Gump, Pasha Publications, 1828 L Street, N.W., Suite 510, Washington, D.C. 20036

Jonathan Miller, Television Digest, 1836 Jefferson Place, N.W., Washington, D.C. 20036

Electronic Sources

Gary Reibsamen, NewsNet, 945 Haverford Road, Bryn Mawr, PA 19010 215/527-8030

Joe Shenouda, The Source, 1616 Anderson Road, McLean, VA 22101 703/821-6660

Thomas Walker, Dialcom, Inc., 1109 Spring Street, #410, Silver Spring, MD 20910 301/558-1572

Rob Elmore, Tymshare Corporation, California 408/446-8899

Ted Bartek, Inc. Net, division of Inc. Magazine, 38 Commercial Wharf, Boston, MA 02110 617/227-4700

Newsletters on Electronic Publishing and Databases

Jeffrey Silverstein, IDP Report, 701 Westchester Avenue, White Plains, NY 10604 914/328-9157

First Steps into Small Computers

"The largest problem for newsletter publishers in adding computer/word processing capability to their operations is getting their people)or themselves) over 'computer phobia,' says consultant Martin Lazar. He recommends beginning with functions like word processing and list maintenance. I would suggest that publishers considering small computer capability stick to one of the bigger names. They have guarantees and service capability you can rely on."

For a small newsletter publisher, a desk top computer with 64K memory is sufficient and is now on the market for under $4,000.

To this you need to add a letter quality printer, probably a daisy wheel type, which will cost another $1800-2500. At this point, you need to consider software (programs). Lazar strongly recommends using off-the-shelf programs which are available in formats compatible with all of these commonly used systems. "Don't start out by getting involved in custom software. You spend thousands, not hundreds, for the programs, and there is usually a long period of getting the new programs debugged after they're written."

Commercially available programs for word processing functions and data base management (lists) are available at prices in the $200-$400 range. "Spend 6 months to a year getting used to the computer before you try to add functions like accounts receivable and payable. Then, when you do, modify your present office procedures again, if necessary, so you can use stock programs ($200-$1,000) rather than having new ones written."

With a small computer system Lazar feels a newsletter publisher can handle word processing editing functions (writing, editing, storing information, information retrieval, etc.) and this type of unit has enough memory capacity to handle list maintenance functions (acquisition, editing, purging duplicates, select names by code, renewal subscription billing, computer letter generation) for up to 20,000 names.

Could You Duplicate Subscriber Files?

Do you have a *catastrophe plan* to duplicate your subscription records if necessary? A publisher recalls the fire in their office building (minor). "It was sheer panic in here when we realized those cheshire cards were our lifeline. We were literally throwing them into boxes, over 2,000—I mean over 4,000 since we had two sets, and running for the stairwell. It took us a week to get things back into order."

Are you better prepared than they were? NAA wasn't. We had a computer service producing labels for fulfillment, but they contained no coding information about dues status or renewal date. All that is in journals and card files in the office. We made this a priority project. The labels on *Hotline* envelopes now carry the month of membership renewal and dues information is also now in the computer. (A duplicate master tape is kept in the editor's bureau at home.) It doesn't cost a great deal, and for a business like newsletter publishing which is absolutely dependent on ability to fulfill and renew, this kind of "insurance" seems mandatory.

What about those journals and office records? We should probably have a safe or at least a fire resistant file cabinet.

CHAPTER V
How to Develop an Appropriate
Editorial Style for Your Newsletter

This may be one of the shorter chapters in the book. There are no rules about appropriate editorial style for a newsletter. Successful newsletters reflect as many different editorial approaches as can be imagined. In the beginning, newsletters tended to be personal vehicles. The *Kiplinger Letter* is the best known example of this style, if not the originator. The publication is a personal letter from the editor to the readers even when, as is the case at Kiplinger today, about 14 associate editors contribute to the development of material for the product. Austin Kiplinger reviews and rewrites every item in the final copy, and it is structured as a letter from him to the reader. Kiplinger says newsletter editorial structure should be "utilitarian, reader-minded, forward-looking and serve as an aid to the decision-making capability of the subscriber."

A number of other publishers today adopt this personal approach to their journalism. As a caveat, it appears to be workable only when the publisher/editor has an established name in the subject area that will make readers care about his opinion. Larry Ragan publishes the *Ragan Report* for "communicators—editors and public information people." He writes his newsletter himself and has become well enough known that he allows himself to insert personal opinions and not necessarily related comments into his newsletter when the mood strikes him. Ragan says, "Comments from readers indicate that sometimes this is the most appreciated part of the newsletter. Once for no particular reason, except that it occurred to me, I commented that I had not met a women who enjoyed Erica Jong's book *Fear of Flying*. I got quite a few letters in response to that comment, all from women and many remarkably obscene, telling me precisely how much they liked the book. Some of my peers on the NAA Board of Directors tell me they never get Letters to the Editor, and I couldn't help thinking that while I was answering all those letters, they were probably starting or buying newsletters. If you want to build a big company in the newsletter business, I'm not sure it's a good idea to put your name in the title of the first one and write it yourself in your own inimitable style."

Straight News Reporting

Probably the dominant editorial style in successful newsletters today is "straight news," quick, concise, even telegraphic in its approach. For example, "Meeting in a closed mark-up session late Tuesday, the Subcommittee cut $15 million from the Administration's recommendation for Title IX funding." The reporter remains anonymous. When authoritative sources are quoted they are usually not those of the publication. "A Senate staff source told the *WIN Letter* he would 'be very surprised if that action (the House) stood up over on this side.'"

This kind of reporting is difficult for the beginning publisher because it requires a lot of time and leg work. It appears to be done best by the larger newsletter operations where the editors work full time at their craft and are separated from worrying about promotion, renewal, office management, etc. A general consensus of veteran publishers appears to be that a reasonable output level for an editor/reporter is 200 pages of final copy a year. (An 8 page bi-weekly for example.) One senior editor qualifies that to say, "Within our usual framework, which assumes about 25% material based on original news reporting, 25% more or less adapted from our other publications, and the remainder gathered from other sources."

If it isn't reasonable to expect that one person can put out a bi-weekly 'news-type' newsletter alone, what can a very small operation do? The answer is, it can do things the larger media cannot. The secret to success in newsletters is offering a type or depth of coverage of a subject not available anywhere else. If the *New York Times* has done an excellent story on a subject in your area, there isn't really much point in rehashing it at length in a bi-weekly newsletter. You can go into additional depth on one aspect or development that hasn't gotten the attention of the other media. Interviews and opinion pieces can be effective for the small publisher. One veteran told NAA, "Anything to set yourself up as an oracle," adding, "if the *Times* does cover something which I have done previously, I will mention that."

Many successful newsletters also serve a type of "digest function." More information is being produced currently in every field than anyone can keep abreast of. You know this. How many of the professional magazines and journals, etc. which come across your desk do you actually read (although you know you should)? One important function of your newsletter can be to call your readers' attention to books, reports, articles, etc. of special interest. The newsletter should provide all the relevant information, including where the piece in question can be obtained and, if necessary, a name, address and phone number of a key contact. As Frank Martineau, publisher of *Association Trends* says, "I do all that in self-defense so my readers don't call me to ask where they can get a copy of, or more information about, any item which has appeared in our publication."

More unusual is the newsletter which serves as "journal of record" in its field. Fred Henck, its publisher says people subscribe to *Telecommunications Reports* because they want to know "everything" that went on in the field last week, and want it in complete detail, (which is why the newsletter often runs to 48 or more pages weekly). "Fred, your newsletter violates every rule of success in newsletter publishing," Henck was once told. He believes that illustrates the point where we began. There are no "rules" governing newsletter editorial style.

As far as general guidelines to style and editorial rules, there still isn't a better book than Strunk and White's *Elements of Style*. Several larger publishers find the UPI Style book quite usable to establish uniform usage for several newsletters.

Newsletter editors and publishers seem to revel in unique approaches to their craft, but they all have an underlying message—make sure the subscriber gets the message he's paying for. Here are some examples from Hotline.

Developing NL Editorial Style

"In the thirteen years I've published *Plastics Focus*," Joel Frados comments, "I've talked to a tremendous number of editor/reporters who wanted to get into the newsletter business. One question no one ever asks is 'How do you write for a newsletter?'"

Here are some writing/editorial techniques which have been effective for Frados. These are all subsidiary to three givens:

1. If you have a sharply enough defined subject and it's hot, it will probably be successful regardless of the quality of writing.

2. The editor has to *know* his subject and audience. If he doesn't, no amount of 'good writing' can cover it up.

3. Newsletters are unique. One person's style, albeit good, is not necessarily another's.

How to Position Your NL Editorially Via Competition

Plastics Focus is a weekly. "We have competition and it's damn good. Most of it is monthly magazines so I work to sell our timeliness." My readers know we're 6-8 weeks ahead because I tell them over and over:"

"Word just came from Dupont"

"It happened last week"

"We expect it to happen this Thursday"

"As we predicted in last week's issue"

"I try to achieve a slightly breathless style; including asides like, 'let me digress just a moment,' or 'give me a second to explain.' I write for the ear. Newsletters use more 'auditory style'—leaving a number of nouns and verbs out and using 'ands' and 'buts' to start sentences. It's personal journalism. I use a lot of 'we and us' and write to 'you'."

Three More Keys to Newsletter Editorial Style

● Interpret. Interpret. Interpret. This is what people buy newsletters to get.

● You have to use press releases and industry stuff. (When I started, I thought I'd have all scoops every week) but *insert your newsletter into the material.* Comment editorially on what they claim; if you have to run a lengthy item because it's news, interrupt with phrases like "This is the key—if they produce what they claim," wherever appropriate.

● 'Maybe' can be a magic word. Writing a weekly, you don't have to be omniscient. Use items like "stay tuned for more" or "more to come later".

As you get established, you don't have to worry as much about "exclusivity" because what you say about something becomes 'news' because you say it (and no one else can have that first).

Plastics Focus Publishing Company, Inc., 96 Madison Avenue, New York, N.Y. 10016 212/679-7902.

11 Ways to Manage Editorial Product & Quality

Washington Business Information Inc. (WBII) publisher David Swit makes eleven suggestions for editorial quality in a multi-newsletter operation. (Note: Many apply equally to one-newsletter firms.):

● Make corrections stand out. Readers appreciate your willingness to admit errors.

● Do not join associations. You are independent journalists. If they insist you become associate members to attend their conferences, don't.

● Give editors renewal rates in as much detail as they can absorb. It makes them part of the overall marketing effort.

- Strive for bright, colorful writing which gives personality to your product.
- If you give conferences, use your editors as speakers. It enhances their credibility in the industry.
- Hire experienced journalists to cover technical subjects. "I find you can teach an experienced reporter a specialty, or you can teach journalism. If you have to try to teach both, you're asking for difficulty."
- There is no substitute for shoe leather. It's the non-public stuff you can get which makes your newsletter more valuable to the reader than the *New York Times.*
- Be damn careful what you do with confidential material. "In Washington, you only get to screw someone once. At WBII, we have a 'glass in hand' rule. Anything we hear at social functions is off-the-record . . . we often go back by phone the next morning to say 'You said something about XYZ last night, I wonder if you're willing to discuss it.'"
- Regularly reread your back issues. "I try to go back on the first Tuesday of every month and read the issues from six months back. You find a lot of material for followups."
- Don't overestimate your readers' information, be especially careful of abbreviations and jargon.
- Invest in word-processing as soon as you can. It's remarkable how much less unwilling reporters are to rewrite when it's a matter of pushing buttons to add and delete. "Frankly, I don't know how I ever survived before there was plastic money and the Wang machine."

Washington Business Information, Inc., 235 National Press Building, Washington, D.C. 20045

Shaping Your Editorial Product

"You are in business to serve your readers, not yourself," says Ash Gerecht, publisher at Community Development Services in Washington. Gerecht makes the following suggestions for control/improvement of editorial product.

- Don't try to make your writing too tight. Don't skip too many articles ("the"), and don't use too many abbreviations ("abbn's").
- Don't assume your reader knows anything.
- Avoid redundancy. "We blue pencil fiercely. 'In order to' becomes 'to', 'prior to' becomes 'before'."
- Go for a colloquial style (this is part of why people enjoy reading newsletters)
- Correct errors fast. It enhances your credibility to admit promptly when your publication has been in error.
- Do post editing. "Editors don't always enjoy it, and it does smack of Monday morning quarterbacking, but I think it's invaluable. I try to be positive whenever I can, 'You did a good job here.' 'Will we be following up this one?' It does wonders for the staff to know that someone (me) is looking at everything we produce."

• Stress your independence. "My newsletters are produced by journalists. We are not 'members' or 'part of' any industry which we cover."

• Get feedback from your readers. We occasionally send questionnaires, perhaps 300, and get a 10% response. I also encourage each of my editors to call at least five readers a month.

• Be yourself, and don't ask editors to do anything which you find distasteful.

How to Work with Contract Editors

"Publishers can expand their range by entering contract arrangements with off-staff editors," says Emily Harris, Senior Vice President of Capitol Publications in Washington, "but there are plusses and minuses in the operation."

On the plus side

1. You can move quickly into new subject areas in which you have no in-house expertise.

2. If you contract with a "big name" in the area, your newsletter acquires instant credibility.

3. You will save money because contract editors don't require employee taxes and fringes, nor take up expensive space.

On the minus side

1. No matter how you arrange it, you have less communication than you have with an on-staff editor, which leads to:

2. Less in-put and control over editorial product

3. You usually have no back-up staff if your contract editor is hit by a beer truck.

Before entering such agreements, Harris recommends going through a disaster scenario when you discuss what you will do if and when the enthusiasm of your outside editor runs thin.

As further precautions she adds:

1. Always test-market the newsletter before you make a contractual commitment.

2. Make sure the prospective editor knows precisely what results are expected from the test to make the "go" or "no-go" decision.

Factors to Learn about Your Outside Editors

1. Is he/she reachable by phone?

2. How experienced is he/she in meeting deadlines?

3. How much is he/she counting on this outside income? (How important is your newsletter in his/her overall business operation?)

4. Can he/she write? (especially important with "big names")

How to Make Working with Outside Editors as Smooth as Possible

1. Designate an in-house honcho who is in charge of the publication at your shop.

2. Install a Quip system (a facsimile system which allows transmission of copy materials over telephone lines) for your editor to communicate with your office.

3. Make sure your editor is aware of your promotional department.

"Very few people outside of the newsletter business," Harris observes, "are remotely aware of the magnitude of marketing effort which is required to sustain a successful newsletter."

NAA has available copies of a sample contract between publisher and outside editor which Harris prepared. Major points of interest in the contract include:

1. Establishing that the publisher owns the newsletter and all rights

2. Establishing the publisher's right to edit copy as necessary

3. A non-competition clause written to protect the publisher

4. A definition of effective term which begins the contract with publication of Vol. I, No. I (allowing an out for the publisher if the test bombs) and providing for automatic annual renewal unless cancelled.

The contract also includes compensation schedule. Capitol bases their contracts on total circulation. "It's clean and easy to calculate," says Harris, but adds the figures on the sample contract are hypothetical and completely subject to negotiation in every instance.

Improving Telephone Interview Results

Since economics often dictate that news sources can only be contacted by cold telephone calls, learning to handle such interviews efficiently can improve your editorial content.

● When at all possible travel to industry conferences etc. to make contacts. Nothing can improve future telephone contacts more than having had a prior face-to-face meeting.

● Trade Information. Store up a couple current industry goodies to drop into your conversation with sources; people enjoy the idea of trading "inside information" more than being "pumped by a reporter."

● Keep Conversations Short. Make a list of questions in advance, cover them, say thank you, and get off the phone. Nothing dries out a source more quickly than making that source believe that the reporter has a lot of time to waste his time.

● Call During the Off-Hours of the Business Day. It's usually easier to reach people during the early morning hours. Higher executives, in particular, are likely to have more time to talk before the traditional workday begins.

● Follow-Up Your Telephone Conversations. Find something to send to a new source by mail to follow-up a phone contact. A copy of the issue containing the article in question is fine to secure an otherwise fleeting contact.

Salary Surveys Boost Readership

Salary Surveys are an editorial feature that boosts readership. Newsletter publishers should consider running a salary survey for the industry they cover editorially if it is in any way feasible. "Salary surveys are the one editorial feature that will maximize the readership of a business magazine whether the surveys are conducted well or poorly," John F. O'Connor of *Purchasing Magazine* says in a recent issue of *Folio* Magazine.

NAA is receiving a strong response to our current Editorial Salary Survey. When the editor was with another industry association the salary survey was our most popular annual feature; the American Society of Association Executives as an example has expanded their study to 64 pages covering about 30 position titles and sells it for $35 to its members.

The most valuable salary survey, from the publications' point of view, is one which can be aimed at a level where the recipient wants to participate and receive the study both so he can see "what I'm getting compared to peers" and also evaluate "what my subordinates are getting before I risk losing someone I want to keep." If your office has computer capability, it is also not an insurmountable task to make the results fairly comprehensive, breakdowns by geographical areas, sales volume of companies, etc.

An Index to Clear Writing for Newsletter Editors

Is the text of your newsletter written in a manner which is appropriate for the educational level of your audience? Robert Gunning, who died recently, published the "Technique of Clear Writing" in 1952 and developed what he called "The Fog Index," designed to evaluate the level of complexity in a piece of writing.

Gunning explained that his Fog Index was developed by averaging the number of words in the sentences of a passage and then counting the number of words with three or more syllables in every 100 words. The two figures are then added and the sum multiplied by 0.4. The resulting figure is said to equal the number of years of education needed to understand the passage. Applying the index formula, he gave John Milton a rating of 26, Harpers Magazine a 15, and the Gettysburg Address a 10. Gunning believed that a rating of 16 to 20 was appropriate for newspaper journalism.

Taking the February 25th issue of *Hotline,* we evaluated the article of "Appropriate Editorial Style" for newsletters (page 2) at 11.6. Realizing that this article contained a number of quotes which tend to shorten sentences and words, we also checked the article on collection practices (page 5). It scored 16.6.

The first two member newsletters at hand, *Creativity in Action* (Sidney Shore, Editor-Publisher, Sharon, Connecticut), and *Education of the Handicapped* (Capitol Publications, Washington, D.C.) scored 14.4 and 20.4 respectively on their page one articles.

This article scores 16.0.

Are Readership Surveys Worth the Money

Many newsletter publishers believe in the value of doing regular readership surveys. Others believe in them even if they don't always get around to putting one together.

In a recent issue of *The Ragan Report,* Larry Ragan takes a contrary view: *Never Ask Readers What They Want.*

"A mistake many well-meaning editors make is to ask their readers what they want to see in their publication. They shouldn't. The readers don't know. It's not their job to know. It's the editors'. But how can the editors know without asking? One way is to ask themselves what they would like to see if they were reading the publication instead of editing it.

"Strangely, most of us have heard the advice never to write something we would not read, but we seldom transfer such good counsel to the publications we edit. And when editors, reacting to such seemingly idealistic advice say that they are different from their readers, that they are better educated, have different interests, see the world different ways, they are in more trouble than they know.

"When a writer asked *New Yorker* Editor William Shawn how he sees his readers, he said, 'We've always had the view that our readers are people like ourselves...We don't think of them as a separate group...We've never changed a word because we're thinking, 'we understand this, but what about our readers?'

"...Shawn's point is a good one to remember. It requires us to imaginatively leap a gap that may sometimes separate us from our readers and to provide content that will answer a question like: "Were I on the assembly line, were I at the typewriter, or the keypunch machine, were I in the sales office or engineering department, what would I want to read?' The answer to that question will provide an editorial formula superior to all the readership surveys they don't have a budget for."

The Ragan Report, Lawrence Ragan Communications, 407 South Dearborn, Chicago, Illinois 60605 (312/922-8245)

Writing the Effective Story Close

Spend more time considering the impact of the close of your newsletter stories. Most newsletter journalism is written in traditional "inverted pyramid style" with most of the information emphasis and effort going to the lead sentence and paragraphs.

If your article doesn't have a memorable close, all the effort expended could be for nought, and readers will lay our work aside with a shrug and wonder why they read the piece.

Seven Suggestions For The Close

1. Repeat the theme of the lead (or rewrite the lead with added information.)

2. Summarize the purpose of the article by restating it in "one succinct paragraph."

3. In a feature story or lighter article use a play on words or aliteration to highlight the conclusion.

4. Save a startling statistic or a new piece of information for the close to make the main point.

5. Use an amusing quotation or antecdote from your main source.

6. Give advice on dealing with the problem raised in the article.

7. If you've made all your points, stop.

Impact, 203 N. Wabash Avenue, Chicago, IL 60601 312/263-2313.

CHAPTER VI
Everything You Wanted to Know About Fulfillment but Were Afraid to Ask!

One of the things newsletter publishers tend to have in common is that when they got into the business, they didn't give a great deal of thought to fulfillment. They thought about editorial coverage and, of course, about promotion, but once you wrote the newsletter and sold a subscription, the rest was presumed to be simple. You put the new subscriber "on the list," and he started receiving newsletters. In practice it turns out not to be quite that easy.

Fulfillment is a complex process involving processing of new orders, trial orders and conversions, address changes, additional subscription orders, renewal series, expires, etc., etc. While, basically, it may be true that promotion sells newsletters and editorial content sells renewals, efficient fulfillment is an important part of the process. Alfred M. Goodloe, President of Alexander Hamilton Institute, when discussing renewal asks, "How many of you still read your subscriber mail? Those of us who started small once did so religiously." He goes on to point out that if your mail includes too much correspondence of the type which reads "This is the fourth notice of address change," "The additional subscription I ordered isn't coming," "I paid, but you keep billing me," this type of fulfillment service from your circulation department will have appreciable effect on your renewal percentage.

The two basic decisions a publisher has to make about fulfillment are: (1) When will I be large enough to efficiently convert to computer operation? (The answer to this question may be 'not for a while'.) and (2) What type of manual fulfillment system is best for my present needs? An NAA study showed member publishers to be using computer fulfillment systems by a 3-2 margin. These data were developed from a survey which concentrated on availability of response from larger publishers. Among all newsletter publishers, the ratio is probably at least 3-2 manual systems.

Among the publishers using manual systems for list maintenance and fulfillment, three systems are the most common. About three-quarters use a Cheshire system and the remainder split more or less evenly between Addressograph and Scriptomatic systems. Each type of system has its plusses and minuses.

(Editor's Note) PACE OF CHANGE: When this chapter was originally drafted, it wasn't economically feasible to maintain your mailing lists and do subscription fulfillment in house with a mini or micro-computer. Now it is. Your author, however, has not as yet done so himself and doesn't pretend to understand computers. We refer you to the articles at the end of this chapter by Herb Messing of Compupower and Paul Levin of Construction Industry Press who do for more information about starting out with an in-house system. The most popular small machines, like the Apple or the Radio Shack TRS-80 are, we understand, quite suitable for this application (list maintenance) with off-the-shelf programming. CAVEAT. What these machines don't do as well, however, is editorial function word-processing, even with commercial wordprocessing packages (programs), they tend to be distinctly less user-friendly than dedicated word-processors.

The Scriptomatic system is the cheapest (a new machine runs about $2,000, takes up the least space in the office and is simple to operate—essentially idiot-proof). It also has drawbacks. The Scriptomatic cards are comparatively expensive (about $70 a thousand) and they wear out after a number of impressions (probably less than 50, certainly less than 100) and have to be remade. Aesthetically, even when the cards are new, they don't produce a very attractive envelope.

Addressograph machines are more expensive (a new machine and plate-maker will run about $4,000. Addressograph plates last forever, but the plate making equipment is very noisy (it's a lot like having a miniature metal stamping plant in your office). Addressograph machines are more delicate to operate than Scriptomatic, and clearing a jam is a far more complicated operation (usually involving screwdrivers, pulling, tugging and swearing—when a Scriptomatic card is bent or worn, it won't run through the machine, but it's easy to pick it out and toss it away).

Cheshire machines are the fastest and most efficient (and most expensive, the basic one-up machine set-up will run about $17,000). Cheshire cards are inexpensive—$10 a thousand—and appear to last indefinitely.

All of these machines are occasionally available on the market used or reconditioned (some from publishers who are converting to computer fulfillment). However, like electric typewriters, the demand for good used machines tends to exceed supply, so it isn't always possible to find one when you want it. There are risks of course, in buying used equipment, but the Scriptomatic and Addressograph machines in particular are pretty durable and should have a fairly long useful life if you can get a good used one.

The big ticket items, the Addressograph and the Cheshire systems are also usually available on a rental or lease-purchase basis. The Cheshire system runs around $300 monthly to rent and the Addressograph about $150. This might be a feasible alternative for the publisher who would like to control his list maintenance internally without committing to the major cash outlay of purchase.

This discussion of hardware has been included because we presume most publishers will want to own their own equipment. Admittedly, it does require a cash outlay, but it gives a certain security in knowing you can control your own mailing lists. In most larger cities both printers and office service firms offer list maintenance facilities. Many of them are very good, but it does involve entrusting your list to them (and hoping they will care as much about getting your newsletter into the mail on schedule as you do). One Washington publisher remembers the time when they were maintaining their lists with a local firm and the lady who owned the firm died suddenly. The business manager sprinted to the office to grab their trays of plates and get them out before the assets of the firm were seized for probate.

NAA talked with another publisher who, for each weekly issue, walks around the corner to an office services outfit, hands them a stack of Cheshire cards and his envelopes and, less than 10 minutes later, walks out with the addressed envelopes at a cost of $.03 apiece. For a hypothetical biweekly newsletter with a circulation of 1,000, this probably comes to about $1,000 a year in total cost (including invoices). The disadvantages are (1) not everyone has an office services firm "around the corner," and (2) when you get there and find out "the damn machine is broken down, I don't know when the service man will get here," you have a problem. Until this point, we've concentrated on the hardware portion of the fulfillment process. The second and more complex part is what could be called "software"—the actual in-office process of developing and maintaining the files and procedures which permit you to efficiently service subscription orders.

Operating a Manual Fulfillment System

The system described is a Cheshire card system, but the principles are basically the same for any system. As soon as a new subscription order is received, two Cheshire cards are typed. One goes in the general file which is used to mail the newsletters and the second card goes in the billing file. The cards can be typed on a normal typewriter.

If the newsletter is to be mailed first class, the subscription file doesn't have to be kept in any particular order, but zip code order is most commonly used. For one reason, if you subsequently decide to make a mailing to subscribers either under a second class permit or third class bulk-mail which requires zip-coding, you already have your addresses in that order.

The billing file is kept separate and filed by month of expiration. In addition to address information, much additional information can be placed on a Cheshire card, usually the date paid and the date of expiration. For example, an initial order is received in April, the card is marked for expiration in April the following year and filed at whichever point the first renewal notice should be generated. By "generate," in this instance, we mean if subscribers normally receive the first renewal invoice three months prior to expiration, come the following January someone pulls the card from the file and prepares the invoice for mailing. If the second renewal invoice goes a month later, during the intervening period this same "someone" has been marking off the cards of subscribers whose checks are received and refiling them for the following year. Then, a month after the first mailing, the same process is followed with a second renewal piece. Eventually, all that remains is the greatly diminished—we hope—number of "expires" which are then removed from both the billing and the mailing files. (In most publisher's renewal series, several pieces come after the date of expiration. Practice varies among publishers regarding whether any actual issues are mailed after the expiration date.)

You can also generate additional information from a manual system. When a subscriber's card is first typed, it can be marked to indicate what list it came from or what promotion piece was used. When renewals are received, the new expiration date is placed on the card, similar information can be entered.

One piece of information should definitely be placed on subscription Cheshire cards. The expiration date of subscription. There have been rumblings of regulatory or legislative action to require publication labels to include expiration date information—presumably so the subscriber who receives a renewal invoice can easily tell when his subscription really expires—while there is no immediate probability of this being required, it could save trouble to already have it in the system. More important, if you anticipate converting to a computer fulfillment operation in the future, it will save a great deal of time and trouble in the conversion process if this information is immediately at hand on the existing card.

Trial orders or "bill me" orders can be handled within this same system. The billing cards are simply placed in the appropriate place in the file and coded to show that they receive a different series of followup invoices or conversion mailings.

From a system as simple as the one described above, you can generate information about percentage response to various prospect lists and promotions, percentage of renewals (and which subscribers by original source renew best), what your results are on "bill me" and what your trial order conversion rates are and much more. One of the attractions of computerized fulfillment is that more proficient houses have programs to generate this type of management information. Essentially you push the button and it prints out. The same information is all there in the manual system described, but it requires a painstaking process of going through the cards by hand and removing the necessary data to calculate the various percentages. Computer fulfillment can be seductive, but isn't necessary for the smaller operation. NAA was shown extensive computer printouts by one multi-letter publisher concerning a new venture. We couldn't help noticing that all these folding sheets, the columns and rows of figures and so forth appeared to tell the publisher that, on this new newsletter, 26 subscriptions had been up for renewal in April and that results of the renewal series had been February, 6, March, 7, April, 4 and May, 2—total renewal percentage to date, 73%. Was all that hardware really necessary?

Most cautious publishers like to keep a third set of Cheshire cards for their complete subscriber list in a remote location (like home), so that, in case of fire or other disaster, they aren't effectively put out of business by lack of records on subscribers billing information.

How much time does all this take and how much does it cost?

For every thousand subscribers, you generate a certain volume of transactions. Some 2,000 or 3,000 cards must be initially typed, a certain number of additional duplicate cards typed to reflect changes in address during the year (a greater or lesser volume depending on whether your letter goes to a consumer or corporate audience). Additional time is necessary to generate and record billing transactions. If your newsletter uses a five part billing series that eventually draws a 70% renewal rate, that translates into a requirement to mail over 3,000 renewal invoices to gain those 700 renewals per 1,000 subscribers. If you accept unpaid orders and bill, and two-thirds of your subscribers take that option, that will require another 1,000 transactions.

In other words, for this hypothetical bi-weekly, a total of about 7,500 transactions are involved (typing cards and invoices), and about 30,000 cards are run through your machine to produce envelopes. Circulation and fulfillment directors NAA has talked with say a competent fulfillment clerk can handle perhaps 100 to 150 transactions weekly. Although this level of activity could probably be handled by one full time person, it probably requires more than one in most small operations because the person who was doing the job originally is also keeping the books and ordering office supplies and, along the way, added an assistant to work on this and serve as receptionist, etc. The 150 transactions a week are probably more than a full time job for one person if it also includes being responsible for generating a good bit of original correspondence—"We're sorry, our records indicate your check #4538 was never received. Would you please check your bank statement and let us know if it has been cashed or replaced with another," etc.

Finally, the great day comes when you are ready to convert to a computer system. General opinion seems to hold that a circulation of 5,000 is the low end of computer fulfillment practicality and 8,000 to 10,000 is a more logical figure. We are repeatedly cautioned to understand that, in general, converting to computer fulfillment will not save money. It may do wonders for your efficiency and staff morale, but it isn't usually "cheaper." (One large multi-letter publisher calculates that for what they pay annually to their service house, they could hire another eight clerks, rent a large room to put them in and continue to do it all manually—they don't imagine, though, that they could get the depth of management and accounting information their computer service offers.)

The first rule in selecting a computer house is get one that understands newsletter publishing. There are lots of service bureaus around. Most are probably competent, but newsletter fulfillment is a different ballgame than magazines, for example, and you should be leery of becoming the guinea pig through which a service bureau learns a new skill. Find out what other newsletter publishers the bureau you are considering is handling and talk with them.

The costs of making the conversion to a computer system.

All service bureaus used to charge a "conversion fee." With competitive developments this is no longer the case. Check bids you receive in this area. A charge of $.40 to $.50 a name for the initial conversion can be a significant factor in total cost (and, additionally, this can be a "negotiable" item before you sign the contract). After conversion is complete, the annual costs of list maintenance can run from about $1.50 per name (for biweekly labels, renewal invoices and list maintenance) to $3.00 per name (which will include various management and financial reports).

The best advice is "take everything they offer initially and see if it is of value to you." You'll probably find there are some reports you don't require so often (which you can change from monthly to quarterly) and there may be some you don't use at all. But it's valuable to see what you could get.

What is involved in the actual conversion?

"Going on to the computer" has replaced "meeting the big, bad wolf in the forest" as the conventional horror story for our times, but it doesn't have to be that bad. The better service bureaus will send you their people to work with yours. The initial process has to be a pain, but if you chucked your cheshire cards and bought an addressograph machine, you'd have to make 5,000 plates at once. Similarly, you have to prepare for the computer the information on your 5,000 subscribers. Without belaboring the 'garbage-in-garbage-out' formula, the computer is only a machine and it can't regurgitate anything it hasn't been fed originally. You may find you have to develop a system to shorten and reformat your addresses to fit the computer. You do have to code in information on "newsletter subscribed for," "expiration date," "number of issues ordered," "what price," "list source," "type of subscriber" (corpo-·

rate, individual, association, etc.). You can sometimes package these into groups—"all of the cards in this bundle fit this description." At a very rough estimate, it takes about 10 work hours to prepare this information for every 1,000 subscribers (one large firm converted 17,000 names, and it took six people—two of theirs and four from the bureau—three days to do it).

At that point you are in business. For at least the first issue that you receive your computer generated labels, we presume you'll want to run your previous system in parallel to cross-check the lists. The computer service bureau will deliver the labels regularly to you (or your printer or mailing house). Then you find your circulation clerk's workload drops dramatically because he/she no longer has to type invoices or mail second notices or prepare labels. All of that is handled by the service bureau. What you have to do is assemble the various orders that come in every week—renewals, new subscriptions, address changes, cancellations—enter the information required on the forms the bureau provides and shoot it off to them. As a rough estimate, this will cut the work load in half, so you can probably double your subscription list with the same in-house staff you had previously.

It takes, as a ballpark figure, about ten days from when you send information to the service bureau for it to wind up reflected on the list. For biweeklies (and possibly weeklies) this means you might have to mail one issue manually to new orders, the cancellations and address changes will receive one more issue before the change is affected.

Every publisher who uses a computer fulfillment system says the same thing. The efficiency is nice, but the real payoff is in the information you can get from the machine for your management purposes. Here are some examples of the types of reports a service bureau generates:

- Payment Rate Reports—show the distribution of time to pay across groups of subscribers starting in various months (distinguished between new orders and renewals).

- Renewal Rate Reports—show renewal rates across groups of subscribers whose orders end in various specified months.

- Expires Inventory—a count of subscriptions due to expire in each coming month.

- Activity Report—analysis of new orders, renewal orders, drops, cancels, and analysis of payments and adjustments made during the period.

- Aged Receivables—schedule of outstanding collectibles.

- Earned Income—can be produced for each regular issue showing the dollar value of the issue services. Takes into account the value of the issue for each subscriber.

- Subscription Liability—shows the dollar value of issues yet to be mailed to each subscriber.

As we said towards the beginning of the article—you could do all this with a manual system. All the information is available to you, but evidence shows you won't get it. There simply isn't enough time for most small publishers to sit down and figure out this sort of information. With the computer fulfillment systems, all you have to do is ask for it (and pay for it) and there it is.

Most publishers, as they grow, become sophisticated about their promotion track records (which list pays off, which promotions work, tests of premiums). With a computer fulfillment system you can become just as fancy with renewals. Most publishers on a manual system use the same renewal series for all subscribers. On computerized systems you can generate different messages for different groups of subscribers. You can easily test different messages, timings or premiums against splits of your lists. You could find out that how you massage your renewal series pays as many dividends as working with your promotional packages.

One More Alternative.

As we said at the very beginning of this chapter, many small publishers are eager to know when their operations will be large enough to make "going to computer feasible". It turns out in some instances, what they really mean is "When can I stop fooling with cheshire cards or get rid of that damn noisy addressograph plate machine?"

If all you really want is to have the convenience of computer-generated pressure-sensitive labels, you can place your mailing list "on computer" for a fraction of this cost. There are a number of smaller service bureaus around which will take your mailing list, put it on a computer and generate labels for you on demand. The cost for this is most reasonable, often less than $1.00 per 100 labels run.—The cost usually includes making whatever address changes you have and the additions and deletions. You don't get any of the various management and accounting reports a full service bureau offers, but you do have attractive labels and an end to some of the problems associated with various other types of equipment.

Five Circulation Management Problems

An old publishing industry bromide says it is easier to maintain a current subscriber than to sell a new one. How important is quality of subscriber service in circulation and fulfillment management to a successful newsletter publisher?

Beth Early, circulation manager at Capitol Publications (one of the largest newsletter publishers, with more than 30 newsletters and over 50,000 total subscribers) gives views on the importance of this area.

She identifies 5 areas as potential problems:
1. Slowness in responding to new orders
2. Difficulty in getting addresses changed
3. Inadequate delivery of newsletters
4. Inefficiency in handling special requests
5. "Remoteness" of the publishing operation.

1. Traditionally, the largest problem which creates order backlogs in newsletter operations is doing promotion and launching new newsletters without considering the staff capability to handle the incoming orders.

On a launch of a new product, she comments, "A major problem is often that people just don't understand that even if they return an order card the day they get the mailing, we didn't plan to publish Vol. One, Number One for 7 to 8 weeks, so we have them on the phone complaining before we ever get an issue in the mail."

2. On address changes or new additions, Capitol Publications has a 10-day turn-around with their computer service bureau. "On our biweeklies, depending on what day the change came in, this usually means one additional issue will go to the old address before the change is made. If people are concerned enough to call we type an envelope in my department and mail the next issue to the new address by hand."

3. A considerable number of "fulfillment" problems may actually be caused by the Postal Service, "Although, in all," Early says, "we don't have that many complaints with USPS. We use first-class delivery for most of our publications and, with the exception of it being almost impossible to get mail into New York City, service is pretty good. Where we have difficulty is with second-class. We use it for a couple of our monthlies and, apparently, delivery is good enough; but we also use the red-tag newspaper handling for *U.S. Oil Week* and delivery on that generates more complaints than all the rest of our publications combined."

4. When handling requests, "We try to respond directly to people who call, but we average about 100 calls a week. Too many of them insist on talking to me because my name is in all caps on all the newsletters and on our welcome letter. It's amazing that people will fight past one of my assistants or stay on hold in order to tell me *personally* of a change of address." Capitol also gets the sort of problems "which are inevitable as organizations get larger; two people from the same company call to change a name and give different new names to receive the subscription," Early added. "When we were small, I would probably have caught it, but if they talked with two different people when they called . . . You also get to know a certain small percentage of "problem cases," you dive for the bomb shelters when this person calls with the seventh change to their school system's five regular and 15 additional subscriptions to four different publications."

5. On "remoteness" of the publishing operation, "I think maybe we worry about this too much in newsletter publishing. I subscribe to a lot of magazines and none of them seem to want to make me feel like part of a family. I don't get 'welcome' letters, or 'thank you for renewing' letters or readership interest surveys.

"One point I try to emphasize with my people is that one thing that Capitol is very good at is taking checks off orders and putting them in the bank, so it's up to us in the circulation department to be equally good at getting those people on the list, making address changes and so on."

Computer Fulfillment for the Smaller Publisher

There is no longer a "magic number" of subscribers a newsletter needs to make computer fulfillment economically viable, according to Herb Messing of Compupower. A publisher who is just beginning can invest $2,000 to $3,000 in a personal computer (an Apple or Radio Shack) and using a canned, commercial program can produce labels for subscription fulfillment and for renewal billings. "There is no point," Messing says, "in starting off with any other type of system because you can continue to expand capability with an in-house system to meet your needs."

Considerations in Switching to a Computer Service

For the publisher who is not now using a service bureau, here are some guidelines from Messing to consider in making plans for a change-over:

• You need to have your records in good shape to start with. Switching to computers will not improve their quality. "I'm trying to resist the temptation to say 'garbage in garbage out,' but it's true."

• You may need a different type of employee to work with computer fulfillment. Manual fulfillment emphasizes "systematic routine, repetitive tasks." The computer does those. You will need an employee who can think. The employees you have now may not be the right ones.

• There is no such thing as 'the way the computer does it' or 'the way the system works.' The system can be set up to work anyway you want it to (accepting the caveat that not every service bureau or system can do everything) but you have to know what you want so it can be properly instructed (programmed).

• What specific features will you need the service handle? People tend to think "Our newsletter is simple. Twenty-four times annually and a 6-part renewal series." How many of these types of things are you presently using? Bill-me's, credit card orders, additional postage overseas, sales tax, binder premiums, paid and unpaid trials, subscription agency orders, purchase orders, advance renewals, extra issue bonuses, special mailing sorts (such as second-class or hand delivery). Each of these creates a need for additional specific programming instructions.

• How much will a service bureau cost? Somewhere between $1 and $5 per year per subscriber depending on how much you want in the way of financial and accounting reports. At the low end you get what you can do yourself with a micro-computer, basically a label generating system which produces mailing labels for issues and renewal notices.

"Is the personal and office computer boom going to put service bureaus out of business?", "Have in-house typesetters put typesetting firms out of business?" Publishers have to decide what businesses they want to be in. Many don't want to be in the computer business.

Most importantly, the cost of the hardware is not the real problem. Software cost is the killer. The industry rule used to be software costs ran 4-1 ahead of hardware—today it's getting worse. Newsletter publishers may also want more service than an affordable in-house computer can produce. One publisher asked me to evaluate his staff study which outlined about seventeen functions they wanted and identified a $12,000 machine they wanted to purchase. "Why did you pick that particular equipment, I had to ask. The answer was, 'that's what we felt we could budget for this project' because, in my opinion, they would have needed well over $100,000 in hardware and custom software for a system which could efficiently handle all of the functions they selected."

Messing's 3 Guidelines

1, Decide what business you want to be in. One newsletter publisher I know subscribes to seven computer magazines and tries to attend at least 2-3 shows a year. If you don't want to become that involved, a bureau is probably the right answer.

2. Start small. If you do decide on in-house, don't over-estimate what you can do. Add functions as you gain experience.

3. Avoid custom software. This cost will kill you. Design your system to use off-the-shelf programming.

Herb Messing, Compupower, One Harmon Plaza, Secaucus, NJ 07904 (201) 866-8600

Designing an In-House Computer System

"For the first month after I bought my computer it sat in its box in our office. I was afraid to open it," says Paul Levin, publisher at Construction Industry Press (CIP). "It came with a handsome instruction manual, bound in leather, but it wasn't written in a language I could read. Finally, I got a consultant who showed me how to plug it in and how to insert the diskette programs. That took a month or so. Then I ordered a printer by mail. By the time it was delivered and sent back to be replaced with a model I really needed, another 2-3 months had elapsed."

The good news is Paul has come a long way since then. The bad news, however, for smaller newsletter publishers considering computers, is that it both isn't as easy and costs more than you may think.

A smaller computer which will handle all common newsletter publishing functions (subscription fulfillment, prospect list maintenance, wordprocessing, accounts payable, general ledger and others) will cost $6,000-$7,000—smaller, lower-cost models may not have the horse-power to handle all the functions leading to unanticipated problems such as:

● Capacity for list maintenance is 3,000 names per diskette meaning your 30,000 prospect list has to be kept on 10 separate diskettes (resulting in ten separate zip order lists of labels).

● Your new high-speed printer (a $2,000 item) has more capability than the computer so it still takes 10-12 machine hours to produce those 30,000 labels. You begin a second newsletter and learn that you can't integrate new subscriber names. You have to essentially start over.

● With suitable hardware to perform all the functions listed above, you need software (programs). Even buying off-the-shelf, programs for every function will run at least $2,000.

● You don't plug it in and start computing. Levin estimates he spent an initial 200-300 hours familiarizing himself with the system, modifying his operation to fit the programs and vice versa. Not every smaller newsletter publisher wants to know that much about computers.

CHAPTER VII
Basic Elements of Successful Newsletter Promotion

Promotion is a key ingredient in successful newsletter publishing. While it is true that financial success in newsletter publishing lies in renewals and that the key to successful renewals is editorial quality, you can't get them to renew until you have sold them the first time. NAA studies reveal that about 90% of all promotion of newsletters is done via direct mail. This chapter will concentrate on outlining the basic elements of a successful newsletter direct mail promotional campaign.

The first element in the campaign is identifying the market for the newsletter. Traditionally, most newsletters have been launched by people who felt they had access to important information in a particular subject area that could make a successful newsletter. Less frequently, entrepreneurs have identified newsletter publishing as a potential profitable area and decided to create a newsletter vehicle to get them into the market. In either case, a basic mistake is selecting a subject and market area that doesn't really have the potential to support a successful newsletter. Conventional wisdom says that any newsletter, however successful, will be fortunate if it ever gains subscriptions from more than about 10% of the potential buyers. Example: A great deal is happening in Washington on both the political and regulatory fronts in the telephone industry that will strongly affect the independent (non-Bell) telephone companies. Is there a market for a Washington letter which gives them the news to react to what Congress, the FCC and Ma Bell are doing to the industry? There are only 1,500 non-Bell telephone companies in the United States (and about half of those are managed by five large holding companies), so while there does appear to be an editorial opportunity, it would be unlikely more than a couple hundred subscriptions at most could be sold. The 30,000 clinical neurologists in the United States look like a more promising market statistically.

How do you find out how many potential readers there are for your newsletter promotions and where do you get their names? The first element in developing a newsletter promotional package is finding and selecting your lists. Basically, lists of names can be obtained in two ways: You can compile them yourself, or you can rent them from their owners for one-time use. Renting is easier. The lists are supplied to you in ready-to-use form, usually one- or four-up cheshire labels. Good list brokers maintain entire categories of lists they are managing, and you can order all or portions of several lists. List rental prices vary widely from $30 to $35 per thousand names to over $100. Most commercial lists rent for under $60 and only the more exotic varieties (i.e. foreign name lists) command the very highest prices. NAA also has done a survey of its membership and has available a publication listing their lists of subscribers, expires, and prospects available for rent or exchange with other publishers. These lists tend to be a bit more expensive, but since they are for the most part composed of direct mail newsletter buyers, one that fits your subject area should be an excellent list for you.

While renting from list brokers is easier, compiling your own prospect lists may be more economical in the long run, as well as more effective. Newsletter veterans say that your own compiled lists are *always* more effective than rented lists—because you know who your real prospects are. (NAA rented a list of associations and found the National League of Professional Baseball Clubs on it.) While rented lists are almost always restricted to one-time use, once you compile a list of your own—admittedly more expensive and time consuming in the beginning—it is yours to use as often as you like.

The caveat here is for the direct response list. If you are planning on publishing a newsletter aimed at the widgit industry, a list of 50,000 widgit industry executives should be full of people interested in your newsletter. A list you compile yourself will probably be better because you can be more selective about who is really a Widget Letter prospect. However, a "direct response list," including 10,000 widgit executives who ordered trade magazines or books by direct mail would probably be best of all, because you know they are actively interested and have responded to direct mail promotions previously.

Where do I find the names to put on my compiled lists? A number of places. For a newsletter aimed at widgit industry executives, you could look at membership lists of widgit industry associations. The associations may also publish directories of widgit industry people and suppliers. *Gale's Research Directory of Associations* (Book Tower, Detroit, Michigan 48226), lists associations you can check for prospects. The American Society of Association Executives (1527 Eye Street, N.W., Washington, D.C.) is another good source of information about associations. You may have to join the association to get the membership lists, but supplier memberships are often nominally priced and worth the expense if the members are really good prospects for your letter. The United States Government may well maintain lists of people in the widgit industry. You might be able to obtain lists of attendees at industry conventions and trade shows. Similarly, industry trade magazines may be willing to rent you their lists.

It is important to remember that you usually face no legal prohibitions against retyping names from a list you rent for your own future use. Names and addresses are not copyrightable. It's a painstaking process to cross-check a list on cheshire labels and type prospect cards from it, but you may use the names you compile this way to build your own in-house prospect list. One caution is called for—some industry directories are sold with an explicit statement that their names, addresses and information may not be reused. Counsel advises NAA that this becomes a matter of contract and not copyright law. Be sure to check for such restrictions on any list you rent and consult with your attorney before making further use of names on it.

Adding names to your in-house list is really a matter of ingenuity. One veteran publisher remembers "having to date the secretary at that agency three times before I got the list of regional offices and officials I wanted."

Designing Your Promotion Package

Once you have your list of names, you're ready to design your promotional package. The traditional basic newsletter promotion package consists of a sales letter, a descriptive brochure, a response device and, perhaps, a return envelope. It may or may not include a sample issue of the newsletter itself.

Volumes have been written on how to design and develop an effective direct mail package—NAA doesn't intend to re-invent the wheel. There are some standard works in the direct mail promotion field. Anyone hoping to make a living in the newsletter business, and relying on direct mail promotion to make it all happen, probably ought to read all of them.

With that caveat, here are a few basics to keep in mind. Your prospect is a busy person. Why are you interrupting the seventeen other things he has on his mind to send him the sales promotion?

How long should my sales letter be? 'As long as it needs to be to do the job and no longer,' is the usual answer. To be specific, most newsletter direct mail sales letters are relatively lengthy, four to six pages is quite common. 'I'd never read a six page advertising letter' is a common initial reaction but, if you think like that, you risk making the common error of designing a promotional effort aimed at the wrong audience. Even with the very best lists, probably 90% of the people who receive your mailing are not really interested. They won't read your four page sales letter. They won't read a one-page letter. The smaller percentage of prospects who are seriously interested in your product want all the information you have to give them. If you have several strong selling points, it doesn't hurt to be somewhat redundant. Mention them more than once. You've got to use the letter to give him reasons why he needs and will benefit from your newsletter. If you have an established newsletter to promote, you have the advantage of a track record. You can cite the outstanding coverage you've already provided. If, however, you are promoting a new newsletter, you have to concentrate on the importance to him and his business of the information you will be covering. Typically, the crucial factors you have to promote are depth and details. Certainly newsletters can be timely—there are dailies in some fields and even a few telex wire information services—but the major factor that makes a newsletter successful is ability to deliver in-depth, specialized information not available to the reader from any other source.

Controversy boils constantly over how you can build the pulling power of your sales letter. Personalizing the address, using typeset instead of typewriter copy, using two-color printing or adding look-alike handwritten extralinear comments—there are experts who believe all of those factors, and others, will build your response rates. You'll have to read the literature and make up your own mind.

Here are some do's and don'ts two veterans in the field have supplied to NAA as keys in your sales prose.

Copywriter Don Hauptman suggests twelve relatively simple steps to preparing newsletter promotional copy:

1. Identify your "Unique Selling Proposition"—the attribute or element that makes your newsletter distinctive, special, unique, exclusive. Formulate it carefully. Write it down.

2. Translate the USP into a creative promotional concept—a provocative headline or envelope teaser that targets and "qualifies" your prospective subscriber, grabs his attention, and lures him irresistably into your copy.

3. Whatever device you used to hook the reader, expand on it, deliver what you promised, and make a natural, logical transition to the newsletter itself.

4. "What are my prospective subscriber's most important concerns, needs, problems?" Never stop asking this question. The answers will help you develop your USP, promotional concept, and copy.

5. Always address the *prospect's* concerns, needs and problems—and explain how your publication meets and solves them, to his benefit or profit. Avoid "manufacturer's copy"—the kind that dwells on you, your company, or your newsletter alone.

6. Back up your claims and promises with *specifics:* names, precise figures, documented facts. Superlatives are often not credible; concretes invariably have the ring of truth.

7. In describing your publication's content, the more the better. Include bulleted lists of articles, departments, standing features, subscriber benefits. You can never be certain which particular items will "turn on" any particular subscriber.

8. Try to project an image of *authority*—the idea that your newsletter is *the* publication in its field. This claim can be reinforced by citing your "scoops," accurate predictions, editor's credentials, third-party quotes, or other appropriate documentation.

9. Your prospective subscribers are people. If feasible, inject (relevant) elements of human interest into your copy: testimonials, anecdotes, real-life experiences, before-and-after case histories.

10. Digging pays off. Superficial preparation usually generates anemic copy. Do some research. Learn everything you can about your subject area and your market. "Brainstorm" ideas with a colleague—or by yourself with a pad and pencil. Then start drafting your promotion.

11. Write with enthusiasm. Far too many promotions display absolutely no interest, involvement, excitement, drama or passion. If the copy is flat and lifeless, how eager do you suppose the reader will be to reach for his checkbook?

12. If you can't do all of the above, find a specialist who can.

Guy Yolton Associates has the following advice for writing a sales letter:

1. Edit for "warm-up." Look out for phrases like "as a progressive businessman, we know you're vitally concerned about . . ." where the writer is just loosening up his throwing arm.

2. Edit for stoppers. Look out for industry jargon, "fulfillment situation," which all your prospects may not know. It may discourage them from reading further.

3. Edit for author's pride. The phrasing you are especially proud of may cause your prospect to stop and admire the craftsmanship of your prose and forget your sales message.

4. Edit for order. Do your points follow in logical sequence? You know what you mean to say, but will the reader understand?

5. Edit for reason why. Look out for "unsupported puffery." "The unparalleled resources of the publisher makes this newsletter unsurpassed"—you haven't proved anything by saying that.

6. Edit to stretch benefits. "Advantages" are within your product but "benefits" flow to the user—design your promotion to stress benefits.

7. Edit for your market. Know as much as you can about your potential reader.

You are never the best judge of your own prose. When you think you have your letter in pretty good shape, let someone whose judgment you trust read it and comment. Try to react positively to suggestions. (If you have a friend who is a newsletter publisher, excellent, but it doesn't really matter if your critic doesn't know a dynamite closer from pass interference—most of your prospects won't know much about the mechanics of direct mail promotion either.)

Should I Design the Package Myself or go to a Professional?

Once again, there is no hard and fast answer. You can spend a lot of money on a professionally-designed package and never know whether the package you could have designed yourself would have done just as well. Similarly, if you do it all yourself you won't know if something a consultant could have done might not have pulled better than your effort (*unless you test*—more on this later).

Like everything else in our economy, prices for direct mail promotion assistance vary greatly. You can get some basic help in writing a letter or designing a package for several hundred dollars, or you can pay ten times as much. Don't go into a contract blind. There are no particular qualifications for becoming a "direct mail consultant." Look for people who belong to their own industry organizations, the Direct Mail Marketing Association and the Direct Mail Creative Guild. Ask to see samples of work they have already done. Talk to their previous clients. NAA knows a publisher who spent a lot of money working with an "expert" who told him flatly "orange and purple are the colors that sell." His promotions all look like the Hobart football team. It didn't work for him, but promotional assistance doesn't come with guarantees. We should add, on behalf of the professionals in the field, that the annual Newsletter Clearinghouse Promotional Package Award (a contest that evaluates the overall package design *and* documented results), usually is won by a package put together by a professional for a client publisher.

List Testing

List testing is far too broad a subject to cover in detail (much more on lists in Chapter XV), but we can offer a few basics. Statistically, say the experts, a valid test requires a large enough universe to yield 30 to 50 positive responses. If you're hoping for an overall return of 1%, you have to have a list of 3,000 to 5,000 to test. If you have 25,000 prospects you could then test your package and the professionally designed package each over 5,000 names and mail the remaining 15,000 the one that pulled more responses. The same applies for testing prices, or premium offers, or including sample issue or what-have-you. If the entire list you are planning to hit with this promotion is only 4,000 names, you really don't have enough to do a valid statistical test, so you are better off simply wetting your finger, sticking it in the air, and going to the entire list with what you judge to be the best package.

If you are testing a brand new publication, the experts suggest you test your absolutely best prospects. Your Christmas card list would be a good place to start. If they can't be induced to order in satisfactory numbers, it is probably an excellent early sign that the market may not be there. For a test of a new list for an existing publication, or a test of a new package or offer, experts normally suggest you test only a random sample of the entire list (every nth name).

One of the most tempting fallacies in list testing is deciding that, for some reason, the list just didn't test as well as you were sure it would, but that you can correct that. The bromide to keep in mind is, "Sick pups don't nurse." If you only received a marginally successful result for a test, you can probably re-test and move up the percentage response closer to your original goal by changing the premium offer or improving the price, but professionals say you are better off to accept the results you got for the first test as indicative of the prospects' response to your product.

John Stewart, the chairman of the Bureau of National Affairs, adds one other memorable dictum: "The only market survey worth a darn is the one which asks the prospect to commit money." He has no faith in surveys which ask, "If we were to publish a widgit industry newsletter, and it contained such-and-such news and cost so much, would you be interested?" This breed of surveys will get you a gratifying percentage response, and a large number of prospects, but it's an expensive way to do business if they don't generate cash orders.

Should I Include a Sample Newsletter with my Promotion?

Most of the industry experts (and the NAA Survey of Industry Practice) say "No." It seems, to borrow a word from George F. Will, "contra-intuitive" to beginners to believe that you can ask people to buy a product they haven't seen, but results indicate intuition isn't always right.

There are several reasons for this.

First is the "representative" quality of any individual issue of your newsletter. You probably have a number of subject areas in which you hope to provide outstanding editorial coverage. It would be very unusual if they were all well-represented in a single issue. Periodically, you hope to get "exclusives" in some area. Again, you usually can't schedule those for the issue you've pre-selected for a promotional mailing.

Some publishers get around this problem by putting together a "compiled issue" for promotion, a sort of all-star line-up of stories from recent issues. Obviously this works best with newsletters whose forte is not timeliness. Others suggest, if your newsletter is normally an 8 to 10 page biweekly, putting out a four-page sample issue with promotions to give the flavor of your normal coverage, but saving printing and postage expense.

Second is the question of expense. Printing a large number of extra issues and paying the postage to get them delivered in a timely manner will usually add 40 percent to 50 percent to your total promotional costs. Some publishers argue that by including a sample issue, they get a sufficiently higher response rate to justify the additional cost, but NAA's study shows they're distinctly in the minority. The 1980 NAA Promotional Practices Study showed that only about one publisher in four aiming at a consumer audience ever uses a sample issue. Newsletters going to corporate markets are more likely to include samples: almost half have done so at one time or another. However, we estimate that probably no more than 10 percent to 20 percent of total newsletter promotional packages regularly contain a sample issue of the newsletter.

If your promotion package is printed by someone other than the printer who is doing the newsletter, you also add a coordination headache. It's hard to sit down with 20,000 extra dated copies of your newsletter while waiting for another printer to supply the rest of the package (and the response card isn't printed yet because the artwork hasn't arrived from the graphics person). Coordination of delivery of various pieces of a promotion, lists, artwork, envelopes is definitely one of the prime "if anything can go wrong, it will" areas.

How to Design your Brochure

In your own mailbox you probably have been noticing not only an increase in direct mail offers, but an increase in the costliness and sophistication of the materials used. People who have the expertise and the money to do extensive testing appear to be learning that spending more on the promotional package helps results. This doesn't necessarily extend to newsletter publishers. The results of the NAA Promotional Practice Study did not show any direct correlation between publishers who used the more expensive promotional packages and the ones enjoying the highest response rates. One rule of thumb holds it isn't necessary to make the promotion more elaborate than the product it is selling. If your newsletter is not a glossy four-color product, your promotion doesn't have to be either.

It seems contradictory, but newsletters aimed at consumer audiences, which tend to be lower-priced, often use more elaborate, expensive promotions. A major reason for this, however, is economies of scale. If you're promoting to a list of 50,000 or more, new printing technologies can permit you to produce elaborate glossy two and three color brochures, which simply aren't viable for the corporate newsletter being promoted to lists of a few thousand at a time.

Often successful promotional brochures use the same basic graphics as the newsletter, sometimes featuring a photo of a first page of the newsletter with additional copy explaining the type of news the letter provides. Testimonials appear to be the stock in trade of newsletter promotion. If Ed Meese has said that he couldn't face Monday morning without your newsletter, of course you use that in your next mailing. (One note of caution: financial advisory newsletters are prohibited from using testimonials in advertising. Even if you aren't sure you may ever have to register as a financial advisory publisher, don't print up enormous quantities of literature including endorsements which subsequent SEC registration may make unusable).

Another reason for using a brochure is that many newsletter publishers are now offering more than a weekly newsletter to subscribers. If your full service will include a reference file with periodic updates, special reports, a call-in hotline, a document service or what-have-you, the brochure gives you the opportunity to describe these additional benefits of becoming a *Widgit Industry News* reader.

NAA had good results with a simple brochure entitled "Ten Reasons Why You Should Become a Member of the Newsletter Association of America." The inside copy of the six panel brochure gave a descriptive paragraph to each of these selected ten benefits of membership (remembering the adage that features lie in your product, but benefits flow to the reader-user). The additional panels (in relatively fine print) gave basic information about the structure of NAA dues and classes of membership, and the last two panels were perforated to become a business reply card membership application. We're not holding it out as an incomparable piece, just indicating that it was relatively simple, low-cost and effective. We've subsequently added additional color emphasis to the sales letter, and graphics to the brochure, and we find this seems to pull better.

As mentioned earlier, Howard Penn Hudson's Newsletter Clearinghouse holds an annual competition for newsletter promotional packages. You might ask them if you can see some of the winning entries for ideas you could use in designing your promotion. If you face competing newsletters already in the field, write and ask for a sample issue. You'll normally receive the full promotional mailing, which will give you a chance to evaluate what they are doing.

One final word about promotional prose. The professionals, the people who make their living writing sales literature, often tend to employ more dramatic language than neophytes might use. You may feel "I'm selling valuable information to a sophisticated audience, not soap." but before the audience can buy your product, you have to catch their attention. Don't be shy in headlining the special virtues of your publication.

The Response Device

The final element in the basic promotional package is the response device that allows your prospect to order your publication. Always remember the first rule of sales—never forget to ask for the order. You have two basic considerations in structuring your response device: (1) Should we include a postage paid envelope? and (2) Are we willing to bill or should we require payment up front?

About two-thirds of the publishers in the NAA survey who promote to consumer audiences require payment in advance and include a business reply envelope (BRE). One NAA member publisher, however, swears he can document that including a nonpostage paid envelope increases his response. (The only reason he can figure out, he says, is that the prospects like "the sense of participation" they get from putting on a stamp—sort of like the Duncan Hines people "improving" their cake mix sales by requiring the housewife to add her own eggs and milk.) Again, in the literature you will find discussion of creating this sense of participation by asking the prospect to "place the gold sticker in the slot to indicate which type of subscription you wish to order" and so on. Some experts believe such devices are effective.

For newsletters aimed at corporate audiences, the percentage of those including BRE's drops to under half. (The thinking is that your envelope will only get lost in their purchasing department. Their check will come back to you in their own envelope—so why go to the expense of including yours? For another thing, the typical corporate or government seven-part purchase order won't fit into your #9 BRE. Among corporate newsletter publishers nearly 90% are willing to accept unpaid orders and bill. Publishers of business newsletters appear not to have significant problem in collecting unpaid orders. In addition, about half of the consumer newsletter publishers will permit credit card billing (VISA, etc.). It costs a small percentage, but it gets money in the door reasonably close to up-front.

Since the response device is the place to print order information, it also offers a place to make special offers for extended subscriptions and special prices for including cash. A number of publishers offer either a better price, an extended subscription or a premium for "cash-with" orders—it's usually worth it to try to get the most cash possible up from and minimize billing and collection expenses.

Normally your response device is the cheapest part of your promotion to print, so some publishers put price information only there.—That way they can change offer, or price structure, entirely without having to change their more elaborate and expensive brochure package.

Put some thought into including a sales message on the response device. If you're including an envelope, you have a whole side of a card to work with. Most publishers hate to pay to mail blank pieces of paper. Include a sales message on that reverse side of the response card. The ideal is to craft the response card so well that it conveys in miniature your entire sales effort, so that when it becomes separated from the rest of the package, it will stand on its own. Certainly, for this reason be sure to include your name and address on every piece.

Don't forget to include a keying device if you're testing. The simplest way to keep records of responses is to put a key—2A1 or BCE—on the card to tell you which list the order is coming from.

How Much Should the Whole Promotional Package Cost Me?

The industry rule of thumb used to be about 25¢ apiece ($250 a thousand) for a bulk mail promotion including: a sales letter, brochure, response device, BRE, envelopes, list rental, mailing house charges and postage. If you were promoting in larger quantities, say 50,000 or more, economies of scale could sometimes reduce that cost to 20¢ apiece or even lower. With today's inflation, publishers reporting to NAA indicate that it is increasingly difficult to keep these "typical costs" under 30¢ to 35¢ for the basic promotion and 25¢ to 28¢ at the larger volumes. Obviously, adding a sample issue of the newsletter (or using first-class postage) adds significantly to the per piece promotional costs. Of the corporate newsletter publishers in the NAA survey, 20% reported spending an average of 54.1¢ on their promotional packages. Overall average costs reported, however, were 25¢ for consumer newsletter promotions and 30¢ for corporate promotions (about five in six fell in the 20¢ to 35¢ bracket).

We should add that veteran publishers stress it isn't really the cost of the individual promotional package that's vital, but the cost per sale. If you are marketing a $375 weekly newsletter, you can spend $1.00 apiece on promotional packages and get a .4% response rate and make money, while if you are promoting a $39 consumer monthly, you have to be much tighter on cost of individual packages and much more concerned about response rate.

Four Other Questions about Successful Newsletter Promotion

a. How do I establish the price of my newsletter?
b. Should my promotions include a premium offer?
c. How frequently should I promote?

d. How about other promotional ideas for direct mail, as well as things like telephone marketing and space advertising?

A. *Pricing*. Pricing a newsletter is a metaphysical exercise. The best price is the one which brings in the most revenue; it doesn't necessarily bear any direct relationship to cost. Having said that, however, we realize it isn't practical to expect you are going to get twelve subscribers to pay $9,000 a year for a newsletter. In the real world, your decision is whether it is more feasible to try for 2,400 at $90 a year or 1,500 at $150 a year. (Not only does the second example bring in $9,000 more income, but you would also save on production, paper and postage). If your prospect list is large enough you can split-test for price and see.

A word of caution here. Pay careful attention to how you split your lists for price testing. Try not to wind up with two executives in the same office receiving widely differing price offers for the same product. One veteran publisher had some problems of this type with a price test, but handled the call-ins most diplomatically by saying, "We're price testing a new product. We'll be happy to have your order at the lowest price offer you received."

Secondly, in a practical sense, your pricing policy has to be dictated to some extent by the market place and competition. Do you have competitive newsletters in the market? What are they charging? At present, for example, biweekly newsletters aimed at corporate audiences run in a price range from $100 annually (the low end is aimed at education and non-profit institution audiences) to more than $400 for very specialized corporate audiences (usually Fortune 500 companies).

Price is only one factor in successful newsletter promotion, but it looks much more favorable initially if the chief competition for what you plan as a $187 biweekly is a $325 weekly than if someone else is already publishing a $127 biweekly. Returning again to conventional wisdom, it is sometimes said that all prices should end in a seven.—We don't know if there is statistical back-up for this, but some publishers believe it. In a more practical vein, if you are publishing a number of similar newsletters, it makes sense to use different prices so you know what has been ordered when you get a check for $127 and a voucher saying "for the newsletter."

One final word on pricing. Don't set your price too low. For one thing, many publishers believe price equates with quality in the minds of readers and higher prices draw a better response. (One publisher who had increased hs ticket $40 told NAA, "I didn't really need that much of an increase, but my competition had gone up and I didn't want to look cheap.") Also, nothing is more frustrating than having a newsletter with a very successful promotion response that isn't bringing in enough money at the current price to make any profit for the publisher. One combination that might allow you to have the best of both worlds is the "introductory offer" (for charter subscribers only $129—full price will be $179). Doing this may not only get you a good cash response in the door up front, but give you built-in subscriber acceptance of your "real price" at renewal time.

Consider raising your price regularly. Most business newsletter publishers have found that increasing price has little effect on renewal rates; readers expect it. What is dangerous is holding the line on prices for several years and then finding yourself in a situation where you need to have a significant jump. That *can* have adverse effects.

Experience shows a smaller increase annually is better received by the market.

B. *Premium Offers*. Eighty percent of the NAA member publishers report using premium offers of some type. About a third of the premiums, however, are price offer variations (three extra months if you order now or include a check). The large majority of "real" premium offers are special reports or books. Again, it is your decision whether you give the special report to everyone who orders now or hold it out for those who include a check. (Or you can have two premiums and offer them both—one to all orders and one only to those who pay now.) Your premium offer shouldn't overpower your product. Admittedly, economics of gaining direct mail subscribers are such that you can afford to give away almost anything to acquire a subscriber, but if you make your premium offer a $40 reference book, you may find at renewal time, when you hope to start realizing real profits, that what you sold a year ago was not a subscription to your newsletter, but your premium, and in order to renew the subscriber you need to offer an equally attractive premium.

Second, your promotion should bear some direct relation to the product you are selling. A copy of "How to Prosper During the Coming Bad Years" by Howard Ruff is an outstanding premium for his newsletter. Experience shows that premiums such as pocket calculators or desk calendars don't really pull as well as "an exclusive special report on the financial structure of the widgit industry, available only from Widgit Industry News for *WIN Letter* subscribers." Many publishers have found that a report compiled from past newsletters can make a most effective premium (especially if their editors haven't knocked off a New York Times list best seller during the past year).

One promotional specialist suggests you put a price tag on your premium and offer to sell it, both making a few extra bucks on editorial product you've paid for and creating an additional "sense of value" for the premium you are offering to give away with a newsletter subscription. This advice is directly contradicted by (a) one publisher who states, in his experience, that given such an option the prospect almost always opts for the lower cost choice, the book or special report, rather than the newsletter, and (b) another consultant who says the point to sell is that your premium is priceless because it comes from sources unique to the *WIN Letter* and is simply not available in any other way than by subscribing. This illustrates probably the most important single point in the entire chapter: PROMOTION IS AN ART AND NOT A SCIENCE—THERE ARE NO FINAL ANSWERS. A promotional concept which knocked the socks off one audience may lie down on the floor and die for you—or vice versa.

How about trial offers and multi-year offers. Quite a few publishers are willing to offer trial subscriptions. The NAA study shows 60% of consumer publishers and 44% of corporate publishers do so. You do create an additional administrative headache for yourself when you do this because you have to set up and administer a duplicate renewal cycle for expiring trial subscriptions as well as your regular program for full year renewals. Interestingly, although they make less use of them, publishers of corporate newsletters report a significantly higher success rate in converting trial offers to full year subscriptions (47% to 25%). Perhaps the old cliche is true, that once you get a corporate client to buy something, it often tends to get established in their purchase order routine and will be automatically renewed.

When designing a trial offer, make sure that your introductory price bears some relation to your regular full year cost. If you are marketing a $150 biweekly, a three month trial for $39 would be about right. If you make the offer too attractive, you may find that you have brought in a number of "browsers" who won't be seriously interested at your full price while you certainly, considering handling and overhead, lose money on trials alone.

Should I try for multi-year subscriptions? This type of offer is well established in the magazine business, but is relatively new in newsletter publishing. Half the consumer letter publishers offer them, but only a third of the corporate newsletter publishers do. In both instances only about one subscriber in ten takes advantage of the offer, even though it usually includes a discount off the full price subscription. Two options for making this decision: (1) You can drive yourself nuts trying to figure future costs including assumed inflation rates and calculations of future value of money, or (2) you can figure that the folks at Time-Life have already done the work with their computer, and if they are willing to give you five years of *Time* at a guaranteed rate now, the numbers must show, regardless of future cost increases, it is worth it to them to have your check today and not have to send a renewal invoice for 4-1/2 years. It may be especially valuable for new publishers who, frankly, need cash now to get off the ground.

C. *How Frequently Should I Promote?* The conventional answer is that you keep going back to a list over and over and over until the returns don't equal the costs of the promotional mailing. NAA has publishers in the membership who promote ten and twelve times a year to their hottest lists. The current industry averages, however, show that corporate newsletter publishers promote to their best lists an average of a little more than four times a year (4.15) and consumer newsletter publishers hit theirs just under two and one half times (2.46).

An important consideration is your financial structure. Large, well established publishers can afford to take a first year loss in start-up costs for a new publication and anticipate contributions to profit from renewals in the second, third and future years. Neophytes are seldom well enough capitalized to afford such a luxury. One multi-letter publisher tells NAA that they haven't launched a new vehicle in the past five years that has done well enough initially to have supported a new newsletter publishing venture on its own. With their financial structure and track record, experienced publishers are usually more than willing to keep promoting as long as results come anywhere near covering costs, and wait to realize profit in later years.

Don't Ever Be Too Poor To Promote. If there was a cemetary for failed newsletters, many of the headstones would read, "We had a good product, our promotion and renewal response rates were pretty good, we just didn't have enough money to do enough promotion." You can't let this happen to your newsletter. An experienced financial man suggests the following order for paying your creditors and committing the cash you do have.

1. Pay your editorial employees—without them you don't have a product.

2. Pay your federal withholding and other taxes.—You don't want to go to jail.

3. Pay your promotion creditors (printers, typesetters, mailhouse, etc.) and keep on promoting.

4. Pay all your other creditors in the order in which they harass you.

5. Pay yourself.

Timing Your Promotions. In timing your promotional campaigns, performance of the U.S. Postal Service is a factor which has to be taken into account. You can hardly plan or design a new promotional effort until you have a reading on the results of the preceeding one. The conventional guidelines used to be: 17 business days after you received the first response returned to your office from a bulk mail promotion, you had one-half of the total response you were going to get. With today's postal service you might add another week to that figure. It takes about six weeks for enough of the dust to settle to see how your last effort did. Many successful multi-letter publishers put each publication on a promotion schedule. They promote quarterly. They don't necessarily attempt to create four all-new different, exciting promotional packages a year, but they realize the basic principle of newsletter direct mail: "If you don't send mail, you don't get orders."

Are There Specific Times I Should Mail? It depends on your audience. Newsletters aimed at education audiences don't mail in the summer or during spring vacations. If literally everyone in the widget industry is at the international widget meeting the second week in October, don't schedule a mailing to be on their desk that week. (Schedule yourself to be in an exhibit booth at the convention taking orders.) Everyone in the world appears to mail the first week in September and January. They do this because industry studies show January and September to be the best months of the year for direct mail results.

You might want to stay away from these months so as not to get lost in the crowd. *The Ruff Times* does its heaviest mailings in the fourth week of the month, because they have found that when people are paying bills they are in the best frame of mind to subscribe to Howard Ruff's philosophy. Try to be aware of any special situation in the marketplace you are trying to reach.

Should I Mail My Promotions First-Class or Third-Class? If you do mail first class you will be in a distinct minority. In all only about 20% to 25% of newsletter promotions (which are likelier to include a dated sample issue) go by first class. Presumably those using first class believe that first class mail gets a better reception—is more likely to get by the "secretary barrier" and onto the prospect's desk rather than be tossed in the circular file as "junk mail."

D. *Other Types of Promotional Ideas*

1. *Sampling.* Identify a list of your top prospects and send them a series of newsletter issues to be followed with a letter saying, "Now that you've seen the *WIN Letter* we know you'll want to become a subscriber." Be careful (both here and in designing your response device) to insure that you are in compliance with postal service regulations governing sending out anything which looks like a bill for material which has not been ordered (DMM Section 123.4). One publisher gets good response with a variation of this idea by asking his present subscribers to give him names of friends to get gift trial subscriptions—"Wally Jones thought you'd be interested in the *WIN Letter*."

2. *Space Advertising.* It works for financial advisory publishers. Very few other publishers report much success with space ads. It's a good way to generate a lot of inquiries to add to your prospect lists, but it usually doesn't bring in many orders. One virtue of space ads is, if you include an order coupon with your space ad, you do get a quick response. You know literally in a few days if space in that publication is going to work for you.

3. *Point-of-Sale.* Is there any way you could arrange to display your material so people could pick it up? One successful newsletter aimed at supermarket discount coupon collectors gets display space at supermarket checkout counters.

4. *Telephone Promotion.* It is expensive and it can create problems in collecting from those folks who said "yes" on the phone. Some publishers believe it works. They find it especially valuable for fast testing on short list segments of AAAA prospects.

5. *"Inflation Fighters."* Like the special charter price mentioned earlier, inflation fighter specials are a way to both give the prospect and customer a price advantage and bring cash in the door earlier. Offer them a special early renewal. "Renew now at the current price and be protected from inflation-caused increases."

6. *Co-op Advertising.* A couple of sources do space ads or produce catalogues on a co-op basis. The theory is that these enable you to reach marginal prospects to whom you wouldn't direct mail. It appears to work better for consumer than corporate newsletters.

7. *Loose Deck Mailings.* The Standard Rate and Data Service Directory lists a number of mailers who put together loose deck promotions. (The prospect gets a series of cards offering different products and services in a related area.) You could find an opportunity to participate in an offer in your industry area. Publishers with experience here tend to caution that this type of promotion works a little better for books and/or special reports than it does for full price newsletter subscriptions.

Check Points in Planning a New Package
A list of check points to consider when you plan to design a new promotional package:

The Basic of Your Publication
● Name—would a new title be more descriptive of where your newsletter is now...or sexier?
● Frequency—it's nice to have "too much news" for your eight-page biweekly, but perhaps a weekly would be an attractive option.
● Structure—could you add a reference file with periodic updates or institute a "telephone hotline"?

Your Editorial Features
● Should you do more interviews?
● Are you able to get "exclusives"?
● Do you have regular features—departments, issue summaries, calendar of events, people in the news, publications of interest, an annual index?

Elements of Your Package
● Envelope design, size, window, teaser copy.

- Sales letter vs. brochure—replace your brochure with a four to six page letter or vice versa.
- Main point. What is the *single most important reason* prospects should have your newsletter—is this your headline?
- Price comparisons. Is your publication cheaper than a couple of hours of a lawyer's time??? Do you have competition? Should you mention them in the promotion? How are you positioning your publication vis-a-vis theirs?
- Editorial inserts. Take the listing of great articles you have published out of the sales letter and let it stand by itself. This is also a good place to use testimonials. If you've gotten some media coverage, some publishers find it effective, albeit expensive, to reproduce the magazine or newspaper article for promotional purposes.
- Editor's credentials—if you've got 'em, flaunt 'em.
- Publisher's letters—think about using one in your package.
- Using a sample—conventional wisdom says "no," but you might have an issue which is so good you would want to use it.

Features of Your Offer
(The real answer is test, but at least think about these:)
- Discount—perhaps combined with a limited time offer.
- Two or three year subscription discounts.
- Premium—add, change, improve.
- Credit card option, bill-me's, should you?
- Double premium for cash with—second can be small, but they pull more checks.
- Trials, short-term or even "free."

These are elementary points, but if you start at the top and work through the list, you will normally come up with a number of ideas for design of a new package. If you're planning to use a consultant, it becomes mandatory because he/she will amost certainly need the answers to all these questions.

Study Completed on Direct Mail Response
January and February remain the best months for direct mail response. Prescott Lists' *List Insights* cites a new study by direct mail consultant Paul Bringe and compares it to a study done by the Direct Mail Marketing Association (DMMA) about six years ago. In both studies January's response rate is listed at 100% and all succeeding months' rates are compared to it. The interesting factor is the amazing similarity between the results of the two studies.

Month	Percentage Response (Paul Bringe's Study)	Percentage Response (DMMA Study)
January	100.0	100.0
February	96.3	96.3
March	71.0	70.0
April	71.5	71.5

May	71.5	72.0
June	67.0	68.0
July	73.3	73.3
August	87.0	84.0
September	79.0	79.0
October	89.9	89.9
November	81.0	81.0
December	79.0	74.0

List Insights gives another interesting table—an analysis of direct mail received by month:

January—9.9%	May—8.9%	September—6.7%
February—9.4%	June—5.1%	October—12.1%
March—8.3%	July—6.0%	November—11.1%
April—9.1%	August—8.6%	December—4.9%

This study covered a mix of direct mailers, the bulge in October/November is probably pre-Christmas mailings to consumer lists, but apart from that, the correlation between the percentage of mail received and the response is obvious. The unanswered question is:

"Are June and July lousy months for direct mail only because everyone "knows" they aren't good times to mail, and therefore stays out of the mail?"
List Insights, 17 East 16th St., New York, N.Y. 10010

How Not to Use Your Head in Direct Mail

Newsletter publishers are often too intellectual, too involved with their subject and business and too rational in their approach to it to be successful promotional writers and designers according to copywriter and direct mail consultant, George Duncan of Boston. "Direct mail is not an intellectual medium, it's an emotional one. It's still exciting to see the mailman coming down your street and the arrival of the mail is an "event" in most offices. What's new, what's happening, what are we getting?"

There are three types of features common in direct mail that most newsletter publishers probably wouldn't use, but which are effective.

1. *Sweepstakes.* A sweep is basically a game; they're used because they still work. "Personally I think they would work if the prize were $5,000 instead of a quarter-million. People just like to play."

2. *Involvement Devices.* "It sounds dumb, but every test I've ever seen shows that including a token or a sticker or what-have-you increases response to direct mail"

3. *Dummy Checks.* "I created some of the first of these in the newsletter business when I was with Ziff-Davis nearly 20 years ago, but I still open them when I get them. I'm sophisticated, I'm a pro, know it's not a real check in there for me—but I still open the envelope."

- One of my first bosses told me always to remember in writing copy, 'tell me about my lawn, not your grass seed.'
- Don't assume the reader will take time to interpret. You have to spin it out for him. Lay out the benefits he'll receive from your newsletter.
- Facts are not necessarily benefits.—You can't simply outline what the content of your letter is—make the step with him to explain how these facts benefit him.

Envelopes. Too often we think, "We're a business publication going to a business audience. A plain #10 dignified business envelope is best." The envelope has two purposes: (a) to get itself opened and (b) to get the prospect's mind started in the direction of your sales message—to help him concentrate on your subject instead of the 17 other things which are going on in his office.

How about the plain window envelope (no corner card, no teaser copy) with the prospect name showing. "Sure," Duncan says, "the idea is the prospect will open it because it looks like a bill—and there's the problem, as soon as he sees it isn't, it has lost the entire message to him. 'Whew,' he says, 'it's not another damn bill.' and tosses it."

Paper Stock and Color Use. Textured paper always outpulls plain, and colored stock always outpulls white. "There is no rational reason for it, it's simply an emotional response."

Brochures. You may think we do not need a fancy brochure for our newsletter, it isn't fancy, it's typewriter copy, no color, just black on cream. "A brochure is a flag," Duncan says, "I don't expect the prospect reads every word in it, but if it's successful, it helps create some interest, helps move him into the sales letter in a frame of mind to think about your subject area."

Sample Newsletters. "It's a terrible risk, unless you're sure every issue conveys your entire sales message. It doesn't matter that you send along a great sales letter, too often the prospect won't read it. He feels he doesn't have to read about why you have a great product, he's got the real product in his hand."

Copywriting. Too many newsletter promotions over-explain about the publisher. "I'm an expert. I've spent 15 years in the field. I've selected this news you can't be without. I'm making this offer for a limited time." Please try to remember his lawn—not your grass seed.

George Duncan, 29 Concord Avenue, Cambridge, Mass. 02138

Checkpoints in Planning a Promotion

Consultant Milt Pierce's rules for writing a smashingly effective direct mail response copy.

1. Write long copy—if the product you are selling is designed to be read.
2. Every letter must have a postscript.
3. Offer 2, 3 or 4 free issues—and let the publication sell itself.
4. Don't put the price anywhere except the order form.
5. Have an insert listing articles that people will want to read.

6. Put in as many pieces of paper as possible without going over the 2 ounce third class limit.

7. Every piece should have the name and address.

8. Use the word "free" as many times as possible.

9. Keep the letter visually exciting as well as verbally fascinating.

10. Don't show the product.

11. Make sure the offer is on page one of your letter.

12. Always use a publisher's letter. It works.

13. Offer people many different ways to buy—Visa, MasterCard, check and an 800 number.

14. Give people the opportunity to charge their purchase to their business.

15. Always include a business reply envelope.

Milt Pierce, 162 West 54th St, New York, N.Y. 10019 (212) 246-2325.

Points to Keep in Mind in Package Design

A potpourri of suggestions from consultant Rene Gnam for designing a promotional package:

• Put a hole in your envelope—let the prospect wonder "What is in that envelope with my name on it?" Put the window (cello-poly, not glassine) to the right side of the envelope; it's against postal regulations for copy to appear right of the window.

• Use teaser copy on the envelope—slant the main headline and put the "action line" (which leads the prospect into the envelope) under the window.

• If you use a return address, put it on the back flap (unless you're really sure your publication or corporate name is going to impress a prospect).

• 80 per cent of the mail received by business customers is in 24-lb. white wove envelopes, 67 per cent of which are #10 size. Be different—different sizes and colors increase attention.

• Tests have shown these types of techniques do work even with "sophisticated audiences."

• A two page sales letter will usually outpull a one pager printed front-and-back (but the difference in response may not be cost effective).

• Get the reader from page to page by breaking a sentence. Don't use "Over" or "More" unless you're writing to journalists.

• Always have a P.S. and make it "as long as it needs to be."

• Never use a P.P.S.

• Don't attach the order form to the letter or brochure. Try never to do anything which makes it more difficult for the prospect to respond.

• Tilt your sales headline on a letter. Don't center it and, especially, don't box it. (The purpose is to lead the reader into copy, not to set it off to stand by itself.)

• Don't put a mini-brochure in the center fold of a four page letter.

• Save the color tints and coated stock for brochures, not the sales letter.

- Put your company logo at the end of the letter, the bottom of the last page; not up front. You're not selling the prospect a logo.
- The most important thing is to get it out, don't spend your life testing. If money is the problem, drop from four colors to two, and get it out.

A Short List of Suggestions to Increase Readability of Your Copy
- Never use ALL CAPS in headlines, always use upper/lower case.
- Don't extend a headline all the way across the page.
- Never hyphenate at the end of a line.
- "Widows" dangling at the end of paragraphs are effective to move the reader along to the next paragraph.
- Use italics in copy only for action lines ("fill out the enclosed order card today...").
- Avoid overuse of all caps except for occasional emphasis.
- Underscore only a few key words or phrases in a letter—not entire paragraphs.
- "elipsis...and dashes — — — are good in sales letters; semicolons don't exist and exclamation points seldom do!"

Results of NAA Promotion Study
How many statistically significant differences would you think there are between promotional practices of publishers of consumer newsletters (aimed at individual subscribers) and corporate newsletter publishers (aimed at businesses and institutions)? Here are some results from the NAA study of promotional practices and results among member newsletter publishers.

- Corporate publishers include a sample issue 250% more than consumer publishers.
- One third less corporate promotions include a business reply envelope or card.
- Consumer letters are much more likely to solicit trial subscriptions (54% to 35%), but corporate letters which offer them report a much stronger average conversion rate (49% to 28%).
- Twice as many consumer newsletter subscribers take multi-year subscriptions when offered (11% to 5.6%).
- While bulk mail remains the bulwark of newsletter promotion, publishers of corporate newsletters are twice as likely to use first class, reporting a total of 30% of their promotions going first class, compared to only 14.4% of consumer promotions.
- Publishers of corporate newsletters will almost universally accept unpaid orders (87%) while only 31% of consumer letters do (about half of consumer newsletter offers are structured to accept VISA or other credit card billing, only 5% of corporate newsletters use this feature.)
- Consumer newsletter publishers do a lot more testing. 90% compared to under 60% pre-test promotions.

- Corporate newsletter publishers spend an average of 40% more on each piece of promotional mail. Corporate newsletter promotions reported an average cost of 29.8¢ compared to 21.2¢ for consumer newsletter promotion.

- Consumer newsletter publishers are two/thirds more likely to raise their price every year. 20% reported doing so compared to only 12% of corporate publishers.

Evaluating NL Offer Strategies & Results

Here is consultant and newsletter publisher Ed McLean's breakdown on structuring the newsletter offer and evaluating the results of various types of offer programs. The example is a weekly newsletter that costs $260 a year for 52 issues. This is the Charter Subscription Rate—as opposed to a listed rate of $312 a year. Here is a schedule of costs used in this example, all of which have a 10% overhead cost assigned to them:

Processing a new subscription order	$1.20
Killing a no-pay or cancel (in batches of 50)	.70
Preparation & insertion of a bill with an issue	.50
Preparation & mailing of a bill	2.00
Total fulfillment, per issue	.90
Premium booklet inserted issue	.75
Premium booklet mailed separately	1.20

Five offers were tested, each to 5,000 names. (Total 25,000)

The first is a "Super Soft" offer. Send no money. Take three issues and, if you like the newsletter, honor the bill that accompanies the third issue. If you don't like it, write "cancel" on the bill and return it. You will owe nothing. And you keep the special premium booklet you receive with your first issue. If you decide you want to continue as a subscriber after your three trial issues, you pay HALF the Charter Subscription Rate—only $130 for 52 issues.

The second offer is "Soft." Send no money. Take three issues and then decide. Premium booklet for replying. Rate is $171.77 for 52 issues.

The third offer is "Medium." Send no money. Receive one trial issue with a bill. Pay it or write "cancel" on it. No premium booklet. Special rate: $199 for 52 issues.

The fourth offer is "Hard." Send no money now, if you prefer. But if you pay you get a premium booklet. A money-back guarantee is offered: a prompt refund on unmailed copies. Special rate: $225 for 52 issues.

The fifth offer is "Super Hard." Cash payment with subscription order. No "bill me later" option. No premium for payment. A money-back guarantee is offered: after three issues are received, the subscriber may cancel and receive a prompt refund on unmailed copies. Charter rate: $260 for 52 issues.

Test results:

OFFER	% RETURN	GROSS ORDERS	NET ORDERS	GROSS INCOME	NET INCOME
Super Soft	7	350	158	$20,540	$17,376
Soft	5	250	125	21,471	19,382
Medium	3	150	105	20,895	19,631
Hard	2	100	80	18,000	17,464
Super Hard	1.5	75	68	17,680	17,648

Since the nature of an introductory offer can affect conversion results, we can track the profitability of these five offers for one year:

OFFER	% CONVERSION	NET CONVERSION ORDERS	NET CONVERSION INCOME*
Super Soft	50	79	$20,540
Soft	60	75	19,500
Medium	70	73.5	19,110
Hard	80	64	16,640
Super Hard	90	61.2	15,912

*All conversions at $260 rate. Before promotional costs.

If we can safely assume that all those left after conversion will *renew* the same, regardless of the offer that introduced them to our newsletter, and this renewal rate (and our charter subscription rate) remains the same at 70% and $260 a year, respectively, a five year renewal-by-renewal tracking might look like this:

OFFER	NET SUBSCRIBERS	5-YR. RENEWAL INCOME**	TOTAL INCOME**
Super Soft	13	$39,850	$77,766
Soft	13	37,852	76,634
Medium	11	32,302	71,033
Hard	13	39,374	73,478
Super Hard	15	45,421	78,981

*Before promotional cost and cancels
**Before promotional cost and cancels

From the figures you can see that while, initially, a "super-soft" offer, as expected, brought in the most cash the net favors the "medium" offer. After the conversion process, net still favors a medium offer but given the assumptions which are made about five-year renewals the "Super-Hard" offer returns the most cash and "Super-Soft" is second.

McLean adds that his personal choice would be the super soft offer, combined with a strong ongoing effort to increase the conversion rate to 60-65% from 50%. McLean also makes three additional points which will affect the choice of offer:

- actual or projected subscriber life
- anticipated income from sales of special reports, data bank access, seminars, books, directories, etc.
- publisher's policy and practice relating to aggressive promotion of "renewal at birth,' 'advance renewals' and regular conversion and renewal programs.

If projected subscriber life is long, perhaps 10 years or more, you may wish to "buy" more subscribers with a soft offer. Similarly, if you have a track record of success in ancilliary sales to subscribers, you will want to sign on as many as possible with an introductory offer. If you have high-powered programs in place with a record of success in conversion and renewals, again you'll want the "number advantage" of a large base of new subscribers.

Ed McLean, Ryan Gilmore Publishing, 5 Snyder Road, Ghent, N.Y. 12075

Designing the NL Offer
Ten Suggestions for Designing the NL Offer

"The right offer can sell almost anything you want," says Jim Kobs, president, Kobs & Brady Advertising in Chicago, and he makes 10 suggestions which seem especially interesting to newsletter publishers:

1. The free trial offer is the absolute best in terms of generating response, but if you don't want to use it, the money-back guarantee is the next best.

2. Charge card privileges obviously include both the advantage to the customer inherent in "bill me" while allowing the publisher to receive cash with minimum delay. Secondly, some experts think, just the offering of a credit card option builds the stature of the publisher in the recipient's eyes and increases the reputation of his firm.

3. Two-step gift offer. If a premium works for you, a second-step premium may work even better, i.e., a small additional premium for including "cash-with" or a second, better, premium for a multi-year offer.

4. Free booklet offers are good to establish your credibility with prospects in your chosen field and, secondly, it's also a good way to obtain names off a rented list that you can reuse.

5. Cash discount offers. This is the basic type of discount offer. In most cases a discount offer will not do as well as a premium with the same value.

6. Price increase notice. It's always legitimate to make a special offer to all current subscribers to renew now at the "about to become" old price.

7. Sample with tentative commitment. Borrowed from the magazine field where it is used extensively, examine five issues free and if you don't like it you mark "cancel" on the invoice.

8. Limited time offer. It's always good to give an absolute deadline on special offers. "This special offer expires on November 20, 1982."

9. Write Your Own Ticket Offers. Give the customer a chance to custom design his offer, i.e., if one year is $96, add on the invoice or order card a chance to get six more issues for only $20 or ten more for $32 or whatever.

10. The bounce back offer. It's always an effective tool to include with the invoice on a "bill-me" order, the first issue or the "welcome new subscriber" letter, an offer to make additional purchases, extended subscriptions, another newsletter, books, etc.

Kobs & Brady, 625 N. Michigan Avenue, Chicago, Ill. 60611

Ed McLean makes a number of additional points of interest:

● "Unfortunately, the answer to every question concerning designing an offer is either 'you have to test' or 'it depends'."

● The "offer" is the combination of all the variables in a promotional campaign, including price, term, premium and billing method.

● The lower the renewal expectations you have, the harder you should make the offer. (There is less point in paying more to get them with a soft offer if experience shows that the list doesn't renew well.)

● The more you go toward a hard offer, the more difficult it is to have a sample issue work effectively in the promotion. (If the prospect is being invited to take a trial subscription, the first issue may whet interest. If he is being asked to make a buying decision on the basis of only this one issue, it's less likely to have enough features in it to be effective.)

● How to handle the problem of the current subscriber who gets a copy of your new supersoft offer discount promotion. Be prepared: have a letter ready to be personalized and send out which reads, in essense, "very clever of you to have noticed this offer—as a valued part of our family we'll be happy not only to have you extend your subscription at this special rate, but as a current subscriber we have a special additional bonus for you if you do so, a special report..."

Some additional points

When designing a premium, often the title seems more important than the content. "The customer is pleased to get the report titled: 'Everything you need to know about...' He puts it on his shelf and feels 'that's accomplished'."

● Certainly think about "Renewal at Birth." McLean finds you can frequently draw 10 percent from new orders by going right back in the mail within a month offering the opportunity to extend their subscription for an additional year at today's low rates.

● Take advantage of being small.—A newsletter publisher should always respond to a complaint with a personal phone call.

- If you want to steal a rental list, do it the legal way; send them a free offer and you are entitled to the names of those who respond. (Please note: some letters have restrictions on use of their lists for free offers.)

Ed McLean, Ryan Gilmore Publishing Company, 5 Snyder Road, Ghent, New York 12075

Ways to Improve Promotion Efficiency

One of the best ways to improve your overall financial picture, according to consultant Van Sternburgh, is trimming your promotional costs while maintaining response. He suggests the following:

The Design of Your Package

1. Consider a shortened sample issue, (or stop using one at all), and/or reprint.

2. Test a lower cost premium (or eliminate the premiums entirely).

3. Try a self-mailer.

4. Omit reply envelopes in promotions to business addresses.

5. Include an envelope, but not postage-paid.

Overall Promotion Management Suggestions

1. Mail less. Don't remail to lists which fail to meet anticipations.

2. Work harder on developing list exchanges and swaps. With list costs going to $60-70/m you can save 25-30% of total promotional costs with a list exchange.

3. Don't clean rented lists. (If you put address correction requested (ACR) on your envelopes and mail a rented list you will pay to get back corrections on a list which isn't yours.)

4. Upgrade your capability to capture prospect names and develop your in-house lists.

5. Always give the customer/subscriber a bit extra; a welcome aboard letter, some complimentary back issues on new subscriptions, an annual index, a special report—something they didn't know they would get when they signed on.

6. Don't use consultants to do work you should do yourself. You know your product and market better than any consultant.

7. Try some of the new ideas you hear about. No more 'business as usual.' Get out there and pry a few more dollars out of these soon-to-be subscribers.

How to Cut Promotional Costs

Consultant Phil Dismukes provides suggestions newsletter publishers might keep in mind in efforts to reduce or control promotional costs. "I assumed when I put this together that everyone knows the basics—test to determine if your response is affected by going first versus third class or by including BRE's—and I didn't want to get into the whole debate over including a sample issue which is obviously costly if you do it. I tried to concentrate on less obvious points, some admittedly pretty minor, which you can keep in mind in doing your promotion planning and budgeting."

Pick Suppliers Knowledgeably

1. Learn enough of the technical details of printing, paper buying, typesetting, mailing, and postal operations to be able to completely and accurately specify your promotion.

2. Visit your suppliers face-to-face in their plants.

3. Match your promotion jobs to your suppliers' capabilities. For example, an 8-1/2 x 11 final sheet can be produced with little or no wasted paper on an 8-1/2 x 11 (i.e. "1250"), 17 x 22, 23 x 25, 25 x 38, and 35 x 45 sheet size press. However, the fixed costs of press make-ready make a "1250" or a 17 x 22 press very economical for runs of about 10,000, while runs of about 25,000 should be printed with a 23 x 35 or 25 x 38 press. A 35 x 45 press is best for runs of 50,000 or more. Never use a small press for a large job or a large press for a small job.

4. Analyze and track all promotion costs *regularly*.

5. Whenever you change suppliers, or once or twice a year (if your regular supplier is doing acceptable work), ask for and compare job estimates from two or more suppliers.

Test Efficiently

6. Of course you should always test the various elements of your package, however, the fact is that testing is *always* expensive. Therefore, only test those elements that (1) can significantly reduce your costs or (2) can significantly increase response. Aside from the list, elements such as price, offer, and selling copy will have the most impact on response. Elements such as postage class, paper weight and grade, and the number of inserts in your package will have the most impact on costs. Remember, for small mailers (less than 20,000 pieces per drop) who get average response rates of less than 1%, only radical changes in your package will probably produce statistically significant test results. Don't waste time and money testing "small" things like teasers, headlines, minor variations in price or offer, ink or paper colors, etc. If they look like good ideas in proposal stage, go ahead and use them.

7. Test different package designs that will save money. For example, if you now use a 4 page sales letter and a sample issue package, cost out and test a self-mailer.

8. Analyze your response for the number of buyers using your BRE. If not more than 10% or 15%, test using no BRE. Always use a BRE for newsletters sold to individuals for their personal, rather than professional use.

Lists and Mailing Suggestions

9. The one area you should never scrimp on expenses is lists. Test lists often and then use the successful ones no matter the cost. The list is the most important element in your promotion.

10. When possible, swap lists, rather than rent them.

11. If you get good results from a compiled list, consider preparing your own in-house compilation of the same list.

12. Except in special circumstances, always use only 4-up ungummed cheshire mailing labels.

13. When possible have mailing labels printed in a single zip sequence to avoid the fixed set-up costs for each new list by the mailer.

Paper and Printing Techniques

14. Buy your own paper and supply it to your printer; no matter the quantity you can often save up to 25% on paper costs this way.

15. Test cheaper paper in your package; generally (within reason) paper quality has very little effect on response and a very large effect on your budget.

16. Avoid colored paper stock. Use screens and ink to achieve color in your package.

17. Avoid using bleed prints.

18. Preprint and stock standard promotion package items like carrier and business reply envelopes and order cards.

19. If you mail in large quantities, say 50,000 or more per drop, investigate using a speciality printer like Communicolor or Webcraft.

And Finally...

20. Pay your suppliers promptly to avoid service charges and slow service.

How to Analyse and Improve Promotions, Direct Mail Copy, Renewals and Testing

Guy Yolton specializes in direct mail and has had extensive experience with newsletter publishers. He offers many suggestions:

First some basics:

1. Get the Envelopes. How many promotional campaigns are held up waiting for large quantities of envelopes to be delivered?

2. If you don't get something out, you don't get anything back.

3. The success of many enterprises is due more to having done it, than to the creativity or sophistication involved.

Seven types of promotion which might work:

1. *Sampling*—send a series of newsletters to top prospects and follow up with a letter, "Now that you've seen the *Widgit Industry News,* we know you'll want to become a subscriber."

2. *Short Term Introductory Offers*—best for well-established newsletters. If you are putting out a $100 newsletter, offer a rate in direct proportion ($25 for three months) to "introduce yourself" to new prospects.

3. *Get an Inquiry*—Yolton is dubious of efficiency of promotions designed to solicit queries ("send me a sample issue") rather than hard orders.—"It might be a way to make a payoff out of space advertising."

4. *Cut Price Offers*—Good perhaps for a launch of a new publications. Offer two months of a $100 newsletter for $10 and you can get indications of level of reader interest.

5. *Include the Newsletter with the Promotion*—(He does not recommend this.) Yolton feels this is only good if you're confident it is the "perfect issue"—includes all of your editorial strengths, etc.

6. *The Pass Along Subscription*—mail a second copy to each subscriber and ask him to pass it along to someone else who should be interested.

7. *Use a Premium*—most effective, if (a) premium is closely related to product (a special report from newsletter) and if (b) premium does not over-power basic offer. (If you make the premium offer too good, you'll find renewals are poor unless you offer another premium which is just as exciting.)

16 Tested "Openers" for Direct Mail Copy

For those who find the hardest part of creating a promotional letter is writing the first sentence, consultant Rene Gnam offers a laundry list of tested ways to begin promotion letters.

● *The direct approach*—state exactly what you're selling and what the offer is.

● *Open in "conversational" style*—get the reader's interest with an antecdote.

● *The premise trap*—get the reader into the letter by stating a premise with which he must agree.

● *The double premise trap*—the same approach with two questions in a row demanding 'yes' answers. (Make sure the questions are reasonable and relevant to the product being marketed.)

● *Use a very long "usefulness" headline*—Rene says the headline can go half way down the first page (and lead right into the copy without a salutation in some instances).

● *Personal ego approach*—any more sophisticated version of "You have been selected to receive..." which plays on the status needs of the reader.

● *The "great announcement" technique*—a charter-offer for a new publication is the most obvious.

● *The big mystery approach*—What do presidents of 70% of the leading companies in widgit marketing have in common?

● *The future life style approach*—most effective for consumer oriented publications—usually a variation of "you too can learn how to make big money playing the option market," etc.

● *The bold all-convincing headline*—"Make One Decision Today!"

● *You can discover...*—followed by an explanation of the key area of information featured in your newsletter.

- *The big comparison*—usually a way of stating all of the vital information the person who responds to the promotion will have compared to the cluck who doesn't.
- *The invitation*—tried and true—"This is your invitation to save $40 on a charter subscription to ..."
- Put the premium in the lead sentence—"Get your copy of our invaluable book *75 Ways to Create Better Direct Mail Copy* by ordering today."
- *The "Sure I Can" approach*—ask the prospect something he can certainly do, "Can you afford to spend an hour a week to achieve, etc., etc." and finally ...
- *Get someone else to write it for you*—if you've been doing it too long, you are probably getting stale and would benefit by seeing some fresh approaches.

How to Start and Finish Good Promotion Letters

The beginning and the end—the headline and the P.S.—seem to be two of the trickiest parts to good direct mail copywriting. Consultant Rene Gnam offers these guidelines to help you draft promotional copy.

There is very little difference between a headline on a letter and a teaser on the envelope. They both attempt to fulfill the same function, get the prospect's interest and move him into the body of your copy receptive to your offer.

Three basic points which should be covered in every headline:

- Identify the interest of the readers
- Promise of a reward
- Call for action

In a recent seminar, Gnam was asked, "Isn't it true that seven words is always the length of the most effective headline? "Ridiculous," he answers, "there is no rule about length."

He does offer several general rules:

- Don't write a headline in a question format which the prospect can answer "no" (and stop reading).
- Generally stay away from competitive references ("your chance to subscribe to the WIN Letter at $50 a year less than XYZ").
- For headlines in question format, multiple questions will usually outpull a single question.

About the Question of a Postscript

A good promotional letter should "absolutely always have a P.S." (Gnam adds he only ran into trouble once, when he did a project for Navy recruiting, where his copy was initially rejected because "Admirals don't have afterthoughts ..." He convinced them to test two versions, and the version with the P.S. was the winner.)

Include a Guarantee in Every Promotion Package

Every effective direct mail subscription promotion offer should include a guarantee. To make the most effective promotional use of the guarantee, it should be developed to include as many of the following features as feasible:

• Make the guarantee strongly and clearly worded. Leave no room for doubt that you mean what you promise.

• Have it signed by a company honcho. If your promotional letters are signed by the newsletter editor or the marketing director, have the publisher sign the guarantee.

• State the period for which the guarantee applies. A long period is more attractive as a marketing device. A customer is less likely to remember he has a money-back guarantee as he gets further into the term of the subscription.

• Make it look like a "valuable guarantee." Have your package include a guarantee statement which can be retained by the subscriber. Design it with an engraved border and give it an impressive title, "Certificate of Guarantee." Some publications have gotten impressive test results by making the guarantee a separate document within the package.

• Conversely, don't hide it. Too often after you've gone to the trouble of building a strong guarantee, the graphics person gets hold of it and thinks, "here's a spot where we can save some space" and the guarantee, which should be a strong selling tool, winds up in six-point Baskerville—unseen and unread.

• If your cash flow can stand it, consider the "We won't cash your check for 60 days. If you're not satisfied with *Widgit Industry News,* just let us know and we'll return your check to you" approach.

• Include the name and phone number of a live person in the guarantee. "If you experience problems with delivery, address change, etc., contact Mary Margaret Evans, Circulation Manager, 202/347-5220" is much more credible than "Fulfillment Department."

A strong guarantee is a promotional tool that should cost very little to develop and administer and should bring in a measurably stronger response to promotion.

Designing the Newsletter Order Card

The first thing to work on in creating a new package is the order card.

• Make the card a contrasting color. Many people, when they open a piece of mail, shuffle through for the order card to find out what is being sold and what it is going to cost. Make it easy for them to find.

• Put a headline and sales message on it. This message is for the people in point one above, who haven't yet looked at your sales letter.

• Put your name and address on it. When the rest of the package and the return envelope is lost, they will still know where to send the order form and check.

• Decide what your offer is going to be. The two all-time best newsletter offers are the *Free Trial* and the *Half Price Subscription.* If you don't like either of those, consider a second year half price offer (with check). It's equivalent to a 25% discount.

- Separate the order information. Put it all in one place so the prospect doesn't have to search around the form for billing options, etc.
- If you have a short-term offer or trial, mark it clearly "Lowest Price Available."
- If you are offering a number of terms, select the one which has the lowest cost-per-issue and mark it with an arrow: "Best Deal Available."
- The best "hooks" for newsletter orders are premiums and deadlines. If your special offer is only good until June 1, make sure it says so clearly on the order form. If you get your special *Widgit Marketing Report* only if a check is enclosed, say that on the order form.
- Include a picture of the product. If you can find space, show what an issue, or a stack of issues, of *Widgit Industry News* looks like.
- Include a guarantee certificate. Make it detachable so the subscriber can keep it. Put an ornate border on it so it looks like a stock certificate.
- If a guarantee works for you, try a double or triple guarantee. (1) If at any time you're dissatisfied, we'll return your money. (2) As a charter subscriber you will always be entitled to the lowest rate available to any one for *Widgit Industry News.* (3) Even if you subsequently decide *WIN* is not for you, your premium is yours to keep with no obligation.
- Add the two most powerful lines of copy possible on a guarantee certificate:

    _____ Date Ordered

    _____ Amount Paid (Check #)

- Make a decision on offering credit cards. Studies show credit card options will increase response on consumer newsletter offers from 8%-18%.
- Never use glossy or coated stock for the order form. Felt tips or ball points may not write on such surfaces.
- Put four little boxes over the address label headed ☐ Mr., ☐ Mrs., ☐ Ms, ☐ Miss, and extend four lines next to the address label for "change of address" information. You want to create involvement and if the prospect picks up a pen to make an address or title correction, half the battle in getting him or her to fill out the order form is won.
- ●☐ Yes, I want to receive 24 information packed issues, etc. Use this format to make a strong positive restatement of benefits. If you don't like "Yes," use "Sure," "OK," "Certainly," "Oui."
- When asking for a final action, don't be polite. Shout "MAIL TODAY." Don't ask "Please complete and return this form with your check."
- Make it easy for people to fill out the order card. Don't ask for a signature except for credit card (you have to have those)—it isn't necessary otherwise.
- If you're selling to education or institutional markets that use purchase orders, put a place on your order form for purchase order instructions.
- If you sell to an audience of "pedantic people," put three or four little "computer-like" boxes on the card captioned "For Office Use Only." You can use them for recordkeeping. You don't have to do anything with them.

- Your entire effort has been made to create a "sense of urgency," to get action *now*. Don't ruin it by printing "Please allow 6-8 weeks for delivery of your first issue" on the card.
- If you're afraid the order form is becoming too complicated, number the steps to lead the prospect through. The order form on Consultant Rene Gnam's self mailer for his direct marketing seminars includes 8 numbered steps:
  1. select city and date;
  2. your name;
  3. additional delegates from your firm;
  4.-6. correct mailing and billing address;
  7. choice of payment terms;
  8. Mail Today to...

"It works. I have people say to me at seminars, 'That's the way I did it Rene, I followed the numbers.'"

Guidelines on Writing Guarantees

A guarantee is widely used in newsletter promotions as a selling tool, but there are Federal Trade Commission regulations/restrictions on what you can promise.

- Guarantees must clearly and conspicuously disclose the nature and extent of the guarantee, including (1) duration of effective time, (2) manner in which the guarantee will act... refund, partial refund, credit, etc., and (3) what creditor claimant must do before guarantor will fulfill his obligation under the guarantee.
- If the guarantee is, in fact, for a pro-rata basis, "refund the amount of the unfulfilled period of the subscription," the guarantee must clearly disclose this fact.
- A general guarantee such as "Satisfaction Guaranteed or Your Money Back" without further definition will be construed as a guarantee under which the full purchase price is to be returned at the buyers option... limitations such as "for a period of 60 days," must be clearly disclosed in the copy.
- Since a guarantee generally constitutes selling points or product claims (for example, "The information in XYZ Report will enable you to increase your earning power by thousands of dollars annually."), the maker of such a claim undertakes the responsibility under law to prove the claim is truthful.

Should "Live" Sample Issues be Used in NL Promotions?

Despite 'conventional wisdom,' sample issues can be used effectively in newsletter promotion. Robert Kahn, publisher of *Retailing Today,* has a continuing promotion effort which includes "live" sample issues.

Kahn continually compiles in-house lists from a variety of sources. Using these lists, he mails about 1,000 to 1,200 promotional copies monthly. Each package includes an order card and a sales letter. The following month he follows with another sample and a "somewhat different letter." Again, conventional wisdom says don't include a sample because no single issue contains all the editorial features you will include over a year—or, as Kahn restates it, "It is entirely possible that one type of retailer may find nothing of interest in one issue and yet the next may be of great interest."

Recently he tracked results closely for several months and discovered the following:

- On first mailings they got an average 1.0% return,
- On second mailings (after cleaning the list of new subs and nixies), they they get a .65% response.

"I have always felt, that many of the second time subscribers are people who read it on the way home and intended to subscribe, but somehow misplaced the card. The second copy a month later prompts them to action."

At this level of response, RT can mail first-class to prospects with a one ounce package and get a satisfactory return even with a relatively low-cost publication ($30 annually).

Retailing Today, P. O. Box 249, Lafayette, CA 94549

Ten Keys to Writing a Strong Letter

1. Learn about your proposition before you write anything.

2. Organize your material from the viewpoint of the buyer's interest.

3. Decide to whom you are writing. Remember, it is a person, not a list. You are writing a letter, not a speech.

4. Keep it simple. That does not mean writing down to anybody. Avoid high-flown phrases.

5. Use meaningful words and phrases—words that stir the emotions, make the mouth water, make the heart beat faster.

6. Don't try to be funny. To try and fail is tragic. Few people can write humorous copy, few products lend themselves to it. Remember, the most serious of all operations is separating a man from his money.

7. Make your copy specific—names, places, what happens to whom.

8. Write to inspire confidence. Prove your points.

9. Make your copy long enough to tell your story—and quit. No copy is too long if it holds the reader's interest.

10. Give your reader something to do and make it easy for him to do. Tell him where to get what you have to sell, how much it costs, and why he should do it now.

Milton Pierce, free-lance copywriter, 162 W. 54th Street, New York, N.Y. 10019

Increase Response from Inquiries

"Information You Requested Is Enclosed"...these five 'magic words' can add to your response on mailings to inquiries.

NAA finds inquiries to be the very best prospects on our list. We've begun typing "Information You Requested Is Enclosed" on the Order Card so it shows through the envelope window of our package of information.

NAA also received a promotional mailing from a newsletter publisher (sample issue, letter, order card) and an envelope teaser (pre-printed) saying "Here is the Sample Copy of _____ You Asked Us to Send You."

Maybe this is more effective in getting mail past the "secretary barrier" but considering we hadn't requested a sample, it doesn't seem quite cricket—and the metered bulk-rate indicia is another giveaway to the observant recipient.

Effective Envelope Teaser Copy

Whether to use envelope teaser copy and, if so, how to effectively use it, has been the subject of recent testing.

- Teaser copy outpulls a blank envelope—assuming the teaser copy is well done.
- Teaser copy can be successful by employing the elements of mystery or intrigue.
- Teaser copy can be successful if it emphasizes immediate benefits.
- All successful teaser copy is related to the self-interest of the recipient.

Establishing Mystery—"Why is this man the world's highest paid financial advisor. Read inside how he's going to raise your income in 1981...The envelope included a picture of the individual with the statement "$50 a minute man" and the note "Postmaster: Do not return to Switzerland."

Implying Benefits—"Now, direct from South Africa, your own personal gold advisory service. Full details inside." Again, the note on the envelope—"If undeliverable, do not return to South Africa."

Envelope Design—The key is successfully including the key elements without cluttering the envelope. In one test, they matched an envelope with light earth colors and very little copy against a solid-colored envelope with teaser copy in reverse type. The light colored envelope outpulled the dark solid-colored package by 99%.

Of course, if the envelope doesn't get opened, nothing else matters. Insure:

- Your teaser copy doesn't trick the recipient,
- Nothing in it makes him/her feel cheated when they open the envelope.
- The envelope teaser copy flows smoothly into the headline or lead paragraph of the sales letter.

Designing & Writing Subscription Promotions

The *absolute first law* of newletter promotional copywriting, according to consultant Rene Gnam, is "Your prospect does not care what you think about your newsletter." Make sure all your copy is oriented to stressing reader benefits.

A corollary to the first law is "Thou shalt not attempt to be funny or cute in direct mail copywriting."

- If your package fails, don't try to rescue it with 'cosmetic changes.'
- Next to "FREE," "Half Off" is the best offer for newsletter promotions.

You can express this many ways (Half Price, 50% off, 2nd Year Free, etc.). Studies show "SAVE HALF" is the best way to state it.

• Gnam cites a series of test results which, in brief, indicate using typesetting, colors and textured stock outpulls a "plain vanilla approach."

• Avoid overly trendy usages such as "business persons, chair, him/her," they appear to create a backlash among many readers which depresses response.

• Don't reduce typesize to fit space. 12 pt type is probably best for promotional letters. Reducing to fit will cut response.

• Make sure, whoever writes your copy, your editor reads it to find any misusages of jargon or "taboo" industry words or phrases.

• Avoid 'Spouse Copy.' If your prospect happens to be a female executive, copy like "With the savings ideas you get in every issue of — — —, you'll be able to treat the little woman to a fancy dinner." is not going to sell. Similarly, current studies all show that whatever market you are targeting, today 10% of the audience is gay...don't use "code words" which offend. (To test these kinds of things, it's useful to have someone read the copy aloud. That can also help pick up items you missed—like using the same verb six times in four paragraphs.)

9 Common Errors in Mailing Design

Nine common errors which create delay and expense in mailings:

1. *Extra Postage Expense.* Too often mailers don't realize until all components are complete that the mailing goes "just over the line."

2. *Production Schedules.* The customer, printer and mailer always have different ideas in regard to how much time it should take to produce the product. Make up a schedule which includes dates all along the way—art boards, mechanicals, copy, okayed proofs, etc.—not just a final date for mailing.

3. *Shortages.* This is the biggest problem for mailers. Don't rely on "printing trade customs" to give you enough extras. It's much easier to order a couple hundred more than reschedule part of the mailing.

4. *Errors in Postal Requirements.* Errors involving indicia are common. Using the wrong indicia format or positioning the indicia in an improper position can result in the package being non-mailable.

5. *Surcharges.* Make sure you don't design anything which fails to meet USPS standards.

6. *Wrong Sizes.* There is simply no way a 6 x 9 brochure will fit into a 6 x 9 envelope. Be precise with all your specifications.

7. *Uneconomical Stock Sizes.* It's fun to be creative, but it will cost you extra if your printer has to custom-order stock or cut it to size, and your mailer has the same problem if your package doesn't fit his equipment.

8. *Special Stock.* Before you fall completely in love with a special stock in the printing salesman's book, make sure it isn't (a) discontinued, (b) prohibitively expensive, (c) difficult to print or (d) work with at the mailers.

9. *Impossible Job Specification.* There are always examples of the beautifully designed mailing packages that has the impossible fold, ink that won't dry on the chosen stock or printing and bindery requirements that can't be done on the printer's or mailer's equipment.

Promotion: 13 Results-Building Ideas

- Offering a number of options on an order card, especially to business audiences, will generally outpull a single option.

- Again as a rule, consumer audiences prefer subscription savings, business audiences prefer premiums.

- When creating an offer, consider changing the term to take advantage of price break points. If your biweekly newsletter is $125 annually, test offering introductory nine-month subs for $95.

- When launching a newsletter, always offer a "charter subscription." It adds 30% to pull.

- You can get source code information on telephone orders. Change the phone instructions on the order card, "Ask for Jane Kompir, etc., etc. (Of course, the same person takes all the calls.)

- Editorial premiums reprinted from past issues are excellent. Don't call it the "Best of Hotline" and risk creating the impression you had to scrape to come up with a few decent stories from amidst the dross. Give it a sexier title.

- When mailing to Canada and Mexico, remember they are "Americans" too. Tests in Canada appear to show Canadians prefer 'extra issues' offers to other types of premiums.

- City Magazine subscribers are wonderful lists. Many of them are brought in by direct mail to lists of *Business Week* and *Forbes* readers.

- For bulk mailings, central U.S. is the best drop point.

- Deadlines are effective in direct mail offers. Make them specific, "Order by November 30, 1982." Ideally, the prospect should have not less than two weeks or more than three, to respond to deadline offers.

- Don't worry about overstating reader benefits. You can use the "You Get" formula repeatedly, and can vary it with "You Receive,", "You Learn," "You Discover," "You Uncover," etc.

- Don't worry about extending strong guarantees. If you have to write refund checks to more than 2% of the orders, you have serious problems with your editorial content.

- When you send a package out to an inquirer, mark it "Information You Requested Is Enclosed." Rubber stamp it on the envelope; type it on the order card so it shows through the window; print it on pressure sensitive labels, but do it. Tests show it will increase pull from your inquiries as much as 31%.

Designing a Newsletter Space Ad

With the exception of financial advisory newsletters, very few newsletter publishers have found space advertising to be successful. Some publishers find that space advertising in the right publications can be effective for gathering leads—if not for many direct sales. Here are a number of suggestions for designing the space ad.

● *Flash Headline.* Studies show a reader will turn the page in 2 to 4 seconds.

● *Product Photo.* Show your product or service in use. One large photo gets more attention than several small ones.

● *Split Headlines.* If your sales message lead-in is long, split it in half to break up the density of appearance while continuing to allow it to read as one sentence.

● *Subheads.* Design them into your copy to give the highlights of your complete message to the 'skim and scan' reader.

● *Over & Under Headlines.* Use with the main picture to (1) get the attention of the reader, and (2) move him into the body of the copy.

● *Borders.* Very valuable in smaller ads, fence in the reader once he starts on your copy.

● *Coupon Borders.* If you want the reader to clip the coupon and return it to you, make it obvious in the layout that he is to "cut out this section."

● *Coupon Options.* Especially in a small space ad, you don't have room or time to confuse the reader. (Give him/her one or two choices at most.)

● *Logo & Nameplate.* Downplay these. The prospect is looking for benefit for himself before identifying you becomes important.

● *Brazen Impact.* Put the message right up front in the headline and continue it strongly throughout the copy and the coupon.

● *Make an Offer.* If you want response, make the prospect an offer to increase his benefits and then promise to deliver something that he/she will want.

Successful Newsletter Telephone Marketing

"It ain't what you don't know that kills you," 19th century American humorist Josh Billings once observed, "it's what you know for sure that ain't so."

Newsletter publishers "know" a number of things about the effectiveness of telephone marketing:

● Telephone marketing isn't effective to cold-sell new prospects;

● Telephone marketing isn't effective for high price newsletters;

● Part-time employees on hourly basis are the most effective telephone sales employees;

● A script for effective telephone marketing has to be short and direct;

● You can't use a "hard-sell" over the telephone;

● Telephone marketing, when it is successful, really only cannibalizes prospects you could have sold by direct mail;

● Prospects sold by telephone are: (a) poor renewers, or (b) have to be renewed by telephone as well.

Some experts dispute, at least in part, all of these statements about telephone marketing in the newsletter business.

- A telephone marketing program can be used to sell to cold prospects, although in most instances the threshold of economic cost justification is about $100 per year subscription price.
- Full-time employees are the most efficient. Use experienced sales people with background in selling intangibles. To keep them from going stale, you vary the work assignments so that, during a day, they may work selling different newsletters or different products. Use some type of commission basis. You pay minimum wages, and you get minimum performance.
- Telephone marketing scripts can be longer than you would think. The key point is to establish cross communication with the prospect. Open the script with a question which both qualifies the prospect (is he/she the person within the called organization to whom you want to be speaking) and initiates dialogue.
- You can use a "hard sell" on the phone. No, you can't get people to send money through it, but you can ask for credit card number and certainly can always close by asking for the order and repeating the terms—telling the prospect that he'll be billed for the subscription.
- Telephone marketing works best in combination with direct mail. The best time to utilize it is on the heels of a mail effort.

More Keys to Success in Telephone Marketing

Many publishers believe only they, or their editor, could know enough about the product to sell it by phone. With surprisingly little experience, good telephone sales people will know as much about a subject as the prospect, and will be experienced in handling problems. The toughest hurdle is the, "Why don't you send me a couple sample issues and then I'll decide?" The key is to convert this objection to an order for a short-term trial. "Judge our publication for a few months on a 'real time basis'."

If you do send a sample copy, accompany it with a dynamic package. Don't assume the prospect remembers the conversation. When you renew by phone, ideally have the same person call who made the sale. If they are really good, they will have notes which remind them what was discussed and what features clinched the original order.

How to Handle a Price Increase

One of the largest problems which newsletter publishers face is *announcing the price increase.* If at all possible, combine the price increase announcement with an "inflation beater" special offer to renew now and continue present rates. Consultant Rene Gnam says when he has been involved in efforts of this type, he has never seen less than a 14 percent response in early renewals and has seen the rate go as high as 40 percent.

A sales letter should accompany the early renewal announcement and it should contain the following points:

- *The price is definitely going up.* Give the effective date and amount of the increase
- Your subscription price will never again be lower than this offer.
- Set a specific deadline on accepting the offer.
- Emphasize in percentage figures or dollar amounts (or both) how much the subscriber can save by ordering now.
- Include specific instructions on how to order—how to take advantage of this offer.
- Emphasize how special the offer recipient is.—"Only our current subscribers are being offered this chance to renew at the current low rate and save…"
- Emphasize some of the editorial features and/or special reports, etc. that will be coming during the extended subscription period.
- And don't forget—"Why not double your savings by renewing now for two additional years?"
- If you're willing to accept "bill me" orders for early renewals, the percentage of acceptance will go up even more dramatically.

On the other hand, in the situation where you've determined you are not going to offer an early renewal option on your price increase, just go ahead and do it. Don't bother to try and smooth it with a sales campaign. You can send a letter with the renewal invoices, but those are tough mailings. Find some benefits, some additional value that the subscriber will be getting, but don't say or imply that what you wrote in past issues was lousy. Don't tell the reader how hard inflation is on you in the publishing business, he has his own problems. Stress benefits to the reader.

Finally, what do you do with the check that comes in at the old price? Do you accept it or return it? For how long after the change of price date? First and foremost, *you put the money in the bank.* You can send a special letter explaining the situation and include an invoice for the remaining $20, or you can just accept it as a 9-month or 10-month renewal and place the subscriber accordingly in your billing cycle.

Gift Trial Subscriptions Pay Dividends

Make money by offering your subscribers a chance to give their friends gift trial subscriptions. Wally Lynch of Lynch-Bowes of New York sent out black and white "Give a friend a gift subscription to the *Lynch International Investment Survey* at absolutely no cost to you" brochures. (It's a 7 x 11" six-panel brochure with detachable BRC order form.)

The first mailing brought 821 responses. It cost him just about $1 apiece to fulfill the five-week subscriptions, including postage, computer charges and a complimentary copy of a special report. From that first 821, they've recorded a 3% conversion to paid subs (either six month or annual) bringing initial revenues of over $2,000. In addition, the gift trial subscribers have also contributed another $1,500 in orders for subsequent trial subscriptions, purchase of special reports and subscriptions to Lynch-Bowes other newsletters. "I would expect the yearly revenue to be about $6,000 contributed by these 821 gift subscribers." Lynch concludes.

An important caveat: "There was a large amount of duplication between the first and second gift subscription promotional efforts. Despite the fact we mentioned that a person could only be nominated for a gift subscription if he had not had a subscription in the past, a large number of nominees were recorded in both the February and May results. Our computer system easily rejected those which had already come in. Quite frankly, we would not have been able to handle this volume and insure that a person was nominated only once if we were on a manual system."

Lynch International Investment Survey, 120 Broadway, New York, N.Y. (212) 962-2592

Using Headlines Effectively in Direct Mail

A headline on a direct mail sales letter has two purposes, to attract attention and to encourage the reader to move into the body of the letter. It usually does so by stating a promise and convincing the reader he or she is on the verge of discovery.

Some Useful Headline Techniques
- Set the headline in typeface; not typewritten.
- Use bold, sans serif type to deliver message without being arty. Helvetica Bold, Avante Garde and Futura Bolde are all good for headlines.

```
XXXXXXXXXXXXXXXXXXXXXXXXXXXXXXXXXXXXXXXX
X      This is a "Johnson Box" which can serve     X
X      as an alternate headline format and is      X
X      useful for typewriter copy headlines.       X
XXXXXXXXXXXXXXXXXXXXXXXXXXXXXXXXXXXXXXXX
```

- Put the headline in a second-color—limit it to eight words. Both factors affect reader recall.
- If you begin the headline as an envelope teaser it is probably most effective to repeat it in the inside copy, particularly for promotional pieces going into a business environment where there is a strong possibility the envelope may be removed before the prospect receives the letter.
- If you have an attractive logo, consider moving it to the bottom of the last page of the sales letter rather than having it distract attention from the headline and sales message.

Using Subscriber Testimonials Effectively

Testimonials can be one of the most powerful selling tools available in direct mail, but they need to be used correctly.

Some suggestions:
- Always try for a recognizable name in the field. The bigger the better. (All testimonials should include the name, company and address—this is much more effective than "blind" testimonials or "R.R., Washington, DC".)
- Have the testimonials be a meaningful endorsement of the publication, not just a vague generality.
- Specific dollar consequences, when cited, are excellent. "We drew $11,600 in new orders for $440 total cost when we tried the promotion technique suggested in your newsletter," is certainly more powerful than, "I read every issue." Be doubly careful, however, with this type of specific endorsement to be sure you (or the endorsee) can document such claims should they be challenged. *Reminder:* SEC-regulated financial advisories may not use testimonials in promotions.

Prospecting for Testimonials

Testimonials can be gathered in two ways: (1) By reviewing your file of "fan mail" and selecting quotes, or (2) Planning from whom you would like to have endorsements and seeking them out.

Be prepared with what you'd like the testimonial to say. The more important the person whose endorsement you seek, the more difficult he/she is likely to be to contact. If you only expect one chance, be prepared when the prospect agrees. "All right, what would you like me to say." Have a draft quote ready.
- Stress exclusivity. Let your "celebrity prospect" know that only a select group of industry leaders are being contacted. It will increase response.
- After the endorsement has run, send the endorsee a framed copy. She'll probably hang it in her office where it can serve as a billboard for your publication.

Always get permission. Even though, in the case of compliments you've received, you have it in black and white, by writing and requesting permission to use the quote in your advertising, you (a) eliminate any possibility of difficulty and (b) often the prospect will rewrite and return a better testimonial than the one you had in the first place.

Opinion is that you don't require permission to run "implied testimonials." "Among the subscribers who have already renewed Widget Week are IBM, AT&T, Xerox, etc." (This also could create a practical problem because your actual subscriber(s) at those companies—unless it's the CEO—will probably decide he isn't sure he has authority to give permission to put the company's name in your endorsement, even if he does have the authority to subscribe.)

Structuring Your Sales Letter

"A good direct mail sales letter normally contains seven or eight basic components," says consultant George Duncan, "placed in a logical structure to guide the prospect."

1. *The Lead-in or "Hook."* Gets attention. With the headline, it's the most widely read part of the letter—can make or break your whole proposition. The lead-in should follow logically from the teaser copy and the headline and should address major concern or benefit to the reader. Probably two-three sentences.

2. *The "Segue" or "Product Intro."* Switches your reader from the interest-grabbing initial statement to the product itself. How will he save money on taxes...increase investment earnings, etc. by reading *this* newsletter?

(a) This is the point at which to make reference to an especially "soft offer" such as a free trial, special low price or "send no money." Relaxes the prospect's concern that what he is reading is going to cost him money. Remember, he's looking for a reason to say no; not to buy.

3. *Product Sell.* Sell! Sell! Sell! With benefits! benefits! benefits! Leave nothing unsaid. Back benefits with features. Anticipate questions and answer them. Use testimonials. Quote surveys or tests. Support promises with proof.

4. *Offer.* Lay out the offer in detail, make it easy for the prospect to say yes...as difficult as possible for a reasonable man to say no.

(a) A hard offer, cash-only high-ticket, is best held to the end of the letter when you've had maximum opportunity to break down sales resistance with benefits.

5. *Guarantee.* Publishers seem to feel a guarantee cheapens their product. It has nothing to do with the publication but with you as a businessman. A guarantee in direct mail gives the prospect an opportunity to take the product into his home to hold it and feel it with "no obligations." It's a selling edge. Don't give it away.

6. *Call to Action.* Ask for the order. The surprising dynamic of direct mail is people don't do anything more than they are told. They will not draw conclusions or infer anything. Direct them to the order card. Tell them how to fill it out, detach the stub, enclose the check in the postage-free envelope. Lay it out for them. Options are helpful. If it works, you've shifted the prospect from a yes-no buy decision to consideration of positive options. "Choose the low-cost six-month trial or the full-year subscription with two exclusive special reports absolutely free."

7. *The P.S.* The second most read part of the letter. Use it. Always. Reinforce the main benefit. Reprise the initial premise. Add a special bonus to your offer, especially if the bonus is further described in a premium flyer. Underscore your guarantee. Establish the dated deadline offer...but use it.

Copley Mail Order Advisor, 800 Boylston Street, Box 405 Prudential Centre, Boston, MA 02199.

Use A Garbage Bulletin for Immediacy

Add a "garbage bulletin" to your direct mail package. You've designed a professional direct mail package that looks as if you have spent months crafting it, but you can still create a sense of immediacy by adding a "garbage bulletin" intentionally designed to look as if it were "a last minute after thought rushed into print."

●Use the cheapest stock you can find. Newsprint is good. Grocery bag paper is excellent.

●Print only in one color, preferably black.

●Typewriter copy is better than typeset. A few strike-overs can be good.

Use one of several 'hooks' to headline. "Last Minute Bonus." "Deadline for Special Offer Extended." "Special, take $16 off the price printed on the order card." "Our Editors Have Decided To Offer."

All these offers work, and it doesn't matter how expensive the newsletter is. . .

Predicting Response To Direct Mail Campaigns

Is there any reliable way to predict response to a direct mail campaign? John Klingel has developed a formula which provides guidelines.

Klingel provides "explanations" for phenomena which frustrate newsletter marketers. Right after New Years Day, the 4th of July and Labor Day are invariably the best times of the year to mail . . . Why can't you mail at other times and get better response when your package isn't competing with so much other mail?

"This is a good example of how many things in direct response do not make sense. I'm not going to try to explain it. The reason isn't important, and we don't have to know the 'why' in order to test and observe that it is true."

Why does the roll-out never produce results which equal the random sample test? (Klingel posits a 20% fall-off in response.) "I've never heard a good explanation for this phenomenon, but I've seen a lot of actual mailing results which seem to indicate its existence."

Having delivered himself of these hypotheses, he posits five factors which affect response to direct mail:

1. Seasonality
2. List Fatigue
3. New Package
4. Premium
5. Price Change

A January mailing drew a 2.0% response. For a September remail, these factors could be calculated in this manner:

Seasonality—20%	Response—1.6%
List Fatigue—30%	Response—1.12%

(He's thinking of consumer magazines, we suspect that newsletters aimed at business audiences can mail more frequently than this without experiencing this degree of fall-off.)

New Package— +10%	Response—1.23%
Premium Offer— +7.5%	Response—1.32%
Price Increase—20%	Response—1.06%

Obviously this forecasting is a combination of science and gut instinct.

John Klingel, 530 University Avenue, Palo Alto, CA 94301 (415) 321-1771.

As stated earlier, most newsletter publishers find direct mail to be the only effective marketing tool available. Space ads are just too expensive to be effective. In addition, what is normally a fairly expensive product such as a newsletter simply does not sell with a small space ad. Publishers have found that space ads are effective to generate inquiries (for follow-up direct mail), but this is an expensive means to add names to your in-house list. Many publishers, however, have found that is certainly cost-effective to add names gained as a result of free media publicity—a newspaper mention can bring in inquiries and hopefully lead to new subscription orders.—Two schools of thought apply here. These techniques are not equally effective for every newsletter.

One veteran publisher, whose firm produces very technical, narrow-focus, high-priced, industry newsletters comments, "I've been the whole news release route, and we've gotten credit for exclusives in the *New York Times* and with Cronkite on CBS Evening News. Frankly, I'm unable to identify the first subscription order we've ever gotten as a result."

Conversely, a newsletter which covers a broader subject area, of interest to at least a segment of the "general public" (investment, real estate, health, etc.) can find this type of publicity very effective.

Using Media Exposure to Your Advantage

Media exposure is good publicity which can often lead to increased industry visibility and new orders. How often have you seen or heard the phrase "According to a copyrighted story appearing in *Widgit Industry News...*" Almost any newsletter publisher can work that angle without too much difficulty or expense.

Who Wants Your Stuff? Get hold of the standard directories—Ayer for print media, Larimi for radio and television—and compile a list of sources which seem likely prospects for the material you have.

What Is News? These are the types of stories media tend to like: trends, discoveries, studies, predictions and statistics. Learn to help them do their job.

Timing. Send it out to media before your subscribers get it if possible. Make it "news."

Technique. Make it brief, one-half page for broadcast media, a single page for print. Always double space, use short sentences and avoid technical terms and industry jargon.

Avoid Overt Commercial Pitches. Media are usually willing to identify a source. Don't ask for more. It is permissible, if you wish, to include a statement like "From a copyrighted article appearing in *Widgit Industry News,* may not be used without attribution."

Send A Sample Issue. It's a good idea to include a sample copy of the issue in question. You might consider putting your best media contacts on the comp list.

Send A Postcard With The Release. Ask if they used it, would they like more, what would they like, etc. You'll get a lot of good leads from these.

Use Media to Gain Favorable Exposure

Newsletter publishers can increase their industry visibility (and circulation) by learning to use other media to get favorable exposure for their publications. Seven suggestions to follow in efforts to gain additional visibility in your industry.

- Identify a handful of publications that can be expected to have readers who will be interested in your publications.
- Study everything they publish about your subject.
- Phone (don't write) the editors to exchange opinions and ideas on hot topics.
- Send copies of your newsletter with relevant articles marked and accompany them with handwritten notes.
- Maintain contact, recognizing that feedback from your new friends will have a salutory effect on what you publish.
- Call ahead when you know you have a story that you expect the other editor will consider important for their publication's readers to know about.
- Relax, be patient, don't push for coverage. (It will come.)

Become a Celebrity to Sell Your NL

"Become a celebrity in your own field of expertise" is the advice Bill Donoghue, publisher at P&S Publications, offers to build newsletter visibility and circulation.

Donoghue's Money Fund Report of Holliston, Mass. 01746 (the official name) has become nationally known for its coverage of the rapidly developing money fund industry. As money funds shot into public prominence, Donoghue estimates that he has done "over 600 interviews for radio, newspapers and magazines as well as 14 television talk show appearances."

Seeking out media exposure may come easier to Donoghue, who admits to being naturally gregarious, ("At least the people who fired me from the larger organizations I worked for previously kept telling me I had a natural entrepreneur's personality.") than to most publishers, but there are guidelines which many can follow.

1. *Learn what is news.* "At first I kept shooting out releases which headlined 'Money funds go over $5 billion in assets,' and when I'd get calls from reporters asking, 'What does this trend indicate? What's the significance?' I didn't have good answers. I've studied to learn how to frame things in terms which are meaningful to the press."

2. *Learn to translate exposure into cash in the bank.* "It's gratifying to see your name in print as an industry authority, but if the article doesn't give the name and address of your publication, people who are interested have a hard time reaching you." They changed the name of the publication to *Donoghue's Money Fund Report of Holliston, Mass. 01746* to encourage this.

This is easier to do "once you've broken the ice. When you can tell a reporter that the 'Wall Street Journal' or 'New York Times' gave credit and address, you make it a lot easier for him to put it in and point out to his editor, if necessary, what others have done."

3. *Be sure you have the right product to sell.* The money fund report is a technical newsletter aimed at fund managers and large corporations. The price is over $200 a year. The press exposure, was bringing literally thousands of inquiries from consumers interested in the money fund phenomena (but not in the market for a $200 + newsletter). They created the *Donoghue's Money Letter,* a $48 monthly with much more general news focus to have a product responsive to the needs of this marketplace.

Some interesting insights into what type of publicity really translates into business. A recent mention in Jane Bryant Quinn's syndicated column brought over 5,000 inquiries. While, on the other hand, "I was quoted in 'Playboy,' same issue as Bo Derek. I thought it would be dynamite for us, and it drew nothing."

CHAPTER VIII
Sources of Additional Revenues
from Your Newsletter

The largest costs for newsletter publishers are promotion, postage, production and editorial. The first three are covered elsewhere in the book. The honest answer is that there isn't a great deal small publishers can do to control what they have to pay either to Uncle Sam or to their printers. Editorial costs can be "controlled" in the sense that many successful newsletter publishers have found ways to spread costs by repackaging and reselling some of the materials in different formats. Ken Callaway, Chairman of Capitol Publications in Washington, once said, "The happiest day of my life was the day I realized that I had paid a reporter to write a story for me and then sold it four times on four colors of paper to four different audiences."

This chapter discusses vehicles for additional revenue created by repackaging editorial materials which you have already created. Chapter 14 on Ancillary Services concentrates largely on opportunities for related business activities (such as publishing directories), which require more significant increments of creativity (and capital). Often a Special Report can be prepared simply by putting a number of articles already written into a new cover. On the other hand, marketing books related to your subject (or writing them yourself) is a more elaborate project.

Here are several suggestions to stretch your editorial dollar:

• *Special Reports and Books*. Repackage the material you have gathered and reported in past newsletters in special reports and books. Ideally, these can be sold on their own. Less optimistically, they make excellent premiums for promotions.

• *Reference Files*. In the course of developing material and editing your newsletter, you may find yourself with a bulging file of source documents. Newsletters that report on Washington agencies, for example, normally have to maintain copies of legislation that affects the agency and their programs; legislative histories, executive branch regulations (in force and proposed), and court decisions that establishg precedents for the administration of the laws. Some publishers have found they can take all this material, index it, put it in a binder and change the newsletter to a Reference File/ Information Service.—You can update the reference file, perhaps quarterly, with new regulations or legal decisions and, for very little cost, you have converted what was a $137 biweekly newsletter into a $197 information service.

• *Spin-Offs*. Can you identify submarkets within your overall prospect group that might buy a less frequent and expensive publication concentrated on their special interest area? If you want to be fancy, these are called "vertical splits," but basically you're just finding new audiences to sell part of the same materials. For example, your weekly *Widgit Industry News* ($259) might contain enough news of special relevance to international widgit operation, Washington developments affecting the widgit industry and new widgit production technologies that each of those could be developed as spin-off, $79 monthly. Recognizing that the content of the monthlies is entirely recycled from the weekly, the balance sheet picture becomes very attractive for a new newsletter you launch with an editorial cost factor of zero.

• *Document Services*. Less ambitious than a reference file is a document service. Most publishers accumulate all types of documents while doing editorial research. Documents which, if mentioned in a story, some readers will want to see. You have two options. You can give source information so the reader can get it directly and not pester you about it, or you can offer to send it to him, either for free or a small fee. If the average document you refer to is 10 pages, your cost to duplicate and mail it are probably about $2. You can charge $5 for the service and (to the extent you receive requests) find some money in the streets.

Finding Additional Revenues from Present Subscribers

Finding additional ways to gain revenue from a very successful, but relatively small, market base has been the outline of the strategy of Business International. They went into business in 1954 with *Business International,* their flagship weekly newsletter. "It did fairly well, but we realized we couldn't make a living selling one newsletter for $120 annually, so we began to develop spin-offs of related products."

From this, the next logical development was special reports. "We decided, as many have, that we had developed a lot of good material so why not package it as a report and offer it as a premium?" They include a description of all available special reports in promotions within their subscriber lists. "We've found that it doesn't work particularly well to promote them to cold prospects."

Another motive for developing special reports was the realization that, while their newsletters were successful, the market was small. "There just aren't that many companies seriously involved in international business, so we felt we had to find a way to develop products which reached different levels and specialities within our customer companies."

From their special reports, *Business International* developed a further refinement of what they call a Multi-Client Study. It's a much more extensive and detailed (and expensive) research product focusing on a specific area or problem. They send out promotional announcements, but they don't do the report unless response is enough to make it profitable. Their multi-client studies are generally priced from $1,200 to $2,500 and can be quite successful with very few participants. They find it successful to play up the "you are in the select group" aspect of these reports. The promotion doesn't contain order cards, but "sponsors agreements" (sometimes they ask for a 50% deposit).

"Our motive in doing these special reports is to make a buck, but, in addition, we do find it builds our own pride and prestige in doing quality work and builds loyalty among our subscribers who participate—as well as enabling us to earn additional revenue from the existing customer base."

Business International has also been very active in seminars. "A lot of people are saying the market for seminars has passed its peak, and they may be right, but what I see is a demand to make such information constantly more sophisticated and more specific." Business International had a two week basic seminar in international business which they offered for years, but demand eventually disappeared. They followed up with more specialized international finance seminar which did well for a while and then tailed off, but currently is doing surprisingly well again. "I think we will continue to be successful with very

specialized seminars, but I really am not excited about the seminar and conference business. I even hate to write promotional copy for them, because I believe that we really don't make any money on them."
Eleanor Stark, Vice President, Business International Corporation, One Dag Hammorskold Plaza, New York, N.Y. 10017

Planning a Successful Spin-Off

How to profitably spin-off a new newsletter in a related area to your principal product without threatening your flagship letter was the problem successfully faced by Barrie Martland, Chairman of Marpep Publishing in Toronto. Marpep's most successful newsletter is a stock market advisory letter, but they discovered that the main reason which was given to them by cancellations was "I love your letter, but I'm not in the market at the present time."

From this they determined there appeared to be a real market for a related investment newsletter which covered opportunities in more conservative, not stock market, investments. They also decided, given the nature of what the new product would be, that while it would not be directly competitive with their stock market newsletter, the potential certainly existed for siphoning off subscribers to the new product. Here is how they constructed a marketing plan.

They introduced the newsletter over a period of a full year. In advance of expiration each subscriber to the first newsletter received a personally typed, signed and addressed letter from the publisher telling him he was about to receive a complimentary four-week subscription to the new newsletter. Then at expiration, they received another letter. "Hope you have enjoyed receiving the new newsletter..." and an offer to subscribe jointly to both letters for a price $50 off the combined full price of both (or an alternative to continue to subscribe only to the original letter). *Note: no offer was made to subscribe to the second letter alone.*

After offering this for a full year, they found the results were better than they had anticipated—30% of the subscribers took the high-priced option and renewals for the first letter continued high. No one was subsequently renewing only the second letter and foregoing the first (and for the second year, subscribers pay full price for both).

From their experience Martland draws these conclusions:

1. If you have a newsletter which is covering three to four major subject areas, there probably is a real opportunity to develop a spin-off newsletter product.

2. The current subscribers to your basic newsletter can be used to form a profitable base for the new newsletter.

3. Don't overlook your expires on the present newsletter as a promotional list for your new venture. Marpep is getting an 18% response from promotions to their expires list.

4. You may well find a new, larger universe for the new project.

"Listen to your subscribers. They may be telling you where you can find a new opportunity." In answer to the inevitable question, what would you have done if there had been a significant trend to switch from your first newsletter to the new product, he answers, "I don't really know. Raise the price significantly on the new newsletter, I expect."

Barrie Martland, Marpep Publishing, 700-133 Richmond St. W., Toronto, M5H 3M8, Ontario, Canada (416/869-1177).

CHAPTER IX
Renewals

To publishers just contemplating a newsletter it may seem to be starting at the back end, but the most critical component of success is effective renewals. As the chapter on promotion indicates, most publishers are happy to spend a dollar in promotional expense to bring in a dollar in sales. Having done that, however, you also incur additional costs for fulfillment of the subscription, probably, on the average (including editorial) between a quarter and a third of the subscription price. Renewals then are the key to financial success, because a $150 subscription can often be renewed for a cost of $1.50.

First Principle. Editorial quality is the single most important factor in determining successful renewals, not design of the renewal series. By the time your subscriber to a bi-weekly gets his first renewal notice, he has probably received about 20 issues of the newsletter. His satisfaction with those will go most of the way toward making his renewal decision for you. Obviously, you will be working to produce the highest editorial quality possible, so what else can you do to help renewals along? Try to insure that your newsletter delivers what your promotion promised. About every six months, lay out the contents of your newsletter and match them against your promotional piece selling points. If your promotion package is typical, you told the potential subscriber about six kinds of important news and coverage he would get in the *WIN Letter*. How close do you come to delivering what you promised? If you find a variance, either change your editorial mix or rewrite your promotional efforts to reflect what you are actually publishing. Before we get into more philosophy of renewals though, let's spend some time on basic mechanics.

When Should I Start My Renewal Series? The "average" NAA member newsletter publisher begins a renewal series about 10-12 weeks prior to expiration. Many successful publishers say that isn't early enough and recommend beginning perhaps 16 weeks prior to expiration. "If I started my renewal series any earlier," one publisher says, "I'd be sending a notice before they got the first issue." Seriously, one school of thought holds that the best time to get an additional order is when the prospect is in a buying frame of mind. As soon as you receive an order, or within a month or so, may be a good time to send out an early renewal offer "Extend your subscription now at the current low price." (This is called "renewal at birth".)

What Should the First Piece in the Renewal Series Look Like? At this point you should assume that the editorial content you have delivered in the newsletter has been sufficiently good to persuade the subscriber to renew. All you are sending him is an order device that allows him to do so. Send a renewal notice. Many publishers also include a reply envelope. NAA sees an increasing tendency towards including a renewal sales letter with every piece in the series including the very first. Caution: your subscriber has not ordered anything from you and you cannot send him a bill or invoice. Postal regulations are very specific about sending "bills" for material which has not been ordered. You can, however, send a renewal notice. Insure that those words are printed on the statement in a typeface as large as any other used and you meet the basic requirements of the postal regulations.

When Should I Follow-Up With Another Notice? Experts advise waiting at least four weeks to avoid "mail-cross" (your second notice crossing his check in the mail). This depends, in part, on knowledge of your market. Corporations and, especially, educational or non-profit organizations, are notoriously consumed by their own bureaucracies. One publisher whose subscriptions go almost entirely to universities waits eight weeks before sending his second notice—so that they can get their purchase orders processed and returned. With this type of audience, publishers usually find it to be a waste of money to include a return envelope because your envelope gets lost as the invoice makes its way through the subscriber's purchase order labyrinth—and the check always comes back in their envelope. Their seven-part purchase order form won't fit in your #9 BRE anyway. If you have this type of audience, you might be well advised to send a two or three part invoice.—It may make things more convenient for the recipient and speed up return of checks if you provide them grist for their mill. Conventional wisdom says these first two efforts in a renewal series will bring in the largest number of renewals.—About 65% of all the renewals you will get come by this point. (The NAA 1980 study showed that figure to be more like 80%).

What Should Be the Next Part of my Renewal Campaign? The next stage in a good renewal campaign is that of emphasis. Most newsletter publishers begin including a sales letter with the renewal invoice at this point calling attention to the key points which will be upcoming in future issues. In a typical renewal campaign this letter might go out about four weeks prior to expiration.

The Alarm Stage. The next stage in renewal series is "alarm." Just at, or prior to, the date of expiration send another sales letter stating "Your subscription is about to expire. Don't miss a single issue and possibly harm your business by not receiving the invaluable information in the *WIN Letter*. Just mark the card enclosed and return it to us, thereby insuring you don't miss a single issue." It's generally considered good sales philosophy to maintain that the subscriber is an active subscriber as long as possible. Don't give him the opportunity in your copy or renewal effort to think of himself as having made a decision to become a "former subscriber." Some publishers find the alarm stage can be heightened by using telegrams, mailgrams or mailgram lookalikes at this point.

Should I Send Copies to the Subscriber After the Date of Expiration as Part of the Renewal Effort? Veteran publishers unanimously say "no," but don't necessarily practice what they preach. The NAA study hows about 2/3 of publishers do send additional issues after expiration date, but it is almost always only one or two copies.

How Long Should I Continue After Expiration? The theoretical answer is that you should continue to send renewal notices until the cost of bringing in another renewal is greater than your cost of selling a new subscription to a prospect. (i.e. One more sales letter and notice to expired subscribers might only cost $75 to send to 200 former subscribers. If it brings in one order for $150, that is probably more efficient than spending that money on new promotions.) In practice, most publishers send one or two more notices after expiration in the *resignation* state of the renewal series. "We know you have decided not to renew your subscription to the *WIN Letter*, we have taken your name off the active list. Would you take a moment to fill out the enclosed card and tell us why? If you wish to continue receiving it, just check the box at the bottom and return." This type of renewal effort usually brings in some subscriptions and, in addition, the comments from former subscribers can often be of value. We know of publishers who have gotten ideas for successful new newsletters from comments they received from expires. (Although most will tell you your newsletter was wonderful; it, the Bible and *Pilgrims Progress* were the only things they read, but their budget was cut, etc.) One publisher says "I wish they would tell me they didn't renew because I publish a crappy newsletter. Maybe I could do something about it, but when they just say they don't renew because it costs too much, I can't. I'm not about to give it away."

Don't forget your "expires" as a future promotion list. Every study of newsletter promotion ever done shows that your expires list, people who once took a subscription to your newsletter, are your best prospects. They tend to rebuy at a percentage higher than any of your prospect lists, so promote to them regularly — perhaps using a special letter. We know one publisher who offers his expires a chance, every two years, to resubscribe at half price. "It's a cheap promotion, and if the only way I can get these people who seem to have decided that they like my newsletter, but won't pay $240 for it, is to bring them in at $120, I'll do it."

What About Premiums for Renewals? This is another area where the philosophy of newsletter publishers does not precisely accord with their practice. If you are going to offer a premium for renewing, logic dictates that you should offer it up front. You want to not only reward your most loyal subscribers, but to encourage them to renew early and get the cash in, you don't want to encourage late renewals. However, the NAA renewal study shows only 10% of the members offer a premium only at the beginning of their renewal series. (And of course, that conflicts with the logic which says you don't need to offer anything at this point of the renewal series because the renewals you get at that time are from people who are already sold.—Why spend more money on them unnecessarily?) Forty percent of those offering premiums offer them throughout the series, but the other 50% offer premiums only in the middle of the series or only at the end. One publisher has said to NAA, "Why do we assume that our subscribers are different than we are? I never pay anything until I get the final notice which says this is absolutely the last notice you will get. Why should we think our subscribers are any different?" That may be true, but if it is, waiting until the end of the line to offer a premium is certainly encouraging negative behavior (from your point of view). Improving the offer as the series goes along is training your subscribers to renew late, not early.

Should I Accept Unpaid Renewal Orders? Studies show that publishers differ widely on this depending on whether they are selling to consumers or corporate audiences. Seventy percent of consumer newsletters demand payment with a renewal order, and only 30% of corporate newsletters require it. Publishers who accept unpaid renewal orders report about a 95% average conversion rate to paid.

To review the bidding, a typical newsletter renewal series has about six pieces mailed about 12, 8 and 4 weeks prior to, at expiration date and 2 and 6 weeks after. Most contain a sales letter in all efforts after the first one or two, about half offer a premium, but many of the premiums are in the form of extended subscriptions for "cash with." After this, the most common premium is a book or special report.

Do Elaborate Renewal Series Pay Off? The answer in the NAA study would appear to be "no" in that the publishers who reported the most elaborate series didn't report getting significantly better than average renewal rates. Then again, it might well be that with their market, they need to make these strong efforts to get an "average" renewal rate.

Do the Newsletters Which Get the Best Renewal Rates Do Anything Different? Again, the answer from the NAA study would appear to be "no." The renewal series offered by the publishers who record the highest renewal percentages tended to just about match the "typical" series outlined above.

What Sort of Renewal Rate Should I Expect? Your rate of renewal will differ dramatically in the first year and succeeding years. Your subscribers, if they make a decision to renew once, are much more likely to continue to renew in succeeding years. The publishers of the *Ruff Times,* the most successful new newsletter in industry history (145,000 subscribers in 5 years), say that their renewal percentage is usually from 60-65% for the first year ("Occasionally, it drops to 59.5% and we panic a little."), 85% in the second year ("If we said 80-85% we'd be sure of being honest.") and after that point "they almost always renew." These figures are about the "standard" the industry looks for (but definitely doesn't always receive). Most publishers would say that if first year renewal rates were to drop below 50% it would be a warning sign that something is amiss in your promotion, renewal or editorial efforts. *Note:* You should keep track of which prospect lists your renewals come from. Some publishers get carried away and are willing to spend more than a dollar on promotion to bring in a dollar sales assuming they make a profit on renewals. Sometimes examination shows that the marginal lists to which you promote to bring in those last orders don't renew. It obviously doesn't make economic sense to promote at a loss to people who, even if you do sell them, don't renew. Similarly, some publishers have found, by doing this sort of analysis, that they have prospect lists which don't draw many orders on the first promotion, but which, for some reason, once sold tend to renew at excellent rates.

Some Additional Points To Keep in Mind. Don't set your renewal series in concrete. Publishers are never satisfied with promotional efforts; they are always tinkering with the sales letter or the brochure or the offer or the premium, in hopes of finding the magic combination that brings in such a flood of orders that the publisher has to retire to Jamaica for the winter to rest up from the ordeal of opening envelopes and putting the checks in the bank. On the other hand, a renewal series too often tends to be set into place and forgotten. This is especially true of publishers who have gone to computerized fulfillment. It is "automatic" in that the fifth message does follow the fourth, etc., without ever being touched by human hands, but is it still the message you should be sending? Are there new reasons why subscribers should be renewing *Widgit Industry News?* Make sure those reasons are incorporated into the *WIN Letter's* renewal effort.

Stay on Top of Your Subscriber Service. Subscriber service can affect renewal too. Read the mail from your subscribers. If you see too many letters saying "You still haven't made my change of address." or "The additional subscription we ordered isn't coming." or "Last issue came with pages missing.", imagine what effect it will have on renewal rates. Newsletter people, in common with much of the publishing industry, tend to informal business practices. Your subscribers, however, expect your business operations to be as professional as the editorial quality of your newsletters.

Try sending a thank you letter to renewals. Most publishers send a welcome aboard letter to new subscribers. Many feel it's good business practice and doesn't cost much to send a similar letter to renewals.

Do you have different renewal markets? Many newsletters gain orders from distinctly segmented groups that respond to widely differing promotional approaches. They should be approached in a different manner at renewal time. Admittedly, this is easier for publications on computer fulfillment. The machine can easily be programmed to spit out renewal sales letters to category A, and so forth, but smaller publishers can do the same thing manually. You may find it makes a measurable difference in renewal percentages.

A Couple More Renewal Ideas.

1. *Offer an "inflation fighter" special*. If you need cash, offer an inflation fighter special to renew or extend now at the present low price and send cash with the order. With interest rates where they are today, your cheapest source of capital is your present subscriber list.

2. *Renew multi-year orders earlier*. In most cases, your multi-year subscribers are your most loyal readers. A person who has taken a three-year order will probably take another. You could probably easily renew him six months out instead of three. It's been a long time since they got an invoice from you, so it won't seem like you're rushing them.

NOW, LET'S MOVE FROM GENERALTIES TO SPECIFICS

Designing Your Renewal Strategy

The perfect newsletter renewal series contains one notice. As soon as it is sent, 100% of the subscribers immediately respond with a check. In our imperfect world, however, most newsletter publishers find that a more complex renewal effort is necessary to gain the maximum or optimum renewal percentage. In this article we describe a very complex newsletter renewal series. Very few publishers use all of these pieces or techniques, but in planning the renewal effort for your newsletter you might want to consider each of them.

One of the truisms of the business is that most renewal series end too soon. You almost never see a series that couldn't send at least one additional piece at a profit. What does it cost to send one more renewal effort to 100 about-to-be-expires? Less than $50 including postage, in most instances. Therefore, a newsletter priced at $150 would make a profit on a 1% response (or a half of 1% return and even break-even at a return of 1/3 of 1%). We suspect, given these economics, that the reason more publishers don't send additional notices is basically frustration. After sending whatever number of pieces in the current series (3, 5 or 7) the publisher tends to think, "they've had XXX chances to renew. I've tried to sell them everyway I can. It just isn't worth more effort," even in the face of economics that show an additional mailing would almost have to pay off.

Another factor which has to be considered is your cost in comparison to acquiring a new subscriber. If, over the course of the year, you average a 1/2% return on a final renewal notice you're paying 67¢ to acquire a dollar in additional renewal orders. Most publishers are quite happy to do that for a new subscription. But, the argument goes, if you can acquire a new order for 50¢ on a dollar, there is no point in spending more than that to retain a renewal.

In a sense this is true although most publishers would be willing to do both simultaneously (sell new orders at 50¢ and pick up more renewals at 67¢ on the $1). The other consideration is the size of the prospect universe. A great number of newsletters are sold to small, well-defined audiences. If there are only so many Widgit manufacturers in the world—and you have a "mature newsletter" which reaches 10-12% of that audience, the publisher should recognize that holding each existing sub may be more valuable than gaining a new one simply because of the increasingly limited supply of new prospects to sell.

Here are examples of types of renewal efforts which might be used:

1. *Renewal at Birth.* This is a concept borrowed from the magazine business. It operates on the presumption that immediately after ordering or renewing is the period in time when the subscriber is most favorably inclined towards the publication, so why not hit him again. 4-6 weeks after receipt of a new order (or sometimes immediately by return mail) go back with a thank you piece and an additional offer. The offer is usually a rephrase of the multi-year opportunity which was contained on the order or renewal form. If the prospect just renewed for a year at $150 (passing up 2 years at $275 or 3 years at $395)—go back with an offer to "extend your subscription another year for $125" or "2 full years for just $245."

2. *Advance Renewals.* These are done two basic ways. Most common is to pick a time of the year when experience shows renewal returns have been good (although just as often, we suspect, the time is influenced by low points in the cash flow cycle or times when there is a need for cash flow influx to support a major mailing effort) and mail an advance renewal opportunity at once to the entire subscriber list. This piece can be very simple. A card, window envelope and a BRE. (Publishers of newsletters aimed at business audiences are somewhat less likely to use BRE's because, in theory, the statement has to be processed through their accounting department and will be returned in their envelope—your BRE may simply be lost in the process. Publishers aiming at consumer markets are more likely to include one.) The message is usually "Renew now and beat the coming price increase" (the inflation-fighter offer). You can repeat this offer every year. So, in fact, you are simply deferring the price increase a year in each case. If you don't want to increase the price that aggressively, advance renewal opportunities can also be structured around a small premium (renew now and receive this exclusive "Special Report"). Some publishers report success with advance renewal efforts which only offer the recipient the opportunity to renew now and be spared the bother of renewing later. "Renew now and insure you won't miss our dynamite coverage of the XYZ issue in coming months." As one consultant puts it, "I know this isn't entirely logical, they wouldn't miss those issues anyway, but you aren't dealing with a completely rational process here." Experience of publishers using advance renewal efforts show typical responses in the areas of 20%-25%. One consultant says he has never seen one which brought in less than 13%. If we surmise 1500 subscribers to our $150 newsletter, this advance renewal campaign should bring in over $40,000 in cash . . . Yes, this can distort your cash flow projections, but all of the error is on the positive side. You are getting money in sooner than planned. And, secondly, you aren't "eating the seed corn of the future" because the subscriber who sends you a check this October, seven months in advance of when he would have been up for normal renewal, will presumably send you another check next October when you offer him another advance renewal opportunity.

A second, less common, way of offering advance renewals is as a "first piece" to the renewal series—perhaps three months in advance of the normal "A notice." The package and the offer is the same as described above. The difference is only that instead of going to the whole list at once, you go every month to one segment . . . Perhaps that one which is six months from expiration . . . This will even out your cash flow, but doesn't produce the sudden influx of money.

3. *Son of Advance Renewal.* NAA offers a renewal at birth opportunity and an advance renewal offer which goes out 6 months prior to expire. Four months out, one month before initiation of the "regular series," we offer what might be called "Son of Advance Renewal." The offer on the card is "renew now and save us the expense of the entire renewal series and we'll pass the savings along to you." The advance renewal offer is a $15 savings opportunity. The second advance renewal is a $10-off deal.

4. *The First Notice.* In NAA's series, this notice goes out 12 weeks prior to expire. Conventonal wisdom in the newsletter publishing business used to be that the first two notices in the series, A and B, should be just that. A renewal notice—and, possibly, a BRE. This theory holds that a certain number of the subscribers of your newsletter have been pre-sold on renewing by editorial content and they will renew as soon as solicited and it is, therefore, unnecessary to spend additional money on sales letters or premiums, etc., to get their checks. Quite a few newsletter renewal series still follow those suggestions but the increasing tendency is to decide you have to come out selling with the A&B notice. In our hectic society, people's attention-span appears to be becoming increasingly short. A good opening renewal sales letter might restate the principle editorial benefits of the newsletter—the same list of benefits which was used to sell them in the sales piece. Some do's and don'ts about copywriting for the text of renewal letters:

● Don't ever allow the subscriber to think of himself as a 'former subscriber'— write in the present tense throughout the series, *even in the notices which go out post-expire.*

● Don't refer to previous notices—telling the subscriber that he hasn't responded to the last notice (or notices) may only reinforce a tentative decision in his mind not to renew. Write each one as though it is the first-and-only one he will receive.

● For convenience, the renewal pieces in this proto-type series are numbered throughout the article. *Please don't do this in your series.* Receiving something marked "THIRD NOTICE" has to create the presumption in the reader's mind that it will be followed by a "FOURTH NOTICE" and a "FIFTH NOTICE" and, at the least, it isn't an item on which he has to make a decision "NOW."

At this point in our series, with the "A Notice" NAA offers a complimentary binder for renewals received within 30 days of receipt. Opinion is divided about renewal premium offers. The most recent NAA studies show only 20% of publishers use them. Binders are the most common ones—the theory being, having received the newsletter for a full-year, the reader will appreciate the value of the publication and will need a convenient place to store them for reference. It is expensive. Depending on how you account for it, "true cost"has to be $5-$10 to send out a binder and you are, some will argue, only spending $$ to reward people who would have renewed anyway. The response to this is (a) those are the very people you should seek to bind to you and if a premium helps, go to it, and (b) *money now is always better than money later*. In all the early stages of the renewal series, from renewal at birth until this point, it is true that the checks you receive are probably from people who are going to renew anyway but, for every 100 checks you get in advance, *you won't get 100 if you wait until later*. Statistically, this is unavoidable. People die, people transfer to other jobs. People have their publication budgets cut. You write something in the newsletter which offends them—you may get 95 of that 100, *but the other 5 may be gone forever*.

A diversion about renewal series formats appears in order here. NAA's two advance renewal opportunities come in a #10 window envelope which says: "Special Membership Offer Enclosed. Act before the deadline to get maximum savings." A number of publishers send a first notice in a carrier envelope which carries the bold copy *Renewal Information Enclosed*. This attracts that percentage of your readers who are both eager for any savings opportunity and determined to make sure they renew promptly and don't miss a single issue. By this time, however, you will have gotten them. The remainder are folks who, at least subconsciously, know they are up for renewal but aren't in a tearing hurry. If you send four more identical notices, each with envelope copy reading "Renewal Information Enclosed" the probability is they may get chucked without being opened.

Contrast Between Theory and Practicality

To conquer this hurdle of familiarity, some publishers have differentiated the later pieces in their series. They change the envelopes (from #10 to #7 with and without window or copy)—they handtype one, one carries a live stamp. They alter timing so each doesn't arrive on the second of the month. In other words, they are cunningly designed so the recipient doesn't recognize it as a renewal notice until it's open. Unfortunately, in the real world, as newsletters become more successful they usually are using a computer service bureau for fulfillment and renewal. One of the side effects of this is that the renewal notices are generated on a schedule (usually monthly), and they are identical in format, mailed in identical envelopes which are bought in quantity, etc., etc. Most newsletter publishers are not large enough to have done extensive testing on renewal series. If 134 subs are up for renewal in a single month, it probably isn't worth the effort and expense to split-test two groups of 67 to see if varying the approach does better than a standardized format.

How to Format a Renewal Invoice. USPS has specific regulations governing format of invoices which are sent for "unordered merchandise," regulations which should apply to newsletter renewal offers. *You can't send a bill for something the customer hasn't ordered.* USPS regulations are quite specific concerning color and typeface and size of notices such as "This is not a bill. You do not have to pay", etc., etc., which have to appear. We are not aware of any newsletter renewal notice which meets this standard in every particular. The prevailing industry standard seems to be insuring that the invoice is labelled "Renewal Notice," *not invoice,* in reasonably prominent type and carefully labeling the period of the renewal being sought "12 months to expire May 1983."

5. *The "B Notice."* NAA's goes two months prior to expire. This might be a good time to test a small editorial premium. A special report on a topic of interest to the reader (it has to be something all new — not rehashed from the newsletter). Some publishers offer a series of these small reports, the idea is that one of the titles may catch the reader's eye, hit his hot button and motivate a renewal.

6. *The "C Notice."* Goes out one month prior to expire. Now is the time when you let the thin edge of hysteria creep into your voice. "Your subscription has only a single month (or two issues) remaining." Act now, you don't want to miss a single issue of the invaluable coverage of all aspects of the Widgit business. This might be the point in the series where you want to test a "Renewal-O-Gram," an imitation telegram format piece — an effort to convey a sense of urgency to the subscriber, *he needs to act now!!*

7. *The "D Notice."* At expire. This probably is the most effective time to utilize telephone renewal. NAA studies show, in practice, the 15% of publishers who do use the telephone use it "as a last ditch effort when all else has failed" but it's more effective when you can say, "We're calling to insure Mr. Blank doesn't miss an issue of *Widgit Week.*" (Of course, to do this, you need to be set up to accept credit card orders.)

In your mail effort at point of expire, this may be the time at which you are willing to accept renewal instructions (bill-me's). The truism in the business is *"A renewal isn't a renewal until you get a check"* but, if you are willing to do it, you can write copy along the lines of "We know how terribly busy you are as an important Widgit executive. We know you don't want to miss a single issue . . . just sign the enclosed order card and return to us and we'll insure your subscription is uninterrupted."

8. *The "E Notice."* One month after expire. Your "Grace Issue Letter." You reiterate how busy you know the subscriber is. List some of the coming editorial benefits in future issues. This might be the place you want to test a "term break." If the subscriber has resisted sending you $150 for a year, offer six months for $75. *It's important to insure that you don't improve the offer at any point in the series.* You want to train your readers to renew early, not to wait until the end of the series to see if there is a better offer coming along. In NAA's series the "B Notice," which is the final one which contains a discount or premium, states "No later offer in the series will be better, so why not renew today?"

9. *The "Second Grace Issue."* Two issues post expire. This is one of the toughest letters to write. It's very difficult not to slip into "We know you've decided not to

renew, so why not tell us what we did wrong . . ." but you can write a "What have we done wrong" letter which emphasizes the outstanding editorial benefits you've conveyed. The timing of notices (8) & (9) is determined, in part, by how many grace issues you want to send—2-3 is most common among publishers who use them. *Note: Don't call it a grace issue.* In this piece, perhaps a personal letter from the editor could be used—"I've added this issue . . ."

10. *The "Last Issue."* However your series is designed, at some point the subscriber will finally receive his last issue . . . say so. Stamp "Final Issue" on the envelope. Include an invoice (and a BRE for convenience) *and mean it.* A certain number of your subscribers have a mind-set which dictates that they aren't going to renew until they receive the notice which says "this is absolutely the last issue you are going to receive." Make sure they recognize that notice when they get it so they can act accordingly. Then, make sure it is the last.

11. *"We're Holding Your Current Issue."* (The next issue after #10.) Send a letter saying "are our records incorrect? Is your check in the mail? . . . We've had to hold your current issue of *Widgit Week.* Send us your check and/or renewal instructions today and we'll mail it immediately."

12. Finally, *The "We Miss You Already Letter."* Usually, wait two or three months past the last piece in this series and write a "personal type letter" restating that the subscriber is an important past customer of the *Widgit Week* family and listing some of the outstanding coverage you've included recently and your planning for coming issues

13. *Make sure they go back into the prospect file.* Every study of the industry has shown that expires, even those who have resisted a renewal series as elaborate as the one outlined here, respond to new solicitation efforts at a percentage at least double that for new prospects.

Eight Ideas for the Renewal Series

Test a series of editorial premiums with renewals. They don't have to be elaborate. They should have *dynamite* titles like "27 Ways to Increase Your Profit on Every Sale." They have to be new, not reprints which have already appeared in the newsletter. The idea of including a series is searching for the subscriber's 'hot button'— feature a different one with each renewal mailing and, presumably, at least one will pique interest.

• Tests show people like "involvement devices" including top execs. Some publishers are now using lift-off pressure-sensitive labels for renewal mailings.

• There appears to be a mini-trend in renewals away from 800 numbers and back to "call collect." Especially with business/institutional newsletters many will call on their own dime, anyway, they must feel it's 'chintzy' to call collect. Don't use collect for consumer letters; readers are likely to drive you nuts with questions.

• Hokey as it sounds, a picture on the renewal order form of a phone off the hook next to your telephone order instructions increases pull . . .

● Multiple newsletter publishers should have renewal checks made out to the individual newsletter name; don't give the customer a chance to become confused, "Who is National Publications, Inc.? What do we buy from them?"

● Be positive in renewal letters. Don't include any "downers." Restating the guarantee in the P.S. is good in promotional efforts, but your readers know your product. Don't remind them you think they may not find it good enough not to want their money back.

● Conversely, a "We miss you already." renewal effort which goes out some period after the end of the series is a good place to test a term break (6 months for $47.50 vs. $95 a year) and again promote the no-risk guarantee.

● If you want longer-term renewal orders, make that the first and most prominent option on the order form, not buried in the small print.

Suggestions on Renewal Design

The problem with renewals is "they just aren't exciting," compared to new sales and, consequently, get less attention according to Consultant Ed McLean...Here's a list of profitable renewal series hints from McLean.

● Do "Advance Renewal" once a year for your whole list. *Do it in what experience has shown to be your best renewal month.* You can do advance renewal every year, but don't always tie it to coming price increases.

● In addition to stimulating cash flow, tests show that efforts like advance renewal and telephone renewals give a stimulus to your other renewal mailings.

● Sell when you do advance renewal. Feature coming attractions, "Don't Miss It." McLean says, "I know they'd receive it anyway, but you're not dealing with logic here."

● Test your package. You can tint the envelope so that the renewal message inside is concealed...or you can go the other direction entirely and print the entire renewal message on the envelope.

● Renewal letters are the one area in direct mail where humor may well be effective.

● The telephone can be excellent for renewals. Business customers responding to telephone renewals tend to have fewer "no-pays" than consumers.

Note: There are new laws in several states concerning telephone sales. Calls originating in California are required to begin with the name and address of the caller, what is to be sold, the price and a request for permission to make a pitch. Know what the law is in your area.

Trends in Renewals

New trends and practices in renewals:

● At some point, ask for a yes/no decision. "Conventional wisdom" says never make it easy to say no, but at some point in the series, *probably later,* you are really trying to get a decision almost as much as an order.

- Test sending renewal notices included with the newsletter.
- Accept two or three year renewals. A bird in the hand...
- Don't worry about "announcing" or "pre-selling" price increases in your renewal series unless you're offering an "inflation fighter." People don't remember what price they paid. (Certainly if you increase from $97 to $197, you will get comments, but an increase from $127 to $147 usually doesn't.)
- Make your postage an 'add-on' to price. "Annual subscription—$42 for 24 issues plus postage."
- Do telephone calls to cancels.

(a) Some will renew over the phone—30% of expires contacted on one list renewed.

(b) You may get some input into your editorial content you can use.

- Try telephone renewals. Kiplinger uses it and gets 14 times the response they draw from the final mail piece in the series.
- Try 'bill-me' renewals. Research Institute sends a first notice 16 weeks out, asking people to indicate ('for the record') their intention to renew and follows with an invoice close to expiration. (An advantage here is you are freed from worries about USPS regulations about renewal invoice format as you are billing for materials which have been ordered.) They collect on 97%.

Four Stages of a Good Renewal Series

1. *Assumption*—At the beginning act as if you know these readers are going to renew. You simply send them the response device which provides the renewal mechanism.

2. *Emphasis*—At the next stage, your message might point out particular strengths, such as "in the coming issues we'll be concentrating on new EPA regulations."

3. *Alarm*—At the third stage, you shift to "Your subscription is about to (has) expire(d). You'll be doing irreparable harm to your business if you don't renew and continue to receive each invaluable issue..."

4. *Resignation*—As a last effort, "We know you've evidently decided not to renew—We've taken you off the list. Would you please tell us why?"—adding "if, perchance, you've changed your mind, just return the card..." These do surprisingly well.

Publisher Finds 4-Part Renewal Series Works

A successful renewal campaign doesn't have to be overly elaborate, according to publisher Bill Haight of Magna Publishing in Madison, Wisconsin. Haight's newsletter is a monthly to university and college administrators and enjoys an overall renewal rate (first and later years combined) of 75% Haight uses a straightforward, four part renewal series.

1. A renewal invoice three months before expiration. No sales letter. Check with order is required. There is no "bill-me" option. "We get 70% of the renewals we're ever going to receive from this first mailing."

2. Two months later ("College purchasing departments are notoriously slow and we try to avoid as much mail cross as we can.") the second effort is a soft-sell letter. A BRC is included and this one does include a bill-me option.

3. At expiration date, the third piece, a letter headed "Dear Former Sub-scriber" which goes on to explain, "You aren't a former subscriber yet, you're still one of us, but you need to act now ..."

4. One month after expiration (they send no issues after expiration) a postcard headed "We missed you" which says "This month's issue just went out but we held yours aside because we haven't heard from you." No envelope is included.

That's the whole series. Once every two years, however, they offer a spe-cial half-price offer to expires. "It's an economical promotion to do to a small list, and if the only way we can get them back is at a reduced price, we'll take them."

A suggestion: Consider the lowly postcard. It can have a useful and valu-able role in your renewal and promotion efforts.

Bill Haight, Magna Publishing, 621 Sherman Avenue, Madison, Wisconsin (608/249-2455)

The Key to Phillips' Successful Renewals

"We make it hard to get off our lists, you really have to want not to renew a Phillips Publishing newsletter," says Phillips Marketing Vice President Lee Euler.

"One of the things which we are doing which is a bit different, and with which we're having a good deal of success, is an advance renewal program. We go out eight months prior to expiration with a special "advance renewal" notice, telling the subscriber that if he/she renews now they won't have to re-ceive any more renewal series notices from us. We point out that this saves us money and we're happy to pass along a share to them by guaranteeing the cur-rent rate for the period of the new order, even though prices may go up. I saw this cited somewhere in a trade publication as the 'worst direct mail idea of the month' but it certainly works well for us."

The rest of the Phillips renewal series starts five months out and continues until one or two months after expiration (and contains six or seven notices). They do send an after expiration grace issue. "It differs on our various publica-tions. Basically we keep mailing until results don't justify costs, and that point seems to be one or two months past expiration."

Do they follow different practices for renewal series for their professional vs. consumer newsletters? "Not entirely, but we have just begun using a com-puterized renewal notice for the first two pieces in our series for professional newsletters. They seem to expect it. It gives us a more 'official' appearance. I'd be inclined to say 'officious', but with the third notice we switch to a more per-sonalized approach including a renewal sales letter and a BRE. In general, I find that anything we can do to personalize the invoice gives good results. We occasionally use a live stamp on a renewal mailing, again for both professional and consumer letters, and it gets results. Two things we don't do however, are

offer discounts or premiums for renewal. My feeling is the subscriber has seen your product by that time and is going to make a decision based on his evaluation of it. I know some publishers offer their 'expires' a special discount to come back into the fold, figuring the mailing doesn't cost much and if they can only sell them at that price, it's still worth it, but we just don't believe in it."
Lee Euler, Phillips Publishing, (301/986-0666).

Ideas for Renewal Series Timing & Design

Here are some guidelines from Consultant Rene Gnam for a basic seven-part renewal series effort:

- *A Notice.* Three months prior to expire. Simple letter copy, limited discussion of benefits. *Always include instructions on how to send the check.* Be honest. Tell how many issues are remaining.

- *B Notice.* Two months prior. Say there will be no better deal later. Remind them of the increased savings for longer-term subscriptions. *Again, always, instructions on how to send the check.*

- *C Notice.* One month out. Use sense of urgency. Use longer copy. Build in stronger editorial benefits. Copy should include "only one issue (or two) remaining." *POSITIVELY NEVER REMIND THEM OF MISSED PREVIOUS RENEWAL NOTICES.*

- *D Notice.* At expire. This is the best time for telephone. Don't confuse the matter with a choice of terms. Your whole message is *"Act Now."* Excellent time to offer bill-me's. It says to customers, "We know you and trust you."
This is the end of your renewal series. You no longer have a subscriber. You have a former subscriber and you begin your expire series. *It's different.*

- *E Notice.* First issue post-expire. Include a grace issue if you like. Say so. Make sure it is only one. Head the letter "Dear Former Subscriber," it will outpull "Dear Subscriber," "Dear Reader," etc. This notice is also a good time for a mailgram or phony mailgram.

- *F & G Notices.* Send at least three post-expire. Keep mailing until the response is less cost-efficient than new promotion mailings.

Here's a chart of 13 ways in which, according to consultant Rene Gnam, renewal series mailings Do (and Don't) differ from newsletter subscription promotion efforts.

ITEM	PROMOTION	RENEWAL
Brochure	Maybe	No
Long Copy	Yes	No
Guarantee	Yes	No (early in series) Yes (at the end)
Response Device	Yes	Yes
BRE (Paid)	Yes	Yes
Letter	Yes	Yes (even with #1
Envelope Teaser	Yes	Yes (beginning) No (at end) You want them to open envelope not necessarily to recognize it.

Publisher's Return Address	Not Always	Yes (early on) No (at end) same as above
Product Insert	No	Yes (early on) Your most loyal renewals may well order a book at the same time.
Future Features	Yes	Sometimes (later in the series).
Past Features	Yes (Carefully)	No!!
Premium	Maybe	Sometimes (if you offer a binder you have to repeat the offer every year).
First-Class Postage	Usually No	No (early) Yes (late)

Rene Gnam Consultation Corp., Box 6435, Clearwater, FL 33518 (813) 536-5556

How to Increase Renewal Percentages

The wrong newsletter publishers are the most concerned about renewals, those with over 90% and those with 40% or less. The first group won't admit they'll never get that last 10% and the latter publications may be beyond help.

Six Keys to Improving Your Renewal Percentages

1. *Stress the "news aspect" of your stories.* Even how-to and instructional newsletters, which tend to have the largest renewal problems, can develop story leads like "A new regulation. . ." and "The agency's recent decision. . ."

2. *Position every story.* Never allow the editor to forget that a newsletter reports *to someone,* not *on something.* Don't assume your readers know why something is being reported. Don't leave it to the reader to extract significance.

3. *Mention your reader in the text.* "Some newsletter publishers are concerned." Richard Hagan of Capitol Publications points out their *U.S. Oil Week* lead on the pending Conoco-Marathon merger was "Marathon oil-jobbers face no immediate effects from merger." ("That's how we handled the corporate merger of the century.")

4. *Use graphs, charts and statistics wherever possible.* Readers value this type of information more than publishers realize. You may think the charts are "unsophisticated" but use them.

5. *Cover other information sources for readers.* Don't make your newsletter a digest, but do try to devote a page or two to nuggets from other sources (with how to find reference material). This will greatly increase the chance every issue has something the reader values.

6. *Get a content evaluation.* Personal calls to a few people are probably better than results from a multiple choice survey to a larger sample. The best people to call are cancels or expires who have not renewed. They are usually somewhat disgusted and will be more blunt than current readers.

When Renewal Problems are Serious (Way under 50%)

•*Throw in the towel.* Fold or sell the newsletter. Don't increase promotion. Some low-renewal newsletters are making money on books and list rentals, but for others, unfortunately, the reaction to poor renewals too often is "more promotion." (If renewal rates are so low you lose money on each sale, is volume really the answer?)

•*Don't rewrite the renewal series.* A new renewal series may help a healthy letter. It almost never will turn a losing publication into a winner.

•*Don't change the promotion package.* Readers are not canceling because you aren't delivering what you promised, but because what you are delivering is not useful.

Till-Forbid Renewals

Wouldn't you like to lock in a subscriber forever? There are two ways you can do it.

Put a box on the renewal notice which says, 'Yes, Rene, invoice me every year at the lowest rate available to any subscriber.' You don't have to send your expensive series; a simple invoice will suffice (and is legal because the customer has requested it), but you do still have to get the check every year. *Automatic Bank Card Charge*—available from Visa and MasterCard in many areas—(instant charge—you get the money credited immediately). Give the subscriber an option to authorize the publisher to "charge my credit card every time a renewal is due" and you get the money automatically until forbid.

Rene Gnam Consultation Corp., P.O. Box 6435, Clearwater, FL 33518 (813)536-5556.

CHAPTER X
What You Need to Know About USPS

Postal Service

The U.S. Postal Service offers few alternatives to the newsletter publisher. Basically, the only decision which is open to the small publisher is which of his mailings, promotional and regular, will he do using first, second or third class mail.

Regular Circulation Mail

About 80% of all newsletter issues are mailed first class. The remaining 20% tend to be consumer-monthlies (and a few very large corporate newsletters) which can qualify for second class newspaper handling. The beauty of first class mail, of course, is its simplicity. You run the envelopes through your postage meter and dump them in the mailbox. No permits, no sorting, no bundling, no reports. Some publishers used to use air mail in an effort to get better delivery, but domestic "air mail" service is no longer offered. Most publishers who anticipate doing any volume overseas business build a supplemental subscription rate for air mail delivery into their price, i.e. $110 a year (overseas air mail $136). Some few publishers also offer an option of special delivery service. Experience counsels against this, because it isn't really "special" anymore. One publication charges an additional $104 a year (which exactly covers their costs, they don't make a nickel) for a special delivery option, and what they get for their pains is a lot of complaints from subscribers who still aren't getting delivery when they want it. Another word of wisdom. If you are at the point where you haven't decided a firm schedule for the delivery of your newsletter, pick something other than mailing on Fridays for Monday morning delivery. Trying to get the post office to meet this schedule appears to be one of the largest single frustrations faced by all too many publishers. NAA knows of publishers who go weekly to the airport in Seattle at 3:00 a.m. Saturday morning with their sacks of mail for Manhattan separated into individual sacks by zip code and addressed by name to the appropriate shift supervisors at the individual post offices—and they still don't get Monday delivery. Try not to knock your head against a brick wall.

The only price advantage available to the first class user is a discount for presort. It's three cents cheaper (17¢ vs. 20¢ as this is written) but is really only feasible for publishers who have large numbers of pieces going to single zip codes.—It's a boon for utilities, but not of much use to newsletter publishers.

Second Class. The remaining 20% of newsletter subscriptions are mailed second class. You must have a permit to use second class mail, and it will cost you $120. Newsletters mailed regularly to a list of paid subscribers meet all the basic qualifications for a second class permit. (The complex part of these regulations comes when you get into what can be sent as supplements or enclosures with publications mailed at second class rates—including flyers for conferences or books you may be marketing.) Publishers tell NAA that, if you get to know your postmaster personally, especially if you are publishing in an area outside of one of the major metro areas, you can sometimes get favorable interpretations of some of these regulations. You must file a report with every issue mailed second class, and reproduce a special annual report (which must include circulation figures which some publishers object to) in the publication at a stated date. You must have an ISSN number for the publication, and various other items of information must be included on the masthead.

Advantage: Rates. Second class rates are also up for revision as this is written, but at present they are at least 50% lower than 1st class, and in large volumes save as much as 80%.

Disadvantages: Speed of delivery. As a rough guideline, anticipate it will take four days plus one additional working day for every postal zone beyond one or two from your area (delivery to local, zones 1 and 2—four days; zone 3—five days; etc.)

Red Tag Service. Publications mailed second class at least weekly are eligible for "newspaper handling." While still subject to the bureaucratic requirements of second class, the mail is supposed to get essentially "first class" service at the second class rates. The Postal Rate Commission is now considering a surcharge for red tag service so that the publishers who use second class, but are not eligible for special "newspaper" handling, are not subsidizing their larger brethren.

Summary. Second class is used by monthly newsletters and a few very large publications (the Kiplinger Letter is mailed second class). Most publishers of daily and weekly newsletters don't feel that second class, even red tag service, delivers the service it is supposed to. At the prices the publishers charge, they don't think they can afford to delivery by other than first class.

Third Class

Third class "bulk mail" is used for most newsletter promotion. The current rate is 10.9 cents for the first two and a fraction ounces, so an elaborate package, including sales letter brochures, response device, and return envelope can be mailed at the minimum rate. We don't advice preparing and mailing third class yourself. For one thing, it requires a permit. (It's easy to get, and the only basic requirement is that each mailing under the permit contains at least 200 identical pieces. The cost is only $40 or $60 annually depending on whether you want to run the postage through your own meter or take it to the post office and pay by check.) However . . .

Get a mailing house to do your bulk mailings for you. First, you save the $60 because they have a permit they can use for your mailings. Second, properly preparing a third class mailing is similar to washing an elephant; a large job if not technically difficult. Sending out a mailing of 10,000 pieces each containing a sales letter, a brochure, a return envelope and three different response cards keyed to the three different lists takes a considerable amount of collating and stuffing. If you have rented a list on pressure sensitive labels, you can affix them on the envelopes yourself (although this is time consuming) but if your list comes on cheshire labels you need a machine to affix them to envelopes. After you get the mailing assembled, you have to separate the pieces by individual zip codes, two number groups, three number groups, "all for state named" etc. If it's not right, the Postal Service will not accept it for mailing. When you are eagerly awaiting responses, it can be very frustrating to get a call from USPS telling you to come pick up the sacks of mail and do them over.

A good mailing house will do all this for you for about 2¢ apiece. You can't do it as cheaply yourself unless you have a steady source of slave labor (spouse, children, yourself).

Choose your mailing house carefully. Everyone in the industry has heard horror stories about the Postal Service, about whole mailings that have just disappeared, horrendous delivery, etc. Investigation, in a number of instances, shows that these problems were caused by the mail house. They didn't get it in the mail when they said they did (or at all). It sat in a corner for 10 days because no one knew where the labels were for this mailing, etc. It can and does happen. For bulk mailings, insure your mail house provides you with USPS Form 3602 which indicates how many pieces were mailed and on what date. Ask the mailing house to supply you with a list of their clients and talk to a couple. It is probably a good idea to assemble all of the pieces of the mailing at your office and deliver them at one time to the mail house rather than have various suppliers and list brokers send elements of your mailing to the mail house. Some publishers like to have someone on site at the mail house when the package is being processed.

Business Reply Permits

Most publishers believe in including a business reply card or envelope. To do this on a postage paid basis, you need a permit (Form 3614)). The annual fee is only $30. For this amount the postal service will deliver the mail to you and charge you the appropriate postage plus a fee of 18¢ an item. If, on the other hand, you pay an additional $75 accounting fee and maintain a deposit at the post office, they will return the mail for a fee of only 3.5¢ apiece. This means if you plan on getting more than 518 pieces of BRM during the year, it's cheaper to pay the extra permit fee.

USPS Cracking Down on BRC Regs

The U.S. Postal Service is beginning to scrutinize Business Reply Cards much more closely and is coming down on publishers whose cards fail to meet those precise standards. (These standards are set down in USPS Publication 115).

It appears there is a great deal of room for improvement in meeting standards. A recent study showed that an astonishing 97% of the BRC's failed to meet standards (up from 83% in 1979).

The following are the most common errors in the design of BRC's.

1. Failure to make the words "Business Reply Card" at least 3/16" high.

2. Using the legend "Business Reply Mail" on cards versus "Business Reply Card."

3. Company logos on various places on the BRC. (They are only permitted when incorporated into the address.)

4. Failure to leave 5/8" clear at the bottom of the card.

5. Failure to have Facing Identification Marks (FIM) within 1/8" of the top of the card.

6. Failure to have the right edge of the FIM mark beginning 2" from the edge of the card.

USPS is authorized to charge an additional 7¢ apiece as a penalty. If the BRC's are coming back with new orders, you don't care if it costs you 7¢ more;

but if the Post Office were to call and say your 100,000 piece mailing is unacceptable because the BRC doesn't meet standards…

Work with your printer to make sure your business reply mail is precisely correct.

Insure Your Renewal Invoices Meet Postal Regs

Are you certain your promotion and renewal messages are in compliance with USPS regulations about sending invoices for unordered materials?

Effective May 21, 1980, USPS issued an updated regulation on solicitation (Section 123.4 of the Domestic Mail Manual) which spells out what is required to mail anything which "reasonably could be considered a bill, invoice, or statement of account due, but is in fact, a solicitation for an order." Every publisher should be certain his promotional and renewal campaigns are in compliance with this regulation.

Do USPS Regs Affect Renewal Invoice Format?

Newsletter publishers' renewal invoices, especially those prepared by computer service bureaus, are almost certainly in violation of strict interpretation of USPS regulations (Domestic Mail Manual Section 123.4) concerning mailing of articles which resemble bills for materials which have not been ordered.

Very few newsletter publishers include an "invoice" as part of promotional efforts, but almost every renewal series contains an invoice. Many also include a renewal "sales letter." The USPS regulations, however, make no distinction between an invoice which is accompanied by a letter which clearly explains what the invoice is for and one which does not.

According to the USPS regulations, any piece which could be considered a bill, but which is in fact a solicitation for an order, must conform with *all eight* of the following criteria in order to mailable.

- Must carry a notice, in not less than 30 point type (boldface all cap) such as "Not a bill. This is a solicitation. You are under no obligation to pay unless you accept this offer." This must be in a color contrasting to the rest of the invoice.
- Disclosure must be printed either on the diagonal—described by drawing a line from the lower left corner of the page to the upper right corner—or must be printed on each portion of the invoice which resembles a bill.
- Disclosure notice may not be modified to read "legal notice required by law", or other such wording.
- May not be rendered illegible by folding.
- Must appear on all pages of a multi-page solicitation.
- If the pages of the invoice can be torn into sections, notice must appear on each section which could resemble a bill.
- Color used must print legibly.
- Must contain no statement that implies the solicitation or its wording is approved by the Postmaster General or USPS.

USPS Regulations Cover Colors of FIM Marks

Don't get too creative with your Business Reply Envelopes and cards without checking to be sure the colors you intend to use are permitted by postal service regulations. The Facing Identification Marks (FIM) which are required on BRC's and BRE's must be printed only in approved colors.

These colors have been approved for use of Business Reply Envelope FIM's (expense aside, there is no regulation against using additional colors elsewhere on the envelope), Black, Blue PMS 300 or Reflex Blue, Brown PMS 470, Gray PMS 430, Green PMS 355, Maroon PMS 209 and Red PMS 185. Any other color must be approved by your USPS Sectional Center. It would seem unlikely they would approve an additional color, since the stated reason for the restrictions is for "readability" by the USPS electronic scanning machines.

Can NL's be Delivered Second Class?

Looking again at second class since the most recent postal increase? Certainly the rate differential is attractive. How important is on-time delivery to your publication? Red Tag News Publications Association keeps a box score on delivery of second class materials by USPS, both for publications qualifying for 'newspaper handling' (red-tag-weekly or more frequently) and regular second class.

For red tag publications, their most recent statistics show: on time delivery 52%; one day late 28% still later 20%... A city-by-city breakdown shows an apparently random skew. Places like Seattle and Salt Lake City are very bad; yet Wichita and Columbus, Ohio are very good. It must be a phenomenon of individual post offices. The publications surveyed are mostly ones maintaining multiple entry points and flying their magazine around the country for mailing. (Yet Nashville is poor, and Cincinnati which isn't far away is excellent.)

While the stats show 80% of red-tag mail arrives within one day of standard, the picture is a lot different for regular second class. The USPS standard is 4 days for the first two postal zones and one additional day for each zone; 10 days for delivery to zone 8. Here is the results breakdown:

Better than standard	21%
Standard	9%
1-3 days late	33%
4-6 days late	21%
7-10 days late	10%
Still later	6%

Regular second class mail is generally used only by consumer monthly newsletters who can live with this type of service.

Benefits and Problems of NL Hand-Delivery

"Frankly, we started thinking about hand-delivery because we felt our complaint rate was unacceptably high," says Barbara Pratt, marketing director for Television Digest. "I recommend trying it if you can." It is presently quite feasible for many newsletter publishers to use hand-delivery in Washington, D.C. and Manhattan and get guaranteed next a.m. delivery for a price commensurate with USPS rates.

The Major Advantages
1. Timely Delivery
2. It makes newsletters "special" to the recipient.
3. If a reader wants a couple extra copies, they can be sent on a same-day basis.
4. Eliminates worry about weight. "We can go anywhere from two to five ounces, with additional copy, special reports, or inserts without additional cost."

Problems
1. You have to develop a fulfillment system which segregates the subscribers who can get hand-delivery.
2. Your circulation people have to know how to handle new orders—mail versus hand-delivery.
3. You will have to find some of your subscribers. They haven't given you a change of address form—they've moved and USPS has been forwarding, but the delivery service can't find them.
4. You need to know the following about addresses on your list for efficient hand-delivery:
   - *Complete* information: floor numbers, suite numbers, etc
   - Where the P.O. Box address is physically located.
   - In Washington, can you decipher mysterious government addresses?
   - Street addresses for commercial buildings—"Fillmore Building" may not be sufficient.
   - Are there subscribers at home addresses within the hand-delivery area? (Some apartments have security systems which require buzzer access—good service doesn't include waking up readers at 6:00 a.m.)
5. Imprint some envelopes "DELIVERED BY HAND"—otherwise, copies will wind up, somehow, being put in the mail at the recipient's office and coming back to you postage due. Don't let your mailer run the hand-delivery envelopes through the meter at 0.00 postage, because that's the easiest way to seal. It increases your problems.
6. You become involved with the subscriber's internal bureaucracy. When you have non-delivery problems, investigation will show, more often than not, the delivery service got it there. It then disappeared 'from the receptionist's desk', or 'on the way to the mail room,' etc.
7. Handle the non-delivery calls yourself—the service will do it for you, but you want to know how many complaints are coming in. If some of them are 'I got my copy, but three pages are the same' or 'I got an empty envelope,' you know to harass your printer, not the service.

The first thing you should do is give your subscribers plenty of notice of what is going to happen and when.

Publications of Interest

Much of what you need to know about USPS operations is available in government publications.

1. *Memo to Mailers.* A monthly newsletter, free on request (P.O. Box 1, Linwood, N.J. 08201).

2. *Domestic Mail Manual.* Includes information on domestic mail service and a detailed description of each class of mail and special service available to the public. Subscriptions are $17 ($21.25 foreign) and include periodic updates.

3. *Postal Operations Manual.* Detailed information on USPS services such as retail and customer services, mail processing and transportation, delivery services, etc. $34 ($42.50 foreign) includes periodic updates.

4. *International Mail.* Everything you need to know about mailing internationally including an alphabetic list of countries with the specific requirements for mail addressed to each of them. $9 ($11.25 foreign) includes periodic updates.

5. *The Postal Bulletin.* For "those who feel their needs require complete and official postal information." Published weekly, includes current orders and instructions and information relating to the postal service and provides advance notice of important changes in regulations. $35 a year ($43.75 foreign).

Note: Prices for other publications include the updates "as required for an indefinite period."

Publications 2 through 5 may be ordered directly from the Superintendent of Documents, U.S. Government Printing Office, Washington, D.C. 20402

The Office at Home Questions

Many beginning newsletter publishers presume that, at least at first, they can run their newsletter business from their homes. You certainly can begin that way. It does present a couple of postal problems.

Using a Post Office Box Address

Most new newsletters published from a home use a post office box address for business purposes:

The WIN Letter
P. O. Box 1982
Alexandria, Virginia 22305

Some promotion and direct mail specialists feel this creates a credibility problem because you are asking prospects to order a publication from a firm they have never heard of without the "security" of an office address and phone number they can call for information or help with problems. There are several ways you can circumvent this problem.

1. The telephone problem. Put in a separate business phone. You can tell your local phone company it's an additional personal phone. You needn't pay business rates or get a business listing because you probably aren't going to get that many calls from your local area. NAA recommends getting a business line, however, and paying the business rate. We believe you should not go into the newsletter publishing business trying to cut corners. One problem in some areas is zoning regulations that prohibit operating a business (even a mail order business with no traffic) in a residential location. A business phone in your den/office is not a major inconvenience; if you are doing a good job fulfilling subscriptions you won't get that many calls. If no one is available to answer the phone during normal business hours you can get an answering service for about $50 monthly, or invest in an answering machine—around $100. Yes, many people hate talking to machines, but they are becoming increasingly prevalent and accepted.

2. The business address problem. If you decide to give your customers and prospects a business address, you have several solutions. You can use a remail service to give yourself a downtown business address, but this costs money and adds delays to your operation. You can include your street address and post box number in your business address:

High Profit Press
307 Kentucky Avenue
P. O. Box 1982
Alexandria, Virginia 22305

The postal service delivers mail to the address instruction directly preceding the city, state and zip. Material addressed as above will be delivered to your post office box. One caution, this only works well if your P. O. Box is in the same zip code area as your home address. Many correspondents will leave off the P.O. Box number if you give them a four line address. If the zip is wrong for the street address it will create delayed and possibly undelivered mail. Some publishers list two addresses separately calling the street address "business office" and the P.O. Box "mail address" or "editorial office." NAA recommends finding a way to list a business address and phone number in all promotions and correspondence.

Don't use your personal phone number if you don't want your spouse or children trying to cope with business calls. Use of a personal address doesn't create that problem. Most publishers very seldom have a subscriber come visit the office. (NAA does know some financial advisers who don't list an office address because they don't want subscribers dropping in to look for tips.)

New USPS Regs in Effect

USPS has published in the Federal Register several new regulations which could affect operations of some newsletter publishers. They cover: termination of address changes/forwarding of mail, use of P.O. Box and street address in combination and notice of requirement to use zip codes.

1. Under new regulations, a change of address notice will expire after one year. There is a potential for extension of a second year, however, for mailers who face potential economic harm if mail addressed to their former address is returned as undeliverable after expiration of the change order. (Publishers of a mail order catalogue were specifically cited in the Federal Register to exemplify this category of mailers.)

2. Under previous regulations, firms wishing to maintain a box office address and a P.O. number could use a mailing address such as:

> Ms. Meredith Kerry, Publisher
> High Profit Press
> 307 Kentucky Avenue
> P. O. Box 1973
> Alexandria, VA 22305

and it would be delivered to the address shown on the line immediately preceding the state, city and zip code. (Small publishers who have done this want to give the prospects the "security" of a street address while actually having their mail delivered to a P.O. box.—The street address is often their home.) This only works when the zip is the same for both addresses, because correspondents often omit one or the other line from mail, and if this results in mail with an incorrect zip, it can mean delayed or non-delivery.

If you wanted all the mail delivered to the P.O. number, however addressed, you could issue contrary instructions. Now, under the new regulation this option is removed. USPS says that mailers have sufficient opportunity on their return address, order forms, etc. to indicate how mail to them should be addressed, and the majority of correspondents will address mail that way.

CHAPTER XI
Newsletter Accounting
and Financial Operations

Beginning newsletter publishers have some important decisions to make regarding the accounting system and method of business organization they plan to use. Newsletter publishing is sometimes portrayed in "get-rich-quick" manuals as a tax-free operation. This is another assertion that contains an element of truth, but needs considerable amplification.

Selecting Your Accounting System

As a newsletter publisher you should keep your books on the accrual basis, because the basis for the tax advantages of newsletter publishing is the "unfulfilled subscription liability." Here's how it works. Let's say you're publishing a $120 annual price monthly newsletter. On a cash accounting basis, when a subscription order and a check come in, you have earned $120 income. On an accrual accounting system, however, your income is deferred over the life of the subscripton. When you put that $120 check in the bank, you haven't really earned $120. You have the liability to provide 12 months of newsletters, so you "earn" that income as you deliver the service over the full period of the subscription. This is permissable under Section 455 of the IRS Code. To set up your books in this manner you need to inform the IRS during the first year of operation. Later than that, you can also request permission to shift from cash to accrual accounting. (See note at the end of this chapter for important changes the 1982 Tax revisions appear to have made affecting newsletter publishing operations.)

For example, in your first year of operation, you sell 800 subscriptions to the *WIN Letter*. Under the sample income/expense sheet on page 130, you would find yourself with a taxable profit of $29,250. On the accrual system, you would still have the same $96,000 income, but assuming that the new subscription orders came in evenly over the year, you would have earned only an average of 50% of the amount, and you would have a liability of $48,000 for unfulfilled subscriptions on your books. This would make your expense for the first year of operation $114,750, leaving you a loss, for tax purposes, of $18,750.

Let's carry this example forward a couple years to make a point. Assume that your underlying costs remain the same, $66,750 for each of the next two years. You continue to promote and get new orders, but you find you have "skimmed the cream" off of the market. You get 600 new orders the second year and 480 the third. Assume also that your renewal rate is 65% the first year and 85% the second. On December 31 of the third year, you will find yourself with 1,312 subscriptions in effect and a gross revenue for the year just ended of $157,440. Your accountant will tell you, however, under the accrual system your earned income for the year was $145,920. This represents the amount actually earned by fulfilling ordered subscriptions. Your unfilled subscription liability remaining is $78,720. Adding that liability to your other costs, the total expense for the year was $145,470, leaving you an apparent taxable profit of $450.00. The point of this illustration is that unfilled subscription liability does not guarantee a permanent tax free operation for newsletter publishers. Here, a reasonably successful new newsletter operation by the end of the third year is in the black for tax purposes. The unfulfilled subscription liability is great for a beginning newsletter business, but it will only keep the tax man away while your business is rapidly expanding, either by increasing subscribers or by starting new newsletters.

Organizational Options

Basically you have three options for organizing your newsletter business. It can be an unincorporated sole proprietorship (or partnership, which is essentially the same for tax purposes), a business corporation, or a "subchapter S" corporation (which has some special advantages and disadvantages).

Let's take the income/expense sheet for the *WIN Letter* (on page 130) and see what happens under each form of business. Our hypothetical newsletter had a successful launch, showing a tax loss of nearly $20,000 the first year, but a thin profit by the third year. By the end of one more year, we have a pre-tax profit of $12,000.

Proprietorship. The simplest form of business is the sole proprietorship. You own the business and run it on an unincorporated basis. This has a couple of advantages. One is simplicity. You fill out a schedule C to add to your personal income tax return and apply the $18,000 first-year-loss to your taxable income. In other words, you are not only operating a business that is generating a good deal of cash flow, but you can use the loss to shelter some of your other income.

There are, however, a couple of drawbacks. First, when you don't incorporate you lose that wonderful benefit, limited liability. We want to help you succeed in the newsletter business, but nothing is certain. You could wind up in the awkward position of having $10,000 in outstanding bills to printers and mail houses, and $15,000 in unfilled subscription liability (from the 150 or so subscriptions you have sold) and no cash on hand either to continue promotion or to fulfill the subscriptions you have sold. You can't walk away from those debts and liabilities if you are not incorporated. No one incorporates a newsletter business with the intention of being able, one day, to send subscribers a letter saying, "We're real sorry, you won't be getting any more issues of the *WIN Letter,* but we're going into bankruptcy," but a corporation has the legal right to do so. (In reality, publishers whose ventures haven't succeeded most often do succeed in selling them to another publisher, even if it's only to take over the unfilled subscription liability. So the letter to the subscriber is more likely to say, "Hi, we're AJAX Publishing, and we want you to know that we have acquired the *WIN Letter* from Profit Press, and you will be receiving our outstanding publication *Widgit World in Review* for the remainder of your subscription.")

Dismissing the distasteful possibility that your venture will not succeed, an unincorporated newsletter business still shows a couple of drawbacks. When you begin making profit, you have to pay personal income taxes on it. If you are making additional income as a consultant from other sources (and perhaps your spouse is gainfully employed) you may find that the profits from the newsletter operation are being taxed at a fairly substantial rate. (The 50% bracket for joint returns starts at about $45,800.)

A second drawback to the proprietorship or partnership is that it limits your flexibility. Suppose your editor is becoming the finest thing going in widgit journalism and you begin to see him more and more as the key to your operation. You really want to weld him with golden handcuffs to your operation. In newsletter publishing one of the most satisfactory ways to do this is to offer him a share of the business. Journalism appears to be, by nature, a transient profession, and even if you are paying well, your editor may decide in a couple years it is time to seek new horizons. He will probably feel different if he has been made a part-owner of an increasingly successful business. This is easy to do for an incorporated business and hard for a sole proprietorship.

A third drawback of operating a newsletter as an unincorporated business is that it limits a number of the good things you can do for yourself as you become more successful, (i.e. pension programs and deferred compensation arrangements, and smaller benefits like a company car and deductible business expenses). Business expenses are equally legal and equally tax deductible on either a corporate or a personal tax return, but the facts of life are that the IRS eyes such deductions much more closely on a personal return than on a business return.

Why can't I begin my newsletter venture as an unincorporated business and take advantage of the tax shelter opportunities for the early years and then, if success brings me to the point that I want to take on additional owners or do some of these other things, incorporate then and pay lower corporate taxes?

The answer is you can, but note one very significant caveat. If you incorporate a newsletter publishing venture previously operated as an unincorporated business, the total amount of unfulfilled subscription liability you have deducted as operating loss in prior years is subject to "recapture" by the IRS as personal income in the year in which you incorporate. We know of successful publishers who have found themselves caught in the position where they would like to incorporate, but can't afford it because of the potential personal tax liability.

The advantages then of incorporating your newsletter publishing venture are:
- limited liability
- flexibility in issuing shares or making changes in ownership
- availability of attractive options in company paid benefits
- lower corporate tax rates on profits

A third option combines some of the best of both worlds.

The Subchapter S Corporation. Subchapter S of the Internal Revenue Code allows a special type of corporation to benefit from the protections of incorporation and also some of the tax shelters of the sole proprietorship. You probably have capital to invest in your newsletter business, to finance initial promotions, purchase office equipment, and other start up costs. As a Subchapter S corporation, you are permitted to carry over to your personal income tax returns a tax loss from unfulfilled subscription liability up to the amount of money you have invested in the business. In other words, if you invested $10,000 of your own funds in the *WIN Letter* and had the first year tax loss of $18,000 you could deduct $10,000 on your personal return. This benefit is, however, subject to the same caveat as the tax loss deduction available to an unincorporated sole proprietor. If you become a regular corporation later, your Sub S deductions are subject to "recapture" as personal income. You might later want to become a regular corporation because a Subchapter S corporation must use any tax losses in the year incurred. In a regular corporation, you can forward some tax losses to future years.

For a number of reasons newsletter publishing can be an attractive venture opportunity. It is a cash generating business and it offers a number of tax benefits. It is not a "tax-free goldmine," nor is it a realistic way to shelter other taxable income. One veteran newsletter financial man told NAA, "As I see it, making the decision on how to operate your newsletter business is determined by what your real purpose is; are you looking to operate a real business in a business-like manner, or are you looking for creative ways to screw around with IRS?"

Here is a breakdown of the first year's operation of an imaginary new newsletter, Widgit Industry News *(The WIN Letter)*. It's an 8 page biweekly, and the key market is 20,000 widgit industry executives, suppliers, etc. You've set the price at $120 annually which looks competitive. (Figures circa 1980.)

Direct Cost:

Editorial	$18,000	A full time reporter/editor (salary, taxes and benefits). Many beginners plan to handle editorial themselves, but find that running the operation and doing all the writing is a bit much. It may also take more time and effort to put out 8-10 pages of quality news every two weeks than you first thought.
Printing	7,000	To produce an increasing number of copies of an 8-page letter biweekly (including mailing services).
Postage	2,000	Assumes all issues go first-class.
Envelopes and Paper Supplies	1,000	
Art and Graphic Design	250	An attractive layout and envelopes are real pluses.
Promotion	24,000	Four mailings to 20,000 list at 30¢ apiece — conventional wisdom says you can do it cheaper, but at current prices, it's getting increasingly difficult to do so.
Direct Mail Consultant	250-2,500	Prices vary, some will draft one piece for you at a small amount, others are considerably more expensive. If you don't know the ropes of direct mail advertising, it may well be worthwhile.
Total (approximate)	$52,750	

Indirect Cost:

Secretary-Bookkeeper	$ 5,000	Probably a part time person is enough.
Rent	3,000	A small office.
Telephone	500	More if you need to make a lot of long distance calls for news gathering.
Travel	1,000	You may need to cover a couple important widgit industry meetings.
Legal and Accounting	1,000	You may want to incorporate; you may need assistance with tax returns, etc.—This is a low estimate.
Equipment	2,500	Typewriters, desk, file cabinets (You can capitalize this and depreciate, of course, but you need to lay out the dollars up front).
NAA Membership ($175 dues)	1,000	Attend conference, seminars, travel (You didn't think we'd leave this out . . .)
Total	$14,000	

Total Direct and Indirect Cost—$66,750.

Balancing this income from 800 subscriptions at $120 for $96,000.

As we go to press it appears that the 1982 revisions to the Tax Code have made important changes in the tax treatment of circulation expenses (promotion and renewal) for publishers operating as sole proprietorships, partnerships on an unincorporated basis, and Subchapter S corporations; changes which may cause beginning publishers to take another look at the question of initial incorporation.

It appears (final regulations have not yet been drafted) that circulation expenses for NL publishers are deemed to be 'tax preference items' and the publisher has two choices: (1) amortize circulation expenses over ten years or (2) deduct all circulation expenses in the current year (this has been the practice of most publishers and, combined with deferring subscription income over the life of the order—permissable under accrual accounting under Section 455 of IRS code—has created the attractive tax losses during initial years which has made publishing an attractive venture).

In the case of a publisher continuing to choose to expense all circulation items immediately, he/she will be liable for a 20% alternative minimum tax on the amount in excess of the deduction that could have been taken had he elected the 10 year amortization. Persons filing a single return pay the minimum tax of 20% on tax preference items that exceed $30,000 while those filing joint returns pay on tax preference items exceeding $40,000. So, a publisher incurring $100,000 in circulation expenses must pay a 20% tax of $12,000 for a single return (after subtracting the $10,000 which could have been amortized and the $30,000 exemption) or $10,000 tax on a joint return. The exact computation will only be clear when the Treasury Department issues regulations.

Should a Newsletter Business Incorporate?

Incorporate initially if you're serious about operating your newsletter venture as a business, is the advice comptroller Allie Ash of Capitol Publications in Washington has for newer publishers.

"The attractions of operating unincorporated are obvious," says Ash. "It's simple, you only have to file a Schedule C with your personal 1040 and you can take real tax savings in the beginning by flowing through the paper losses you will doubtless have on an accrual accounting system (from unfulfilled subscription liability)."

There are four large drawbacks to operating in this manner:

1. You lose the protection of limited liability.

2. The tax saving features are usually temporary. "Unless the business continues to grow by new subscriptions or new starts, you will be generating taxable earned income in just a few years."

3. You can find yourself "too poor" to incorporate later—People have reached the stage mentioned above and decided it's time to incorporate, only to learn that IRS will then "recapture" all of the unfulfilled subscription liability losses you took on your previous personal returns as "income" in the current year.

4. As the business grows, if you want to cement key employees to the company, you don't have the option of giving part ownership.

Sub-Chapter S Corporation—These have all the advantages of the basic corporation plus some aditional features which are useful for the publisher who has invested personal resources in a newletter venture. In a sub-chapter S organization, you are able to deduct business losses from your personal income to the extent of the investment in the company you have made. In a regular corporation, however, losses may be carried forward from one year to another, but in a sub-chapter S organization they are lost forever if they cannot be used in the year generated. (This could mean that a publisher who has organized a newsletter operation as a sub-chapter S corporation might wish to convert to a regular corporation in order to have the option of carrying forward losses, but then you again face recapture of any business losses claimed in prior years as personal capital gains.)

Partnerships—Newsletter publishing ventures are often operated as partnerships. Ash recommends setting up a corporation with specified shares of ownership as preferable. "A corporation has some business advantages, but it appears to me that the most frequent difficulties in partnership operations come from misunderstandings between the partners over roles with the company rather than from the technical form of operation. You should probably also have an agreement for a buy-out formula if you decide to dissolve the arrangement."

"For one thing, if your partner should get killed in an accident or involved in a nasty divorce, this protects you from squabbling with the spouse over company operations." (These buy-out agreements should cover all stockholders of privately owned newsletter corporations.)

Ten Ways to Take $$ Out of Your NL Business

Publishers concerned about their tax situation can look at these suggestions for ways in which they can take tax free dollars out of their newsletter business.

1. *Use a company car.* The business pays for it and deducts purchase and operating costs as expenses. The IRS has not instituted the threatened rules about imputed income from having the use of a company car. The principal user should reimburse the company by personal check on a monthly basis for the personal use of the car. The reimbursement should have some relationship to reality.

2. *Use a company expense account.* The same business expenses are equally deductible legally if they appear on a personal return or on the corporate return. In reality, expenses on a corporate return, properly accounted for, will draw much less scrutiny from IRS. Those same expenses on the personal return are likely to get a much closer look.

3. *Pay club dues or memberships through the company.* The same principle as No. 2. While it is equally legal either way, it is a lot easier to handle by having the company pay. A note of caution, only deduct legitimate business expenses incurred at the club. If the publisher's spouse and/or children sign chits at the country club, take those out of the monthly bills and pay them personally before the company pays the remainder of the bill for business use.

4. *Entertainment facilities.* A lodge on a lake can be a permissable business expense, but rules on this are tighter than they used to be. The facility has to be used exclusively for the employees of the business and be available to all on a non-discriminatory basis.

5. *Tuition payments for dependents.* You can't do this unless you offer education reimbursement to all employees on a non-discriminatory basis. You might, however, employ your children as the sole employees of a small publisher and, if they were going to college in the same location as the newsletter was published, tuition payments could well be permissable.

How A Banker Views Newsletter Publishers

"The newsletter business throws off more cash than any other business I can think of with the possible exception of a Pac Man arcade" comments Lynn Green, Vice President, 1st American Bank in Washington, D.C. That being the case, why is it that so many newsletter publishers, including those not particularly small or new in the business, find it so difficult to get financing for newsletter publishing ventures?

"Bankers are taught from day one," Green observes, "to look at balance sheets and do balance sheet analysis and, facing reality, newsletter publishers, because of the very nature of the business, are simply never going to have the type of balance sheets which are exciting to a loan officer. You, the publisher, have to work to "educate" the banker to understand the cash flow of your business; to move his attention away from the balance sheet and to the operating statement. Bankers are traditionally conservative. Newsletter publishers don't have much in the way of fixed assets. They don't have inventory levels banks can look at. Traditional collateral is simply not there.

"Newsletter publishers look at projected renewal income as equivalent to accounts receivable. From a banker's view, the major problem is your accounts receivable don't have to paid. While you have 5,000 subscribers, they are spread over 50 states and XX foreign countries. If the publisher were to default on a loan secured by anticipated renewals, how would the bank go about collecting the money? They would probably have to sell the account to someone else at a discount to do it and, therefore, the bank discounts in advance the value of the asset for loan purposes.

"For all these reasons, publishers need to understand they are requesting what is usually viewed as unsecured loans for working capital, a type of loan which bankers view as a very high risk. What you are likely to encounter are requests for loan approvals to be coupled with sizeable compensating balances and then to be offered only at rates of prime plus two (or higher)."

"I know of no firm banking industry policy regarding unfulfilled subscriptions—you look at them as a very valuable asset but they certainly don't look like that on your balance sheet. Bank "A" may insist on treating them as liabilities, but Bank "B" may be willing to see it your way which leads me to the positive side of this discussion.

"There still is a positive side. The question is definitely one of education. Move the emphasis from balance sheet analysis to cash flow analysis. The principal thing a bank wants to know is 'how is this guy going to be able to repay this loan or line of credit every month' (or quarter).

Emphasize The Strengths of Your Business

A. Show how your total revenues have grown from year to year.

B. Show the growth in number of newsletters published (or subscribers to your "flagship" newsletter).

C. Show the growth in the prime prospect lists to which you market (coupled with analysis of your promotional track record).

D. Accept some discussion of compensating balances as part of the picture. (One of the reasons aggressive bankers may be willing to finance ventures like newsletters (which wouldn't have attracted them in the past) is that today the bank business is much more competitive. How much of your excess cash which might, in the past, have been in savings accounts or CD's is now in a money fund?")

CHAPTER XII
Legal Questions
in Newsletter Publishing

In our increasingly over-regulated, litigious society, newsletter publishing is practically a bastion of laissez-faire. There are probably fewer legal requirements, restrictions and regulations surrounding newsletter publishing than most other forms of business enterprise. There are legal questions, however, which are of special concern to publishers. Some of the more important are described in this chapter. What the following chapter does *not* do is attempt to cover the legal considerations endemic to going into business—the question of incorporation, filing W-4 forms and withholding returns with IRS, finding out whether your jurisdiction imposes personal property tax on your typewriters, etc. This article will be limited to considerations particular to the newsletter publishing business including:

- Copyright
- Trademark Registration
- Usage of ISSN Numbers
- Libel
- The Freedom of Information Act
- Collection of Sales Tax on Newsletter Subscriptions
- Overtime/Wage Hour Law Requirements Regarding Reporters, Editors
- Anti-Trust Concerns
- Federal Trade Commission Regulations Concerning Direct Mail Offers
- Securities and Exchange Commission Regulation (of Financial Advisory Newletters)

A. Copyright

The overwhelming majority of newsletter publishers copyright their materials (well in excess of 90%). Under the terms of the Copyright Act (revised in 1978), publishers have two options for copyrighting:

1. *Deposit.* Achieved by sending two copies of each issue to the Library of Congress, Copyright Office, Washington, D.C.

2. *Registration.* Along with the copies a Library of Congress form TX and $10 is required.

Having taken either action, the publisher is entitled to place the copyright symbol "©" on his publication: ©1982, Profit Publishing. This entitles the publisher to the full protection of the law. Additional language, which you sometimes see, indicating that violaters will be boiled in oil, has no additional legal significance. There is, however, a significant difference between deposit and registration of a copyright. In the case of an action for infringement of your copyrighted materials, only holders for which the copyright has been registered are entitled to statutory damages as provided by the Act. Otherwise, you are limited to seeking recompense for actual monetary damage which, counsel advises, is difficult to prove. You can register a copyright anytime within three months of publication. In most instances, if an infringement is going to be made, it will occur soon after original publication. If a publisher suspects improper use of his copyright materials, he can register a copyright within 90 days after publication and still receive full protection of the Act.

How much can be used of copyrighted material by another publication? Basically, this is a grey area. It occurs in newsletter publishing both when other publications reuse material originally published in your newsletter and when you may wish to use or adapt materials which originally appeared in another publication. As a rule of thumb, publishers are usually on safe grounds quoting or excerpting from a copyrighted article which appeared elsewhere if proper attribution is made. In the real world, if a newsletter publisher believes another publication has used too much (or too frequently) from his publication, the result is usually a letter from him, or his lawyer, requesting that the second publisher cease and desist. If such an instance were ever to go to court it becomes subject to complicated analysis including exact comparison to determine how much material was used, whether it was verbatim or rewritten and summarized, and how extensively (facts cannot be copyrighted only format).

What about the doctrine of Fair Use? The 1976 Act establishes, for the first time, the concept that there are certain permissible uses of copyrighted materials. Section 107 includes the questions which are to be considered in terms of determining "fair use" of copyrighted materials,

1. Character and purpose of use—i.e., brief usage in reviews or quotations properly attributed, etc., generally are permissible.

2. Nature of the work—a pirated copy of a feature film would probaby be considered a more serious infringement than a xerox machine copy of a newsletter.

3. The Amount of the Work Used—in this case, a copy of an entire issue of a newsletter, for example, might be held to be a more serious infringement than copies of the same amount of material from a larger magazine or book.

4. Most important—The effect of the use on the holder of the copyright—presumably a publisher could overcome a "fair use" defense by demonstrating the use in question of his materials was costing him sales.

In practice, again there is not a great deal of precedent yet established governing this new revision of the Act.

How about people making photocopies of my newsletter materials? They do. One veteran publisher says, "I guess I figure that it's implied in the contract that when they take a subscription to one of our high price newsletters, they are entitled to make a couple photocopies for office use." It is however, illegal, albeit almost impossible to police. In flagrant instances where publishers have become aware of subscribers routinely making dozens, or even hundreds, of copies for distribution within their companies, a letter from counsel accompanied with a bill for an appropriate number of subscriptions has usually been sufficient to settle the issue.

Multi-Copy Rates. Some publishers address this problem by establishing special rates for multiple subscriptions. With others, if you want two you pay for two. Experts advise that it is unwise to attempt to calculate a multi-copy rate which approximates the cost of photocopying, because to the violator those costs (office equipment and secretarial time) are buried in overhead and you tend to discredit your established price if your newsletter is $179 annually and multiple copies are $22.50 apiece.

The Copyright Clearance Center. Along with the Fair Use Doctrine, the Copyright Clearance Center was established in 1978. It is intended to provide a vehicle through which photocopies of copyrighted materials can be made legally and a royalty paid to the holder. Briefly, publishers register their publications with the CCC, establish a per page, per issue, or per article cost for their materials. Potential users are also supposed to register with the CCC, keep records of the photocopies they make and remit the appropriate charges to the CCC which, making a deduction for their costs, returns the remainder to the publisher. As this complicated explanation probably documents, the CCC is not widely used. NAA recommends, though, that publishers register their publications because if for no other reason, you can then document in any instance of infringement that you have made an effort to provide a vehicle for legal photocopying of your copyrighted materials.

While some publishers might prefer an interpretation of the law which permits no copies to be made for any purpose, this is not the apparent congressional intent behind the 1978 revisions.

Work for Hire. As a general practice editorial materials produced by reporters and editors on the staff of a newsletter are considered "work for hire" and the copyright protection and ownership of these materials remains with the publisher. This question can become confused when the publisher utilizes part-time stringers or freelancers. A written agreement spelling out this relationship is recommended for publishers using other than full-time staff to produce editorial materials.

Reprint Privileges. The newsletter publisher, as copyright holder, may grant reprint permission for his copyrighted materials to whomever he chooses and establish such fees as the traffic will bear. The fact that permission has been given gratis to one individual or organization does not prevent a fee being charged to others for the same privilege at the publishers discretion. (Give it to the church magazine but sock IBM)—it isn't recommended, however, to discriminate in terms offered to competitors.

B. Should Your Title be a Registered Trademark?

It isn't terribly expensive although it can be time-consuming, but most newsletter publishers don't register their newsletter names as a trademark with the U.S. Patent and Trademark Office. A quick check of newsletter samples on hand at NAA headquarters shows fewer than 20% carry trademark registration information on the masthead.

If you think that "Widgit Industry News —The WIN Letter" is not only a great name but a competitive advantage to your company, you might be well advised to go ahead to attempt to officially trademark the name. You have a common law right to the name which you establish by using it in commerce, but if someone violates it you have to take them to court and bear the burden of establishing proof. If you are registered, however, the burden of proof is on them.

The process of submitting an application is fairly simple, but publishers might wish to consult counsel in preparing an application. What is required to be submitted is five copies of the proposed trademark in use (issues of your newsletter will do), and a $175 fee. What the attorney will do for you is conduct a trademark search to see if anyone else has the name previously registered. The most common problem encountered in a search is other registered names which are similar, if not identical. There are no firm guidelines on whether your application is sufficiently different to be able to be registered. It may be worth the investment in legal time to get a better judgment on this than to go through the time and expense of filing an application which is refused.

Beyond names which are already in use, trademark restrictions also do not permit registration of names which are: immoral, deceptive or scandalous, include the U.S. flag or any other government insignia, or include the name, picture or signature of a living person without consent.

Note: you can't register your company name, only the name of a good or service. As soon as you submit the application you may include the designation, 'tm' on your masthead which indicates you own a common law trademark and have applied to register. The process of approval can take a year or more and only when approval is received may you upgrade the marking to the 'r'.

To receive application forms and additional information on copyright registration, contact the U.S. Patent & Trademark Office (703-557-3158).

C. Usage of ISSN Numbers is Slow Among Newsletter Publishers

ISSN stands for International Standard Serial Number, a program begun in 1971 by the National Serials Data Program, an arm of the Library of Congress. For their purpose, newsletters are classified as "serial publications" which includes periodicals, newspapers, annuals (directories, reports, etc.), journals, transactions of societies, etc. Serials are defined as "a publication in print or in non-print form issued in successive parts . . . and intended to be continued indefinitely."

Once a publication is assigned an ISSN number, it is permanent. If the publication later ceases to exist, the record of its number is maintained and is never assigned to another publication. (If your publication changes title, a new number is issued for the new publication, and the previous number is "retired.")

How do you get an ISSN number assigned? Send the National Serials Data Program a copy of their "Serial Data Sheet for Publishers," available from: The Library of Congress, National Serials Data Program, Washington, D.C. 20540.

How much does it cost? Nothing.

What benefits are there to having one? The people at NSDP list nine benefits (abbreviated here):

• identifies a title regardless of language or country in which published

• results in accurate citing of serials by scholars, researchers, abstractors, and librarians.

• useful communication between publishers and suppliers

• integral part of the journal article citation used to monitor payments to the

Copyright Clearance Center
- used by libraries
- simplifies inter-library loan systems and union catalogue reporting and listing
- "eminently suitable" for computer use in fulfilling the need for file update, and linkage, retrieval, and transmittal of data
- USPS uses ISSN to regulate certain publications mailed at second-class rates
- all ISSN registrations are maintained in an international data base and are available in the ISDS bulletin

Where do I put it? They'd like you to put it on the top right corner of page one—most users do—but other places, most commonly on the masthead, are acceptable. Typeface and size are at publisher's discretion.

How many newsletter publishers are using ISSN's? A random sample of 100 NAA member newsletters showed fifteen displaying ISSN numbers. While it may be sound business practice for a newsletter publisher to register the copyright for his newsletter materials, trademark his publication name, and acquire an ISSN number, it is not *required* in order to publish.

D. Libel

In the past several years, there appears to be an upswing in accusations of libel in newsletter publications. An informal survey at an NAA seminar showed about half the publishers present had at least been threatened with an action—not necessarily a suit or even a 'lawyer's letter,' but at least an "I'll sue if you print" communication.

The legal requirements of libel have not changed. To be found libelous something must be:
- in writing,
- false,
- communicated to someone,
- accuse someone of a crime, hold them up to ridicule or tend to injure them in their trade, business or profession.

What has changed is the defense. The law encompasses two classes of individuals, public officials or individuals (defined as those persons who push themselves into public view) and private figures. In the past it has been very difficult to libel a public figure, because in addition to the basic tests, the publisher must be shown to have published with a 'wanton disregard' for the truth. A couple of recent decisions, however, have tended to narrow the definition of a public figure. A researcher "awarded" the Golden Fleece for government waste by Senator Proxmire (D-WI) was held not to have become a public figure because the Senator issued a press release about the subject or because he held a subsequent press conference to refute the allegations.

Certain documents may be used with impunity, are privileged; publishers may quote from court documents and congressional reports with impunity. In a story involving a private individual, he/she need only to prove you failed to use "care" rather than wanton disregard. NAA notes that some publishers include "disclaimer" statements in their newsletter (some variation of "we did our best to insure that the material in this issue is true, but . . ."). Like additional language appended to the copyright symbol, this appears to have little legal significance.

Here is a short checklist to help avoid libel problems. Nothing replaces common sense, but a study by Dr. Dennis F. Hale of Bowling Green State University came up with a consensus of 11 checkpoints to use in avoiding the possibility of libel suits against your publication.

- Develop a set procedure for handling sensitive copy which identifies "questionable materials."
- Try to avoid sources with "questionable motives."
- Don't overuse unattributed or confidential sources.
- Always, Always, Always contact the subject of the story in question for their version.
- Have sensitive stories reviewed by two editors and, if necessary, your attorney.
- Seek verification, if possible, of allegations in published documents.
- Preserve all notes and records relating to a "questionable" story you do print.
- Check and double check sensitive facts.
- Avoid judgmental adjectives.
- Be extremely careful with headline copy.
- Remember, negligence may be becoming the predominant standard for liability. The 86 attorneys who participated in the study raised more warning flags about reliability of sources than any other single point. "Be certain of reputable, independent substantiation for every potentially libelous textual assertion."

Insurance coverage to protect newsletter publishers from libel suits as well as damages arising from "errors and omissions" is available. The occurence of such judgments against newsletter publishers is quite unusual. The publishers who have taken such insurance state it helps them sleep better, because while the probability of loss is small, the potential damages assessed can be high.

E. The Freedom of Information Act

The Federal Government is a vast storehouse of information, much of which could be of potential news value to newsletter publishers. In addition to the reams of materials which Uncle Sam makes available as public information, newsletter publishers have successfully used the provisions of the Freedom of Information Act to seek other information from the government (PL 90-23).

There are, however, two major stumbling blocks to gaining news information through FOIA actions, (1) the process is cumbersome and includes quite a good bit of built-in delay and (2) the act itself contains categories of exemption which often include the type of news being sought.

The specific exceptions—The law cites categories which are permitted to the government as grounds for withholding information which may be requested. The act does not apply to matters that are:

- specifically required by Executive Order to be kept secret in the interest of national defense or foreign policy,

- related solely to the internal personnel rules and practices of an agency,

- intra-agency and inter-agency memorandums or letters which would not be available by law to a party other than an agency in litigation with the agency.

- personnel and medical files and similar files, the disclosure of which would constitute a clearly unwarranted invasion of personal privacy,

- investigatory files compiled for law enforcement purposes, except to the extent available by law to a party other than an agency,

- contained in or related to examination, operating or condition reports prepared by, on behalf of, or for the use of any agency responsible for the regulation or supervision of financial institutions,

- geological and geophysical information and data, including maps concerning wells

To deny a request for information, the agency involved must cite one or more of the above criteria and the burden is on it to explain why it is pertinent. The purposes to which you intend to put the information are not relevant, as the Act clearly specifies information may be released "to any person."

The request process—The first step in gaining information is to ask for it informally. If denied, find someone else within the agency or another agency within the department and ask them. Members have told NAA that often they have succeeded in gaining information initially denied in this manner.

If this fails, the second step is to submit a Freedom of Information Act request. This is a simple process, requiring merely a letter to the agency requesting the information and noting that the request is being made under the Freedom of Information Act. A simple process, but time consuming because your request is then a matter requiring official interpretation within the agency.

After submission of an official FOIA request, the agency is required to respond within ten working days. If your request is denied, you have the right to an administrative appeal which, again by statute, must be answered within 20 working days. If the appeal is denied, the law requires that you be informed of not only the reasons for denial and the specific identity of the individual making the decision, but also your right to go to court (there is even a provision in the law for judicial action against the person making the decision to withhold information if the court finds the action to have been arbitrary or capricious). Congress tried to stack the law in favor of the public, but you will note, as many as 30 working days may have gone by before you reach the point of going to court.

The Act also provides that, after notifying you, the agency can take an additional ten days if you've asked for a lot of material or materials involving coordination of several agencies, etc. The government is also permitted a reasonable charge for duplicating, etc., if volumes of material are involved. Despite all of the hurdles, the FOIA can be a valuable tool for seeking information. NAA, for example, was successful in obtaining a great deal of background material related to development of the SEC Commission budget for investment advisory regulation through FOIA actions, but it required persistence—submission of requests, appeal of initial denials, etc.

F. Sales Tax

One tax question which does occasionally arise in newsletter business operation is that of collection of sales tax on the subscriptions sold in the local jurisdiction. To NAA's knowledge, the District of Columbia is the only jurisdiction which requires collection of sales tax on newsletter subscriptions. In all other states, newsletters are exempt on the same basis as magazines and newspapers.

There may be exceptions based upon frequency of issue in many jurisdictions which could affect other products of newsletter publishers such as special reports and books. Publishers should consult local regulations to determine if sale of one-time publications are treated differently than annual newsletter subscriptions.

G. Wage and Hour Regulations

In newsletter publishing there appears to be some confusion about the application of the Fair Labor Standards Act (newsletter firms are, of course, subject to all employment regulations, i.e., unemployment compensation, equal opportunity, age discrimination, etc., etc.).

The short answer to the question of exemption of editors and reporters from the provisions of the Fair Labor Standards Act is, *They Aren't*. The FLSA does create catagories of exemption from overtime requirements for "professionals" but reporters and editors are not classified as professionals within the meaning of the Act.

Persons in "executive positions" are also exempt from overtime requirements and, today, most reporters and editors meet the short test (a weekly salary of $250 or more). However, the complete definition of an exempt executive is one who spends more than 50% of his/her time in managerial functions and or supervises more than one other person. There is also a catch hidden in the definition of an executive which could eliminate from exclusion as an executive a person who spends much of his/her time doing work "essentially similar in nature" to that done by persons supervised.

Don't assume that reporters and editors are exempt from FLSA requirements or that they can be required or permitted to work overtime without pay under casual agreements about "setting your own hours" or "compensatory time."

H. Anti-Trust

In a small business environment such as newsletter publishing where, according to NAA estimates, no single member publisher generates as much as 5% of the total industry volume, it might seem that restraint of trade could hardly be an important consideration. However, while publishers have told NAA that they find the information they gain informally at NAA meetings, chapter lunches and seminars to be among the most valuable benefits of membership, we are reprinting here the following guidelines prepared by the Association of American Publishers for its members as a checklist of "do-nots" which should be kept in mind during meetings, formal and informal of newsletter industry companies and individuals.

- Do not discuss or disclose information about competitive policies or practices such as
    - prices, pricing formulas, bids, mark-ups,
    - discounts or discount schedules,

- credit or freight terms,
- return policies,
- profit or other margins, royalty rates, fees and other individual costs,
- advertising or promotional assistance policies.

● Do not discuss specific customers, suppliers or competitors, their terms of sale, or purchase or whether you will or will not do business with them.

● Do not engage in informal or social conversation about anti-trust sensitive issues. Discourage those who do from continuing, or leave the discussion and state your reason for doing so.

I. The Federal Trade Commission

FTC regulations impact newsletter publishing in two areas, establishment of the guarantees commonly used in direct mail promotion and test marketing of new newsletter launch ideas.

Guarantees—A guarantee is a strong selling tool in direct mail and it is generally recommended that your promotional package include one. There are FTC regulations governing what you can promise.

● Guarantees must clearly and conspicuously disclose the nature and extent of the guarantee, including (1) duration of effective time, (2) manner in which the guarantee will act... refund, partial refund, credit, etc., and (3) what creditor claimant must do before guarantor will fulfill his obligation under the guarantee.

● If the guarantee is, in fact, for a pro-rata basis, "refund the amount of the unfulfilled period of the subscription," the guarantee must clearly disclose this fact.

● A general guarantee such as "Satisfaction Guaranteed or Your Money Back" without further definition will be construed as a guarantee under which the full purchase price is to be returned at the buyers option ... limitations such as "for a period of 60 days," must be clearly disclosed in the copy.

In addition, promotional hyperbole, such as the "information you receive in *XYZ Report* will enable you to increase your income thousands annually" could be construed by the FTC to constitute selling points or product claims for which you are required to undertake the responsibility to prove the claim is truthful.

New Products—The FTC requires that products ordered by mail be delivered within thirty days of the receipt of the order. This can create a problem on launch test mailings since, due to the delivery of bulk mail, within thirty days of receipt of initial orders the publisher may not yet have produced Vol. 1, No. 1, or even made a go/no-go decision. Two recommendations, (1) the promotional materials should indicate through such language as "charter offer," "pre-publication discount," etc., that the solicitation is being made for a product which is not yet in existence (it is not necessary to be so blunt as to write, "If we don't get enough orders we aren't going to print."). (2) Send each new order a welcome letter, within thirty days, which explains when the first issue of the new newsletter should reach him. Should a second thirty days period expire prior to publication, you may send a second such letter, but the second letter *is required* to contain a clearly-stated option to receive a refund. Within 60 days of receipt of order, however, the newsletter will normally be in production or a decision to return orders received has been made.

J. The Securities and Exchange Commission

We reserved until last the single government agency which specifically regulates newsletter publishing. The SEC, using what NAA finds to be a strained interpretation of the exemption for publishers contained in the 1940 Investment Advisory Act, considers publishers of financial advisory newsletters to be within the purview of their regulatory authority.

What is a financial advisory newsletter? Despite a 40-year plus history, the SEC has not yet promulated a satisfactory explanation of what can or can not be published in a newsletter to determine its status vis-a-vis SEC regulation. Materials on regulation of investment advisors are available from the commission, but they are not definitive. Publishers may send descriptions of their intended newsletters or sample issues to the commission and request a ruling (or a no-action letter), as to whether such a publication would be required to register. If a publisher receives such notification from the SEC, they reserve their right to change their minds later. There is, NAA is informed by counsel, no penalty for failing to register with the SEC as an investment advisory until requested to do so. Note: to many publishers these registration requirements appear to be an infringement of first amendment rights. There is no precedent established to determine this, and a publisher choosing to refuse to register on such grounds can anticipate an expensive legal struggle.

State Regulation—Most states have little SEC's or State Banking Authorities. Some such as Wisconsin, Connecticut, Pennsylvania and New York are quite aggressive and publishers will probably find it necessary to register and comply with state regulations to do business in those jurisdictions. Again, it is advisable to consult counsel with regard to specifics of state regulation of financial advisory newsletter publications.

How to Set Multi-Copy Prices

To most people who may be copying your newsletters, you have to remember that Xerox is essentially free. It isn't really worthwhile to try and establish a price for additional copies which reflects cost of xeroxing. The person who is doing that figures the secretary is already on the payroll and the machine costs are buried in overhead, so the actual cost is nothing.

Basic approaches to the multiple subscription question:

1. A lot of publishers simply don't offer them. If you want two copies, you buy two at full price.

2. If you give duplicate subscriptions, set a fair price for the duplicates, perhaps 20-30% off of list. Your price establishes a value of your newsletter to subscribers. If that price is $165 a year, it just isn't right to offer duplicate copies at $35. A few publishers have set scales, 20% discount for 2 to 5 copies, 25% discount for 6 to 10, etc.

Capitol Publications in Washington lists "Multiple subscription rates available on request" on some of its newsletters. *Hotline* asked publisher John Wills what they do when rates are requested. "It doesn't happen very often. Mostly we get inquiries from associations saying, 'Could we have 500 copies of *Education Daily* ($325 per year) to distribute to our members?' I say, 'Sure, for

$80,000 a year!' and we never hear from them again. A number of years ago, we did make a serious effort to get multiple orders on the dailies; we set a price that was ridiculously low—our out-of-pocket incremental costs for a new subscription (printing, postage, fulfillment aren't that much) and promoted 'Wouldn't you like the convenience of having your own copy of the newsletter for each key person?' It didn't do well at all. We found we get more revenue by spending the same money promoting, 'Wouldn't you also like these other fine Capitol Publications newsletters?'"

CHAPTER XIII
Sources of Finance —
Buying and Selling Newsletter Properties

What can you do if you believe you have everything you need to begin a successful newsletter business except a dynamite idea for a newsletter? Buy an existing newsletter. Purchase of an entire newsletter publishing business is unusual because (a) you can be talking big bucks and (b) most successful newsletter publishers are not interested in selling their companies. The newsletter business hears constant rumors that big book or magazine publishers are "looking seriously into newsletters" and are "about to crash into the field by major acquisitions." So far, however, that hasn't happened. Ken Callaway, chairman of Capital Publications in Washington, told the *Washington Star* during the 1980 NAA International Conference that his company would gross between $5 million and $6 million in that current year (a company he began 15 years ago with a $700 Christmas bonus as seed capital). "I get phone calls, once in a while," Callaway has told NAA, "and if XYZ Publishing conglomerate were to offer me $10 million for the company they'd real sure have my attention, but it hasn't happened." Since then Capital Publications has made a major acquisition of another publisher and the figure which would "real sure have his attention" is now considerably higher.

You have a better chance of buying an individual newsletter. It is, however, very definitely a sellers' market. A number of well-established newsletter publishers are seriously interested in acquisitions, and a beginning publisher would have to be both fortunate and financially able to act quickly in order to get an attractive property ahead of one of those companies. Howard Hudson's *Newsletter on Newsletters* and the NAA *Hotline* newsletter both occasionally list newsletters for sale, and you sometimes see ads in the *Wall Street Journal*. As the following chapter indicates, the old industry rule of thumb that a fair price for a newsletter property was one year's gross revenues has pretty well gone by the board, but it's still a useful guideline for how much capital you need.

If you do consider buying a newsletter make sure you and your accountant are comfortable with the financial information you get. Pay particular attention to documentation of the promotional response and renewal rates.

Where Do I Get the Money?

One of the questions would-be newsletter publishers ask NAA is, "Where can I get the money to finance my new launch?" NAA has no easy answer. The most common source is your own bank account, or those of your friends and relatives. As indicated elsewhere, the direct cash outlay to test the water — to do some promotional mailings and look for response — is not too high.

Sources Other Than Your Own Bankroll

Commercial Banks. It's not necessarily true that if you ask your friendly local bank loan officer for financing for a newsletter that he will gape at you as if you'd tossed a toad in his in-box; but banks traditionally aren't particularly sympathetic to would-be publishers. They understand publishing is a high-risk business and, more important to them, one that has few physical assets. Banks traditionally are happier financing something like a men's store because if it fails, they can hope to get back some of their loan money by selling the remaining merchandise and display fixtures. A publisher will have spent the loan funds on printing and mailing promotions and newsletters, and if the venture flops, the publisher will have very little to sell. Seriously, the normal rules for attempting to gain loans apply. The more expertise in the field you can demonstrate, the more impressed the bank may be. The greater documentation you can present in draft budgets, income projections, etc., the better off you will be. Demonstrating sincerity by investing a chunk of your own assets in the venture also inclines banks to look more favorably.

Government. At this time, NAA knowns of no government programs for financing newsletter publishers. The Small Business Administration does not make loans to publishers, believing government financing of opinion vehicles might create First Amendment questions.

Existing Publishers. Probably the second most frequent question along these lines is, "How do I find a publisher who will produce this great newsletter I have in mind?" While it may seem logical, this approach doesn't often work. Look at the proposition from the publishers' viewpoint. You are asking them to undertake all the financial risks of a new venture; promotional costs, overhead, printing, fulfillment, etc. Quite logically from their viewpoint, they want at least a significant share of such a newsletter. They might offer the would-be publisher a contract to edit a newsletter for them for a set fee or for so much per subscription sold, but the ownership and most of the future profits would stay with them.

Venture Capital Groups. Some financially sophisticated newer publishers have approached venture capital groups seeking backing for their projects. The same considerations outlined above under commercial banks apply. The more persuasive a case for the project you can make, the better your chances might be. However, we understand the sources of that type are usually looking for places to put larger amounts of capital than are required to launch a newsletter. The scale for a newsletter launch may not be interesting to them and, of course, there is the question of giving up ownership or control. Second, several publishers have structured limited partnerships to gain investment funding (with themselves as general partners — see your CPA to explore this possibility). The 1982 revision to the Income Tax code, however, may have made major limitations to the ability of the beginning newsletter venture to generate the tax losses which are the initial attraction in these instances.

How Do I Go About Buying a Newsletter?

One of the most salient features of the newsletter business is its "portability." A newsletter product, either very successful or less so, is a very marketable commodity and the publisher has, at any time, the option to sell. Similarly, a publisher interested in expansion of his operations quite frequently has the opportunity to acquire a new newsletter. In fact, the IRS code is structured so as to encourage successful publishers to look at new ventures, either started internally or by acquisition. (You might as well risk capital to build the business as pay it to Uncle Sam.) The would-be seller's problem is, in a sense, simple. He wants the highest possible price and, if possible, he'd like it in a cashiers check at time of sale. The buyer has more problems to consider.

The recurring question, ''what is a fair price for a newsletter property?'' continues to be asked often enough to insure that no generally agreed upon formula has yet been reached.

Evaluation of a Potential Acquisition

Here is a short list of *key points* to learn (and or decide) up-front about a potential acquisition opportunity.

● The price which you should pay to acquire a newsletter is determined by (a) *your knowledge of what it will cost you to publish the newsletter,* (b) your assumption of what returns the newsletter will enjoy (promotion response and renewals) under your 'enlightened management', and (c) your decision on what rate-of-return you want to earn on the money which you invest in the purchase.

a. You have knowledge of your own costs. How much it will cost you to publish this newsletter? What your costs are to put 1000 promotion pieces in the mail. Your fulfillment cost per sub. Your cost for the renewal series and your allocated overhead, etc. Figures the current owner may supply on his costs for the items mentioned above may not be of more than historical interest to you. One publisher made an acquisition of a substantial newsletter property for which the previous owner, located in a different labor market, had been doing fulfillment adequately with minimum-wage employees on a manual system at a cost which the new owner couldn't touch. If the current publisher is using 3-4 editorial types on the newsletter, before you simply assume you can do the job with a single editor, some more research into the field and the news-flow may be in order.

b. Again, you know what level of promotional response and renewal rate your other newsletters are experiencing. As a rule of thumb, *it is usually recommended not to assume that the newsletter in question will enjoy either higher promotion/response or better renewal rates under your management.* Publishers who have made a number of acquisitions usually find that doesn't occur.

c. Buying a new newsletter is only one potential use for your capital. When, as in the past several years, you had the option to put the money in certificates of deposit or money fund accounts and earn interest of 15%, what rate of return is reasonable on a similar amount of money expended in acquiring a new newsletter property? Some amount of ''premium'' over current investment rates: 3%? 6%? 10%? This is a decision which is strictly up to the potential buyer but, obviously, the assumed rate-of-return selected will very much effect the amount which can be offered.

Using the rate-of-return selected in (c) above, one way the price a buyer can offer for a newsletter can be determined is constructing a five-year income and expense projection, and discounting the resulting cash-flow back to present value. (Discounted present value tables tell you, for example, if you project a margin of $100,000 on the new newsletter over five years, and you have selected a rate-of-return of 20% on your investment—what amount of cash you can pay *now* to acquire this newsletter which will yield that return over the five-year period.) There isn't anything sacred about a five-year period. One publisher explained three years seemed too short, and going beyond five seemed a bit conjectural . . . He also suggests discounting inflation for the purpose of this analysis by assuming that the subscription price for the newsletter can be increased as necessary to maintain the existing balance between income and expense. (More about discounted present value in another section of this chapter.)

● Make your assumptions on a 'worst case' basis. When you contract the pro-forma income-expense statement, always assume "how bad can it be?".

● Work from statistics, not statements. The promotional response rate and renewal history of the newsletter will tell the potential buyer a good deal more about the property than the financial statements of the present publisher. When examining the records of the current publisher make sure you have an agreement, or at least a mutual understanding, about terms. One publisher considered an acquisition on which he learned the present publisher counted a name as an "active subscriber", until the final end of his renewal series—which came about four months post-expire.

● Make sure you compare the figures you develop with the statements. You have the figure for beginning year circulation, the promotional track record and the renewal history. Do these figures match the year-end circulation? Is there anything which you should know about advance renewals? Early bird renewals? Multi-year offers? Short-term trials? Special premium offers?, etc., etc., which may tell you something you need to know about the 2,134 subscriber names on the list?

How to Price a Newsletter Property

Let's look more closely at a potential acquisition which you are considering. This hypothetical newsletter has a circulation of 1,000 for a biweekly; the price is $100. The current publisher is asking $100,000 (probably figuring one times annual gross is a fair price because that's what he has heard is "traditional" in the newsletter business — more about this later). Let's look at the numbers and find out how the price you should be willing to offer can vary as much as 100%, based on the promotion and renewal records of this newsletter. (without changing its 1,000 subs — $100K gross.)

Your Embedded Costs

How much will it cost you to fulfill those subscriptions? Here is an assumed cost breakdown:

Editorial Costs	$18,000	(a full-time editor, salary plus taxes and bennies)
Support Staff	7,000	(about one-half person for production typing, proofreading, etc.)
Printing, Postage, Paper Costs	6,000	
Fulfillment	3,000	(list maintenance, renewal, management accounting statements)
Contribution to Overhead	10,000	(marketing department, business taxes, allocated executive salaries, office rental, etc.)
	44,000	

For purposes of demonstration, we've tried to keep all of the examples in this chapter as simple as possible. In real world situations the decisions are often more complex. Suppose, in the example being discussed, the purchaser planned to triple the editorial investment, change frequency to weekly and raise the price from $100 to $167 a year?? He still will be able to calculate his costs for production and promotion, but the historical figures from the present publisher on response and renewal rate are pretty much out-the-window since what will be offered is essentially a new product.

While these costs may not change, you do also have variable costs which are subject to change based on promotion and renewal results. Making an analysis of the newsletters operations you determine that:

Average promotion record	
response rates—	1%
Renewal Rates	
Conversions (first year renewals)	60%
Second Time Renewals	80%
Longer Term Renewals	90%
Subscriber History	
First Year Subs	400
Second Year Subs	400
Longer Term Subs	200

This gives an overall renewal rate of 74% but the figures are much more valuable broken down as above. Given these figures, how many subscriptions will you have to sell over the period of five years to maintain the present circulation level of 1,000 annually? If you schedule out the renewals as listed over a period of five years, you will have to sell a total of 960 new subs to maintain the level of 1000 annually.

Given your promotion response rate of 1%, this will require mailing 96,000 pieces. If your promotion costs are $300 per thousand this is a total of $28,800 over the period. Add this to the direct cost for the five year period, $220,000, and you have a total cost of $248,800 with assumed income of $500,000; an average return of $50,200 per year. Your decision is to seek an annual gross return of 20% on your money. This is the point to turn to discounted present value tables. What is the value today of $251,200 profit over the five years at a return of 20%? This return is what the purchaser is buying — anticipated future profits — not the subscribers' names, not the unfulfilled subscription liability and not inventory of unsold special reports, although these all come with the deal. Discounted present value tables tell you that to acquire an anticipated annual profit of $50,200 for each of five years, you can pay $151,300 today and earn 20% return on your money for the period.

In this case, you could offer, as it happens, 1½ times one year's gross and meet your own assumption for return. Obviously, if your assumed return is more or less, the amount you could offer would change accordingly. Let's look, however, at another example. The newsletter described above appears pretty successful. In fact, newsletters with promotion and renewal rates similar to the ones we postulated are not offered for sale everyday. More commonly, a newsletter property which is available for purchase has a less enviable track record. Let's make some new assumptions. Everything about our potential acquisition is the same; number of subs, frequency, price, annual revenues, except:

- the average promotion response rate is . . . *0.5%*
- and the renewal experience is, for first-time conversions . . .   *50%*

                   for second-year renewals . . .   *60%*

                   longer term renewals . . .   *70%*

(Given the same subscriber history this works out to an overall renewal rate of 58%.) Your embedded costs will be exactly the same. So is your promotion cost. Maintaining a subscriber level of 1,000 for five years, given these new assumptions, will require selling — not 960, but 2,027 new subs over the period at a promotion cost of $121,600 — (more than twice as many new orders to be gained, and at a response rate half the previous assumption). With these figures, the assumed gross profit over five years is reduced to $159,000. If the required rate of return on your money is still 20%, going to the tables you find that what you can offer becomes $95,100.

In these two examples, two quite realistic sets of assumptions change the offered price 40% for what, on the surface, could appear to be the same newsletter property.

Well, that process is, while complicated, understandable enough. Why the continuing debate over what is a fair price for a newsletter? Several reasons: (1) The process described works best for a larger, well-established publisher who *knows his costs accurately* and what change (usually fairly little) adding one additional newsletter may make to his operations. A smaller publisher, or even someone who is considering an acquisition to get into the newsletter business is not really in a position to have the cost figures necessary to make that kind of judgment. (2) Without sounding too much like your college Economics 101 course, a newsletter transaction involves two parties, a buyer and a willing seller. They have to be able to come to some mutually understandable agreement on a purchase price. One experienced publisher has described his first venture at a newsletter acquisition as the closest he has ever come to buying a 'pig in a poke.' "Finally, we met with them (a still larger publisher), and pushed our certified check across the table to receive in return a list of names and the responsibility to send them newsletters." A beginner in newsletter publishing recently asked NAA, "On this newsletter, which I understand is for sale, they have about $150,000 in unfulfilled liability . . . shouldn't they be willing to pay me if I'm willing to take that liability from them?" Both of these people share the same misunderstanding. What they are purchasing is not subscriber names or the obligation to fulfill prepaid subscriptions, what you are really acquiring when you buy a newsletter is the rights to all future year's profits. (It isn't like buying a men's store where you get fixtures and inventory and a lease and, what is usually the arguable point, a certain amount of established "good will.") So the process of determining the value of the newsletter really is based upon what those future profits are assumed to be.

Several Other Ways in Which Newsletter Values have Been Calculated

One Times Annual Gross Revenue. Like most simple 'rules-of-thumb' there is a reason for it. There are several methods by which the value of a newsletter can be calculated, as we already have indicated, but we will find the values so calculated often come rather close to good ole' ''one times gross.'' A reason for this is that most newsletters available for acquisition are probably grossing under $100,000 annually. At that level of receipts, the amount of profit generated is probably such that a reasonable price to acquire those future profits *happens* to approximate one year's gross. Let's explain this by looking at multiples of earnings. How much should a would-be purchaser be willing to pay for a newsletter currently generating $15,000 annual profit? In the past, experts commented that for a small business which is relatively high-risk (newsletter publishing certainly qualifies) five to seven times annual earnings was not an unreasonable level. Interest rate inflation, however, has overcome the conventional wisdom in this case. That formula would say for a newsletter generating $15,000 profit, an offer price of $90,000 to $100,000 would be reasonable. For the past couple of years, investing $100,000 in a CD or in a money fund would have returned $15,000 with no risk. How much less, then, should a publisher offer to pay to acquire a newsletter generating $15,000? Today, three to four times earnings appear to be ''in the ballpark'' for a newsletter. What is this $15,000 profit newsletter grossing? If the current publisher is running a tight ship, perhaps $60,000. If expenses are somewhat higher, $75,000 to $85,000. In either event, as you can see, the multiple of earnings formula also results in a price somewhere vaguely in the neighborhood of ''one times gross.''

Sum of Two Year's Renewals. This method is mentioned occasionally, an obvious reflection of the fact that, as with our first example — two newsletters — each grossing $100,000 annually, may be quite different properties. In the first example, with an overall renewal rate of 74% the sum of two years renewals would be 128.8% while, in the second instance, with an overall renewal rate of 58%, the sum of two year's renewals is 91.6%. Once again, not too far from one year's gross, and pretty well in line with the figures produced from income/expense analysis and discounted present value tables. One large drawback to this system is the special problem it presents for the "mature newsletter," one which has been published for quite a while and which has a significant market share (perhaps 10% of the prospect universe.) In this case, it may be increasingly difficult to sell new subs and the total subscriber list may be slowly declining but, in most instances a newsletter of this type will have a very high renewal record from its core of loyalists — sometimes 90% plus. The sum of two years formula makes such a newsletter a premium property, worth perhaps one and three-fourths times gross. There are also newsletters which sell well, but don't renew. A newsletter with an overall renewal rate of 46%, if it sells like rabbits and turns first-year profits even with that low renewal record, is probably worth a good deal more than two-third's of a year's gross, which is what the two times renewal rate formula develops.

Weighted Averages. A weighted average is really a quick and dirty method of approximating a combination of discounted present value and multiple of earnings, recognizing that what the purchaser is acquiring is putative profits.

Here is the formula. Multiply the assumed future profits for each year as follows:

1st Yr.	*2nd Yr.*	*3rd Yr.*	*4th Yr.*	*5th Yr.*
x 9	x 8	x 7	x 6	x 5

Let's assume that, in the example above, on the newsletter presently generating $15,000 profit, the current publisher assumes a slow but steady progression in profitability over the coming five-year period.

1st Yr.	*2nd Yr.*	*3rd Yr.*	*4th Yr.*	*5th Yr.*
15,000 x 9	17,500 x 8	20,000 x 7	22,500 x 6	25,000 x 5
135,000	140,000	140,000	135,000	125,000

Taking the sum of all those figures, $675,000, and dividing by the sum of the key numbers, 35, gives you a "weighted average" for future profits of $19,286 a year. Yet again, a potential buyer willing to pay three to four times earnings is going to offer somewhere in the vicinity of one year's current gross revenues.

Discounted Present Value. While the concept sounds complex, it isn't difficult once you make the necessary calculations to determine the anticipated future level of profit and your assumption on return on investment (ROI). For example, look at the situation above. Using discounted present value tables and an assumed return of 20%, you could pay $59,800 for that newsletter (assuming you buy the present publisher's anticipated future profit estimates). If your necessary rate-of-return is only 15%, you could offer $67,000.

What About Making an Acquisition to Fold in With my Present NL??
This is often the case. It changes the picture because it changes your future costs. Going back to our first example, let's assume you intend to merge this newsletter into your existing publication which is its direct competitor. For purposes of argument, we'll assume you learn that 50% of the subs are duplicates. There is a tremendous body of information-seekers out there; people who subscribe to everything which is offered in the field. In this case, therefore, you have to be able to analyze the list in advance to see how many net new subs for your newsletter you will gain. Not only do you gain just 500 new subs, but you also have an obligation to fulfill an average of six months extension for the other 500 subs who were already readers of yours. (You can't tell them that for the remainder of their sub they are going to get your great newsletter instead—but you can extend their present sub by the amount necessary to reflect what they paid for the previous publisher's newsletter.)

In this instance your variable costs, if all factors remain the same, would be only about $18,000 (to sell enough subs to maintain those 500 annually plus $2,500-3,000 in extra fulfillment costs for the 500 duplicative subs). Your new embedded costs are negligible, perhaps $11 per year/per sub for fulfillment, (editorial and overhead being taken care of already). These 500 new subs would gross 1/2 what the 1,000 did in the original example, but the reduced cost would mean, following the same exercise, that you could offer $106,000 for this newsletter.

In the real world, a competitive newsletter which you can purchase is most often a dying swan, without impressive records of circulation promotion response or renewals (or it's a $79 a year monthly and you'll be stepping its conversion up to your

$197 weekly which will probably depress renewal rates), so that it may not be quite as attractive an opportunity. It's usually desirable, however, for the buyer because of reductions in his cost of production to acquire and fold in a competitor.

Words of Wisdom for the Seller

We haven't said anything about the seller since page 148 when we left him seeking the highest possible price and 100% payment in cash. Here are some suggestions for the seller to make a deal for his newsletter as attractive as possible. Selling a newsletter is often not a happy experience, because, if the property had been as successful as the current publisher hoped, it wouldn't be for sale . . .

Keep Good Records. As should be obvious from the foregoing, the prospective buyer is going to want to know a heck of a lot about your operation. Everything that you can produce — promotion history, list use, response records, renewal rates by source of orders, cost per sale, etc., etc., — will be useful to him and, further, the more easily you can provide this information and the more professional its presentation, the more confidence it will engender in you and your operation.

Don't 'Inadvertently' Conceal Anything. There are all too many folktales going around the newsletter business about potential newsletter buyers who learned only by accident the present publisher had recently done a large advance renewal effort, sold a number of two-year subs, carried expires on the rolls, brought in an influx of new orders with low-ball trials, etc., etc. A buyer learning something like this for himself is probably not going to make the offer the seller is looking for.

Most Important, Keep Publishing. If you are going to make the decision to sell a newsletter, do it. Don't let the situation drag on to the point where you discontinue regular publication. The nature of the newsletter business being what it is, when you start missing scheduled issues, you don't have a product to sell any longer.

Terms of the Deal

Certainly, the certified check approach is nice, although perhaps not always not best for the seller's own tax situation, but certainly you should be willing to consider a graduated schedule for payout.

A very solid publisher who is willing to offer $150,000 for a newsletter may well not have that amount kicking about loose in checking. If the seller's willing to take $50,000 down and four subsequent annual installments, the buyer might be willing to add perhaps $20,000 to the final price (considering he will have the use of substantial portions of the total price for several years). The major worry this type of arrangement creates for would-be sellers is, "How do I know they'll make a go of it. I don't want to be left holding the bag a couple of years down the road."

1. As a seller in this situation, you're entitled to considerable financial data about the buyer's company from which you should be able to decide their ability to generate the necessary cash-flow to meet the payment schedule.

2. It's a matter of contract. You and your lawyer should be able to get them to agree to pledge whatever collateral is satisfactory as surety for their completing the terms of the contract.

How About Going Through a Broker?

A third-party intermediary or broker is not at all unusual in newsletter transactions. For the seller, listing your property through a broker rather than taking it on yourself may be attractive. In the first place, selling a newsletter can be an emotional experience if the seller is the founding editor/publisher. A broker can cast an experienced eye over the product and help evaluate what the market price should be. Second he/she is probably far better connected in the publishing world and able to locate the most satisfactory potential purchaser. The customary fee for such service is 5% of the sales price and, we suspect, in most instances, as in real estate, the seller tacks enough on his asking price to cover the broker's fee.

Guidelines for Seeking Acquisitions

David Swit, publisher at Washington Business Information, Inc. (WBII), which has acquired several newsletters offers suggestions to other publishers who may be seriously interested in expanding through acquisitions.

How do you learn of publications available for sale? Swit takes a direct approach, "We write and tell them our company is interested in acquisitions. Use the NAA membership list and send a letter. When we did this after the NAA conference we got a number of responses, got into serious discussions with a couple, and made one acquisition."

- *Look for newsletters you can sell for a lot of money.* WBII's success has been with limited circulation high-ticket newsletters, the average price of their eight current publications is $231. "Your operation may be different, but we aren't set up at WBII to publish and market a $37 consumer monthly."

- *Do the negotiations yourself.* Try your best to keep the lawyers out of it.

- *Have a checklist of things to know.* The list prepared by John Wills of Capitol Publications in the NAA Guidebook is an excellent starting point — I've added about 37 points which are particular to our operations.

- *What is the market?* How much of the realistic circulation potential does the present publisher have? Are there related markets in which you think you could successfully market this newsletter.

- *What is the competition?* There may usually be room for another newsletter in any field, but if the reason the acquisition you're considering hasn't been as successful as the present publisher would have liked is due to well-established competitors, you certainly need to know those facts to negotiate intelligently.

- *What is the information flow?* How much news is there in this area? You certainly have to know before you arbitrarily assume you'll buy a 4 to 6 page biweekly and upgrade it to an 8 page weekly.

CHAPTER XIV
Ancillary Products and Services

One of the more controversial areas among newsletter publishers is the question of ancillary services. The debate is, should the successful newsletter publisher look for new profit opportunities in ancillary services such as books, list rentals, conferences, seminars, directories, consulting services, etc? Judging from the actions of successful publishers and the program participation at the NAA conferences, the answer is "YES" to all of the above. Consider the minority viewpoint, however, before any further discussion. What newsletter publishers do best, is publish and market newsletters, and they should tend to their lasts, not look for new worlds to conquer. The time, effort and money needed to design, promote and administer a conference, for example, could be used to build a new newsletter that would, in the long run, be more profitable for the publisher than a seminar. With that in mind, let's take a quick look at some of the ways successful publishers have cashed in on something besides newsletters—and some of the pitfalls in each of them. Remember, these projects require a different type and concentration of effort than those discussed in Chapter 8.

Books

Some publishers have done well in the book business, usually in one of two ways. The best way is to have your editor write a best seller like Howard Ruff's "How to Prosper in the Coming Bad Years" and use it to promote your newsletter. McGraw-Hill has a successful incentive program that encourages the editors of their highly technical industry newsletters to write books in their subject areas (nights and weekends). McGraw-Hill then markets them on a commission basis with the editor/authors.

Here is where other publishers have come to grief in book marketing efforts. Publisher A locates a few professional books in an area related to his newsletter subject (i.e. $40 trade paperbacks in a narrow, highly specialized field). He discovers he can get them from the publisher at 40% off list price. He spends just a couple dollars printing an insert flyer to go to newsletter subscribers. The cost of the promotion effort is almost nil. The expense of filling the orders (usually on a cash only basis) is also pretty low. The rest is gravy. "Where has this been all my life," he thinks to himself and plans to expand his efforts in book marketing. Before you know what has happened, he has expanded until he is selling a sizeable list of titles. He has added office space to warehouse this inventory. He has also spent a fair amount of money on designing a catalogue of "Books Available from Profit Press, Publishers of the *WIN Letter*" and is mailing this promotion not only to his subscribers but to his prospects as well. He is taking in a gratifying amount of gross revenue on book sales, and it is a shattering moment for him when his financial person tells him that, considering all the costs and overhead, they aren't making any money. This has happened to several major newsletter publishers. You may be able to do it more efficiently. Some publishers do. The word to the wise in this case, however, is that beyond a casual effort limited to merchandising books in flyers with your regular subscriber mailings, it's becoming increasingly difficult to make profits in book marketing.

Conferences and Seminars

It's a natural connection for publishers to make, to move into the conference and seminar business. As a publisher in the field, you have several things going for you.

1. You are acquiring a reputation among your readers and the industry in general as an authority.

2. You have the mechanisms in place to create and design promotional packages.

3. You have contacts in the industry to get the best people as speakers for your conference.

4. You can use the conferences as excellent opportunities to market the rest of your services (newsletters, special reports, etc.).

Here are some of the negatives in operating conferences:

1. Every new conference you design is an entirely new project. The fact that your last seminar on "International Market Opportunities for Widgit People" turned out to be a big success doesn't mean the next one you dream up won't be a complete bomb. — You start from ground zero each time. (It's this spending time on concepts that the folks who oppose ancillary services say could be better placed in developing new newsletter product.)

Many in the business suggest having a couple of basic seminars

● "Understanding Washington Regulatory Impact on the Widget Industry" — to offer over and over and over for everyone in the industry. This is a profitable, low risk way to get into conferences.

2. Managing a successful conference is not as easy as it looks. Costs can get out of control any number of ways, and you can find yourself in the classic position of having operated a "successful conference" but not made any profit.

3. You should also worry about how running a poor conference or having to cancel will affect your reputation. You can limit your risk on a seminar. (If not enough people pre-register, you simply return the money of the five you have gotten.) While you're out whatever you spent on promotion, you won't lose any more actual money, though your image may be tarnished.

List Rentals

This is an excellent source of income for many publishers. As you get into the business, you will find you own a number of good lists: subscribers, prospects you have compiled from directories or inquiries, book buyers or conference attendees, etc. Normally you have to be able to deliver the lists on computer labels, or computer magnetic tape, to be able to rent lists. The market place determines price, but lists of newsletter subscribers are usually priced at least $50 per thousand names. The Standard Rate and Data Services directory carries a free listing of lists for rent. Yours should be listed there. The Direct Mail Marketing Association will give you a list of list brokers who will handle your lists. Try to keep your subscribers happy, too. Despite the publicity given to "privacy" of mailing lists, you aren't required to have permission from the people on your mailing list to rent the names. NAA strongly recommends, however, that at least once a year you publish a notice that the publisher will occasionally allow other firms promoting quality products or services to use its mailing lists. If they don't want their names to be used, ask subscribers to tell you. Experience seems to indicate that only a very few subscribers will take you up on this, but you save a disproportionate amount of trouble by getting their names off your rental lists. This coding obviously is most easily done once you're big enough to maintain your lists on computer.

WARNING — Don't ever rent your list to anyone without requiring prior approval of what they intend to mail.

Directory Publishing
There may well be an opportunity for a directory in your industry. You may find that in the course of compiling your prospect lists, you already have on hand more information about the Widget Industry and its people than almost anyone else. There is a lot of competition, however. The Gale's Research directory of directories can tell you who is already publishing what in your industry.

Consulting
As editor of your newsletter, you may become known as an authority in the industry. You may be offered consulting opportunities. The temptation is to take the money and run. After all, it's a quick return cash (and an ego-gratifying business). NAA would only point out, as one specialist did to us, that an hour of your time devoted to consulting can only be sold once. Using that hour to design a new promotional effort, or a new newsletter idea may give you a considerable multiplier effect.

Considerations in Book Marketing
Using your newsletter as a vehicle to sell books will certainly create revenue, but you have to be honest with yourself in determining whether or not it brings in income.

Stick to people, subjects and industries you know. You can create books from editorial materials in your newsletter or from special reports you have done independently of the newsletter. You can encourage editors to author books, (McGraw-Hill does this) and you can be alert for books of others which would be relevant to your readers. Research organizations, 'think-tanks' and other non-profit groups are good sources. They'll use their expertise to produce a really good report and then sometimes put it on the market for $5. If you can get there first, you can sell it for them for $300.

Sell books of other publishers. The commission for this usually varies from 25 to 40%. (This can lead to problems when you rely on their ability to fulfill—drop-ship—and/or take on the headache (and cost) of inventorying quantities of books to ship yourself.)

"I don't worry," says Bob Davidson of McGraw-Hill, "about what is a 'book'. I figure if it looks like a book and smells like a book, it's a book. Actually, though, we find if it's called a 'special report' and published in a soft cover or binder format rather than the traditional hard-bound book, you can charge more for it."

"If it moves, stuffer it." You can include flyers for your book list in every mailing. McGraw-Hill includes a list of 18 to 20 books on an insert brochure and has found such an insert mailing returns three for one on cost. "The one caveat," Davidson adds, "is some people are leary about including stuffers in renewal mailings. You might find some people deciding to buy a book and not renew."

Guidelines for Book Publishing

"Should we publish books?"

"What kind of books?"

"How can we recognize a good book idea?"

"How do we put the book together?"

"How will we sell these books?"

"Will we make money?"

Here's a checklist of suggestions provided by Bob Davidson at the book Publishing Center at McGraw Hill in New York. A number of newsletter publishers have learned to develop significant revenues by marketing books related to their newsletter subject area, but McGraw-Hill appears to be the industry leader in developing and producing books from within their own staff capabilities.

Should We Publish Books?

Many of your readers, perhaps most, will never see the inside of a technical book store. Your program can be an essential source of business and professional information. At the same time, you will enhance your publication's image as a total information source. You have at your command a strong base from which to start, namely editorial skills and know-how in subjects of importance to known and reachable constituencies.

What Kind of Books?

Deal from your strengths. Concentrate on your knowledge of the subject areas of importance to your constituencies. Don't underestimate the importance of your endorsement of a book, a virtual "Seal of Approval." No one else has your publication's reputation, no one else can reach and influence these groups as effectively as you can. Profit from, but don't betray, this respect for you, this confidence in you, this reliance upon you. Give meat and potatoes, avoid whipped cream.

• Concentrate on books with anticipated shelf-life. Conventional book publishers seek sales lives of three to five years; 60% of profits may come from the sale of backlist books. A book based on breaking news or passing trends may become obsolete before it's published. (NOTE: If you plan to publish newsy, short-lived books, or high-priced special reports, be sure that someone is relieved of other duties and can provide the TLC required to avoid delays.)

● *Books which repackage the "most read" articles from your publication organized by some common denominator are the safest, easiest, and usually the most profitable.*

● Books created from original manuscript are the most complicated, expensive and risky.

● Automatic obsolescence of essential information on an annual, biennial, or triennial basis can generate almost guaranteed repeat sales; e.g., the *National Electrical Code* is revised and reissued triennially.

How Can We Recognize A Good Book Idea?

A good book is one that people will need and pay for. There is no foolproof fail-safe formula, but there are ways to swing the odds in your favor. Deal from your strengths, concentrate on useful subjects with known life spans, beware of topics that can be outdated by a single unexpected national or international event. Be sure that you know *what* the book is to do for *whom, where* the prospective buyers are, *why* they will need the book, and *how* the book will meet this need. Here are some aids you may wish to consider.

● Start with a one-page summary of purpose, procedure, market potential.

● Prepare an outline or table of contents, with or without annotation.

● Obtain a statement of qualifications from the author or editor.

● Determine the market for the book.

● Create a preliminary description of the book, its audiences, its purposes, etc.

How Do We Put A Book Together?

Start simple, as with a tearsheet book. There's no mystery to creating a book, but there are numerous traps for the inexperienced. If your own staff doesn't have book production experience, find a free-lancer with book publishing experience. Check with other NL publishers already in the book business. Whatever you do, get help as early in the project as possible. It's far easier to plan to minimize delays and avoid excessive expenses if you work together from the start.

Who Will Do The Work?

Plan for your own editorial staff to guide, evaluate, and organize the book's content for relevance, accuracy, timeliness, timelessness...whether it's a tearsheet book or an original manuscript book. Then what? It's often difficult to ask that the day-to-day details of shepherding a book along toward publication be handled by your staff, *unless* there is essential expertise and true slack time. (The alternative, if your program is big enough, is to assign full-time book-program staff.) *You'll save dollars and avoid headaches if you ask your staff to do what it does best, and farm the rest out, even if it costs a few apparent dollars.*

How Will We Sell These Books?

An essential test for any book idea: Can it be sold through your established marketing channels? If not, reconsider. If your own constituencies will not be interested, you are in risky territory. Who are your best buying prospects? Your own subscriber list, those persons who know you best, respect you, rely on you. Sell to them at low cost by space and filler ads, postcards, stuffers, and more. Especially sell to your own lists of past buyers of books and other editorial products.

Will We Make Money?

Yes, if you have a timely topic of continuing need for significant fractions of your constituencies, if you have maintained careful control of costs, if you promote and sell where you are most effective by using media over which you have exclusive control *and* if you take advantage of the numerous additional sales channels from which you can realize cost-effective incremental sales, virtual "found money." *AND IF YOU AVOID TIMID PRICING or OVERPRICING.* Find out what the market is charging, what prices are customary. *Analyze your bottom line:* Consider sales, preparation and manufacturing expenses, royalties, promotion expenses, the cost of order handling and fulfillment, supplementary income from bulk sales, book clubs, foreign rights, etc.

Marketing the Single Book Title

Newsletter publishers can be successful in book marketing, even with single titles which they (or their editors) produce internally. The following are suggestions on marketing a single book title. The basic options are:

House Ads—Your own publication subscribers are the best potential audience. If you include an insert with your regular mailings, spend some time and effort on professional appearance. House ads (in magazines) can vary in pull as much as 500 percent with different copy and graphics. (Make sure the publication is relevant to the audience.)

Trade-offs—If you carry advertising or are willing to use inserts, you may be able to arrange trade-offs with other publications, although most newsletter circulations are probably not high enough to interest magazines in trades.

Per-Sale—Some publications will carry your ad on a cost per-sale; that way, you can use space advertising without high up-front costs. Normally you will have to let them receive the orders to verify the number of sales made from their ad.

Barter—You may be able to trade subscriptions or copies of books for space—i.e. three months after the ad runs, they get XXX copies free to do with as they please.

Paid Ads—Many publications give a discount from list rates for mail order or publisher ads—usually 25 to 30 percent. In any event, if you are using space advertising go with the quality magazines in the field; bargains in space rates are usually not worth it. Check to see what other direct mail or book ads are in the magazine. If there are few or none, it's probably not good space for you either.

The classic space ad for book sales is the full page ad with coupon offering the book and offering free-trial. Books can effectively be sold direct up to about a $20 cover price—after that a combination of space ad and direct mail is usually more effective. Be cautious with satisfaction-guaranteed offers, especially of "how-to" books. Publishers are now being burned with tremendous return volumes. In some cases over 40 percent of the books ordered are being returned.

Bind-in or blown-in order cards, even if they add as much as 50 percent to the cost of the ad, have often tested to be more effective than the printed order form as part of the ad itself.

Smaller than full page ads can be effective. Tests show that a small ad, if run consistently, even the same ad in the same space, will show a building level of response.

Ad Plus Direct Mail—For higher priced books, the most effective selling pattern is a combination of space ad and follow-up direct mail. As a rule of thumb, it is cost effective to make a follow-up mailing per $25 in book price, i.e. a $50 trade book could support an ad and two follow-up mailings.

It is often possible, especially with trade magazines and association publications, to negotiate a deal. In return for running the ad, you receive their mailing list. A word of caution, these lists tend to be terribly out of date. A recent McGraw-Hill study shows that 53 percent of the executive subscribers to their publications have a name or title change within a year.

You would tend to think, "They're getting the magazine every month, the list must be pretty good." The truth is, nobody reads the address label on a publication to note that "Bob Brown, Director of Information" left three years ago; but when a #10 comes in addressed that way, it comes back marked, "no longer here." (Go directly to title only for this kind of business mail—Attn: Sales Manager.)

Never use a list without testing. Make at least 20 phone calls to names at random on the list and look to find 50 percent of the people active in the job and title on the list before using it.

3 More Ways to Generate Inquiries:

1. *Free Editorial*—You can send camera-ready editorial copy to newspapers—a lot of them use it. Two methods which work:

(a) Develop editorial articles on subjects with a plug—"Write XYZ publishers for a free brochure on this subject" buried in the copy.

(b) *Actual canned book reviews of your book* will also be run by quite a few papers and will generate direct response inquiries and orders.

2. *Postcard Publications* and *Loose Deck Mailings*—There are magazines which are in reality nothing but postcard offers for various services and loose deck co-op mailings of related product and service cards. (See listing in back of the SRDS directory for these.) Both will generate inquiries. Books under $15 or $20 can be sold directly off a card, but more expensive titles generally require a follow-up mailing.

4 Tips for Designing Your Book Direct Mail Package:

1. *Use the format of a letter brochure, the illustrated letter,* (often a 4-page 11 x 17)

2. *Rip apart the book for promotion copy*—use quotes extensively and highlight all the best features.

3. *Put a second order form in the package*—If you use a response card, print a duplicate on the brochure. These kinds of mailings tend to have a long "shelf-life," and the second order form will add 10 percent to total response.

4. If you are doing a speculative promotion (you won't print unless you get sufficient response) be sure to let the prospect know.—*Offer a "special pre-publication price."* "We're passing the savings from not over-printing along to you" and some anticipation of when you'll be printing. Be very careful of this if you're asking for payment now, lest you run afoul of FTC regulations on shipping of goods ordered by mail.

Directory Publishing as a Profit Center
for Newsletter Publishers

Directory publishing can be a real profit center for newsletter publishers. Some publishers take in more money from directories than newsletters. All publishers should do basic research to see if there appears to be an opening for a new directory in their field. Gale Research Publications (Book Building, Detroit, Michigan 48226) and the U.S. Department of Commerce are good sources for information on directories currently published.

Here are nine suggestions for successful directory publishing.

1. Be willing to start small if you are in a growing field.

2. Don't be afraid to face competition.

3. Do the job right—your product must be superb.

4. Put a good price on it, and promote the hell out of it.

5. Use UPS or equivalent service for delivery. The customer who orders it, wants it "now".

6. Add new features to the directory every year.

7. Hit the library market.

8. Attend and exhibit at Industry Trade shows. Prospects like to get their hands on the product.

9. To get foreign listings, give free copies of the directory. Otherwise it's "mañana."

More Guidelines

1. Never charge for a listing in the directory.

2. Set a price about 5-7 times your production costs.

3. Always publish an errata sheet.

4. Don't allow commercial use—indicate so in the directory.

5. Don't charge for ads the first year (this is a controversial point—many do charge from year one).—You get a lot in this way, and it makes it much easier to sell the second time around.

The most difficult part of successful directory marketing is overcoming the prospect's view that every third year is "often enough" to buy (because "it's expensive and I don't use it that often"). You have to make all the changes and updates in your book. You know they need the new issue.

Three possible solutions:

1. A sales letter which states it just that way. "The reasons you're wrong in thinking you don't need a new industry directory this year."

2. Go so far as to select a paper which yellows with age for directories, to help emphasize the transient nature of the information they contain.

3. More effective than a discount for ordering in advance, is offering a discount for returning the old copy. The prospect hates to admit the book he paid a lot of money for is now outdated; but, conversely, it's a tremendous psychological lift for him to think he can get a discount on a new issue by just mailing back the old one.

CHAPTER XV
Lists, List Rentals and Marketing

How to Locate and Use Mailing Lists Effectively

It is generally accepted in newsletter marketing that the most important element in a promotion mailing is the quality of the list selection. This is usually stated with some variation of the expression that "the best package in the world won't sell to the wrong list" or "any halfway decent promotion effort will sell reasonably well to a really good list."

That being the case, what does the newsletter publisher need to know about lists. This breaks down into several categories of information. What kind of lists are available? How do you find out about them? Where can you get hold of them? How do you evaluate their usefulness for your publication? How do you develop your own in-house lists for mailing without rental expense?

Sources for Locating Lists

List brokers who manage numerous lists for various owners are located in most major cities, although the largest concentration is in New York. They usually publish categories of the lists available. The Standard Rate and Data Service provides listings of mailing lists available for rent in its directory. NAA's annual membership directory includes listings of member newsletter publishers who will rent or exchange their mailing lists with other members.

In addition to these sources, competing publications (magazines, newsletters) in the field may be willing to rent you lists of subscribers, expires, or prospects. Industry trade and professional association membership lists are sometimes available, and almost every type of business or interest affiliation is covered by a directory.

Gale's Research publishes both a directory of directories and a directory of associations which should help you locate potential list sources. At this point, your problem should really be one of embarrassment of choice. You probably will have located more potentially good lists than you can use. If you haven't, this may be an invaluable early warning signal about marketability of your newsletter. The best newsletter idea for which there are no good lists available is a bad newsletter idea.

What Kind of Lists are There?

The most common type of list is a *compiled list,* gathered by someone from one or more sources. All that is warranted of them is that the records on them share some identifiable characteristic (all bowling alley managers or pediatricians). Response lists are almost always better. They consist of people who have purchased something which identifies their interest (bowlers who subscribed to Bowling Alley Age). Obviously, people who purchased by direct mail are superior prospects for direct mail offers. One experienced consultant ranks lists of prospects in the following hierarchy for newsletters:

1. Subscribers to competing newsletters,
2. Book buyers in the field,
3. Magazine subscribers in the field.

Within categories two and three, those who bought by direct mail are better prospects than respondents to space ads, etc. Everything else — trade show participants, warranty holders, etc. — is less reliable.

Studies show that 20% of the people in the United States have never purchased anything by direct mail. You will find those names included on compiled lists which helps explain why response lists normally outpull them. Research also indicates that of the 80% who do buy by direct mail, 20% of them purchase 80% of the total mail business. Theirs, of course, are the names you want.

How Can I Judge the Quality of a List?

Most list brokers prepare sales cards about every list they are managing. Similar to an advertising rate card, it includes a great deal of information about the particular list. Number of names, price to rent, minimum order requirement, source of the orders (direct mail-space ads), price they paid, special selections available (zip codes, or by state, etc., etc.). You use the rate card to decide whether the list of 50,000 subscribers to Bowling Alley Age looks first-rate for your direct mail promotion.

If you are considering compiled lists, be especially careful to check the source of the names. Over the past several years, NAA has been offered lists of newsletter publishers from at least six different sources and checking has indicated all of them were compiled from the same directories.

Where Can I Buy Mailing Lists?

You should know a couple of points about choosing a list broker. Many list brokers, newsletter publishers have felt, aren't really interested in working with newsletters because of their small volume. There is at least a degree of truth to this. The amount of work a broker must do for a new client who wants to test, for example, four different list segments of 5,000 each, probably exceeds his income (brokers normally receive a 20% commission from the owners for each rental). Talk to at least several firms. Some *are* more comfortable working with newsletters and their type of list needs than others. Beware of ''order takers.'' Any broker can put together some combination of names which meets the quantities you've suggested, but they will be ''secondary prospects'' at *best* for your newsletter.

Two keys to evaluating a broker: (1) does he only ask what lists you want or does he offer suggestions of his own from experience in the market. A professional should be capable of working with you to select the best lists or list segments for your tests and mailings. (2) If he doesn't ask about the size of your mailing plan and budget, turn him down. If the broker doesn't feel a need to know about what you're planning to spend, it's a sure sign you're not dealing with a real professional.

Check Points for Ordering a Rental List

The alternative to using a list broker is to buy lists directly from list managers. The only benefit to this is the control you have over the nagging process. You have a direct contact with each person who is selling a list and can direct your ire. The biggest benefit of using a *good* list broker, is that the broker will stay on top of the situation.

Either route you use you should know about these check points for ordering a rental list:

- Make sure you can get date clearance for the time you want to mail.
- Send a sample of your package immediately upon making the request.
- Ask the owner/broker to protect the mail date for you — preferably a week on either side.
- Don't confuse "delivery date" with "mail date." (It takes longer than most publishers think to get a list and once you have the labels, you need time for your mailhouse, etc.)
- Merge-Purge if you use a number of lists. Ask the broker for an 85% net name guarantee on merged-purged lists.
- Specify the format you want — cheshire, mag tape, etc. Don't wait to be surprised.
- Always put instructions in writing.
- Specify key codes to the broker to facilitate split testing.

Of course, you don't want to rent those 50,000 names at $75 per thousand ($3,750) to test whether this list will be good for your newsletter. How many do you need? (Commonly, the rate card will specify a minimum, usually 5,000, which you must rent.) Here's a simple formula which is used by many newsletter publishers to establish the number of names which they need to test in order to validate a list for their newsletter. Test enough names to yield 50 positive responses, but not less than 3,000 names.

Speaking of Testing. . .

You know what response you need to get from your test mailing. If it's .75%, how many names do you have to mail to get 50 orders — about 6,700. A list segment of 7,000 names should be valid for the list. (If for some reason, you believe you could reasonably anticipate a 2.5% response, you could expect 50 orders from 2,000 names but experienced promotion people would tend not to regard that as a sufficient universe.) Similarly, for a very expensive publication which anticipates only a .4% response, you would need 12,500 names to get 50 orders and validate the list.

In summary, for whatever percentage response you anticipate, test enough names to get 50 orders but not less than 3,000. If you want to be more scientific, a basic college statistics textbook will contain "confidence interval tables" which allow you to determine how large a sample you have to use to achieve what level of confidence in the result as an indicator for the whole (and with what tolerance for error). In any event, don't make assumptions such as "5,000 is always the appropriate quantity to test" or "you should test 10% of the names on the list" (if the list is 1,000,000 names, that's an expensive test).

Once you've determined how many names you need to test a list, how do you decide which ones you want? What you want, of course, to test a list is a random sample from that list. Why would you want to test any segment of the universe for which you find some reason to believe the results would not be typical of the whole?

Most commonly the random sample is done by "nth name" selection. If the entire list is 75,000 names and you need 6,000 for a test, every 12th name of the list will give you a sufficient quantity. Some mailers, however, prefer a zip digit select. On an "nth name" select, you really don't know what you have. It could be "hotline" names of recent buyers or multiple buyers or some other list segment which isn't really representative of the potential performance of the whole list. Second is the question of confusion on the roll out. Because lists change so much with people moving or retiring, no selection of every 12th name will be the same. List brokers keep track of what they use in broad terms. When you rollout, your broker may eliminate every 12th name, but there's no way of knowing if every 12th name on the new run matches your initial group. Some list brokers do keep records from list tests by names supplied, rather than just on list, but these are jewels and not easily found.

If, on the other hand, you ask for all zips ending in "5", you should get 10% of the list (7,500 in this case) and you can easily determine by visual inspection if, in fact, that is what you do have. Also, if you ask for 0-1-2 ending digits you should get a preponderance of business addresses and 7-8-9 should be largely residential zips. One drawback is that lists do not necessarily evenly divide nationwide with 10% of the prospects in every area in each zip digit number.

What to do When you get the List

1. *Check for Zip Codes:*
   - make sure they are on all addresses on the list
   - check to see that they are complete five-digit zips
   - make sure they are correct (i.e., no 10017 zip codes on Texas addresses, that all 500 Chicago addresses you have aren't all zipped 60601).

2. *Check for Complete Addresses:* One person rented an overseas list which left cities off of each address (went directly from "5 Grey Ladies Gardens" to "England").

3. *Ask for a Zip Breakdown:* If New York metro is your best prospect area, check to make sure that a proportionate number of the list are in those zips; if your newsletter doesn't sell in the Midwest, you don't want to see too many 500__ zip codes.

4. *Use Your Special Knowledge:* If your editor is from Denver, have him/her check over the Denver names on the list just to see if they "look right."

5. *Insist on Physically Handling the List:* Some renters will only handle your mailing through their mailinghouse, or will want to send the list directly to your mailinghouse. One specialist told NAA, "I told them if they insisted on delivery to my mailhouse, I was going out there and get the list so I could look at it anyway. They told me a good mailhouse 'automatically' makes all the checks I described. I can only say if you know of one that does, I want to know about it."

6. *Use "Address Correction Requested":* Normally you won't pay to clean someone else's list, but if you put ACR on 500 envelopes in your test, and 150 or 200 of them come back, you've learned a lot about that list.

7. *Do Some Telephone Checks:* One person says when he rents a name/title list (Bart C. Fitch, Sales Manager, XYZ Corp.), he always makes about two dozen ran-

dom phone calls. If, in 50% of the cases Fitch is, in fact, presently XYZ's sales manager, he feels it's a pretty good list.

Multi-List Promotions

Usually you will mail to more than one list on a test mailing. It might be that there is one list of 32,322 widget manufacturing executives, and they are your entire market, but this is very rare. More commonly, you will come up with eight or nine lists ranging from two which should be "absolutely super" (but only have 982 and 1,734 names) to two at the other end which appear somewhat "marginal" (but contain 25,000 and 32,000 names) — a total potential prospect total of over 100,000 names. Since this appears to be the universe, you'd like to be able to get a test reading on the marketability of your new newsletter from a single mailing.

If you are renting several lists and in considerable quantity, it is likely that duplications will occur from list to list. By getting a computer service bureau to merge-purge the lists, (this requires lists which can be furnished to them on mag tape), you save the cost of mailing to duplicate names. Most publishers estimate you need 100,000 names before savings from this equals expense. In the case of large mailings, however, your very best sublist may be the duplicate names. If you were mailing to lists of subscribers from eight different direct marketing publications, a prospect whose name appeared on every one of them would almost certainly buy your product.

Here are some pitfalls to avoid in structuring meaningful tests:

1. Don't bother to test lists of fewer than 8,000 to 10,000. The savings in not mailing to the second half of the list is probably not worth the trouble. Go directly to all of them.

2. Don't test too few lists. For an established publisher, a test of his very best list may give a valid quick and dirty reading on marketability of a new publication related to existing ones. For other types of new launches you need a broader spectrum of information. Probably one of the most common errors in new list testing is the erroneous assumption that if the really good list drew 1.8%, the marginal list "has to" draw at least .6%. Believe us, it doesn't "have to."

3. When testing lists, test lists. Don't assume that as long as you're going to test, you can test brochure vs. sample issue and teaser copy vs. plain face envelopes as well. This is dangerous for two reasons. (a) You become inundated with too much information, and you aren't really sure what it means and/or if response levels reflect the list or the offer. Secondly, to do statistically valid testing for each subcategory rapidly becomes expensive. You can test two lists with segments of 5,000 each, if you need a 1% response. Testing three lists, two offers, two packages and two formats will require 90,000 pieces to cover all the permutations.

What Will I Know and When Will I Know it?

After you've done everything right with your lists and dropped your test mailing, how soon will you know what the result is and how should you act on the information? You can determine this through "half-life analysis." Count the number of mailing receipt days in your office after you *receive* the first return. (Not the day the mailing was made, the day you received the first order.) The half-life period for mailings made first-class is nine to eleven days and for bulk mailings 18 to 23 days (allowing for non-mail days and holidays). On the ninth mail day after you have received the first return on a first-class mailing, the returns should be 50% of what you will finally get. If you have 25 orders, you will eventually get the fifty you need to validate that list. Note: the final 50% will not come in as fast. If you have 25 orders on the 18th mail day from a bulk effort, it may take six weeks or more for the remaining 50% to come in. You can use the half-life information to decide to roll out and get back into the mail with additional promotions to the lists which are working.

Two additional cautions on roll outs:

1. *Quantity.* A general industry guideline is never roll out to a quantity more than ten times your test universe. Go from a 5,000 test to a 50,000 list at most, but not directly to 250,000 names. Conservative publishers might test 5,000, roll out to 25,000, and only then go to the remaining 70,000 on a 100,000 list.

2. *Timing.* One of the things which affects response in direct mail is seasonality. Publishers should schedule list tests for off-peak periods. Then, a list which does reasonably well at an off-peak period can be rolled out in greater quantity at the peak times of the year. (Half-life analysis enables you to speed up test results so you can be in the mail with your larger efforts on January 1st or September 1st, or whatever date has been good for your mailings.)

Building Your Own In-House List

For a number of reasons almost every newsletter publisher finds that the very best prospect list he has is the in-house list he has developed. One simple reason is economic. With list rentals, especially for strong, direct mail responsive lists becoming steadily more expensive, a publisher's own list is the cheapest available.

Sources for Your In-House List

Directories. Get any industry directories available and go through them to add the names of people who are not now subscribers. Note: some directories are sold with a caveat that the information in them may not be re-used. This is a matter of contract rather than copyright law. NAA's understanding is that all that can be copyrighted is format, not information. If you retype a name and address from a directory for your prospect list, you may use it.

Order the new editions when they are available. Most directories are published annually or bi-annually. Although you've been trying to stay on top of the field, you'll be surprised how many additional names you find in the new book.

Don't forget Uncle Sam. The government maintains an astonishing number of lists of people by different categories. Most of these are not only available to the public, but are cheaper than commercial lists.

Inquiries. People who write or call for information about your newsletter are your very best prospects. NAA converts them to membership at a rate five times higher than cold direct mail. Make sure every single one is "captured" and added to your prospect list.

Skim the cream from rented lists. You will not, of course, violate the terms of the list rental agreement you make by using rental names more than once. You may, however (sometimes the permission of the owner is required), offer a free sample issue or low price special report in your mailing to that list. This will normally greatly increase the number of responses you get, and you are entitled to capture those names.

Keep your eyes open. NAA looks for new newsletter names everywhere. Members send us names. Newsletters are mentioned in other media. We sold membership to a publisher whose newsletter we first found in a trash can at Penn Station in New York. Literally hundreds of names a year can be added this way.

Swap lists with your competitors. It takes some convincing, but swaps usually turn out to be very successful for both parties. It helps you reach the segment of your market which will buy anything. Be willing to swap any lists you have, including actives. If your competitor won't swap or rent subscribers, ask for expires or book buyers—they might be willing.

Keep a tickler file of organizations which have turned you down for list rentals or list swaps. Perhaps the next time you call on them they will have had a change of policy or personnel.

Keep an industry conference calendar so that you can, in an organized fashion, go after every attendee list.

Sit down with the last six months of your newsletter and reread it with only marketing in mind. You will be surprised how many source ideas you will find.

Convert your editor's rolodex into a mailing list.

Do a careful analysis of your current subscriber list. Know who they are, where they came from and what promotion they responded to.

Always, always, add your expires to your prospect lists and keep mailing to them.

Maintain records on all your in-house lists. Nothing is more frustrating than coming across a list in your files with no documentation of what it is, where it came from, and how you can update it.

If a potential list supplier is friendly on the phone, try and pump him for suggestions for other list sources you might investiate.

What about those lists you "can't get." Most newsletter publishers are aware of a couple lists they know would be good, but that they are unable to obtain. These usually fall into two categories—competing publications which won't make available their subscriber lists and associations which don't release membership records.

Be creative. Is that competing publication selling subscriptions by direct mail? Try to learn what lists they use and mail to them. See if the association recruits "suppliers" as associate members. If one privilege of such membership is access to their list, it might be worthwhile. Attend their conventions and pick up attendance lists. Ask if they'd be interested in swapping a complimentary subscription for a space ad in their journal or a special discount on subscriptions for their members. In today's society, no one is a direct mail virgin. Everyone's name and address is on a list you can get, even if you finally can't obtain one specific list.

Computerizing Your In-House List

For both efficiency and simplicity, maintain your own lists. Get your in-house prospect list(s) onto a computer as soon as possible. If your operation is like most small publishing companies, your "prospect file" consists of directories around the office and stacks of cheshire cards labeled (hopefully) with source information. It's inefficient both for you and your mailinghouse to handle. If you send your mailer eleven different list segments for a single mailing, you'll either pay one of his employees to zip sequence all of them or end up with your eleven lists entered in the post office as eleven small mailings. Quite probably, you'll send a half dozen pieces to the same guy whose name pops up on all your lists. Very large newsletter publishers with a number of newsletters probably have reasons to maintain several prospect lists. Most publishers, however, can do very nicely with a single zip sequence list which they key code so segments of the list can be broken out easily.

Make some editing decisions. You have to decide how you want your addresses to look. How many lines? Do you include titles? How do you handle overseas addresses? Learning how to format names facilitates development of 'match codes' which permits merging separate lists and selecting out duplicate names. At least once a year send a mailing either first-class or address correction requested (for ACR mail you pay 25¢ for each one returned, but you do get the dead names off your list for future mailings). Some recommend immediately remailing an ACR return in a fresh envelope via first-class. As many as 25% or more may be deliverable.

Get a number of bids from service bureaus. What you'll find is that most of the service bureau people you talk to have programs for list maintenance in place. Their interest is really in selling that program to you. It may well be more efficient for you to switch to the way they would like you to do it than pay for development of a custom system. You're an expert in publishing, not list maintenance.

Know what your costs are. Prices for service bureaus seem to vary considerably. Find out what you pay for additions, changes, labels, printouts, etc. Watch out for fixed costs like "storage fees" or "activity charges" (for keeping your tape on the shelf and for taking it down when you want to use it). Try to get a contract where you pay only a fee based on your actual use for production of labels.

Visit the firm you select. One publisher discovered the firm whose proposal impressed them most, in spite of the embossed letterhead, was a one-man operation who planned to job out the actual work to a third party.

Three more rules for successful computer list management:

1. Use outside consultants and services where applicable. You probably don't want to be in the computer business and you can learn a lot from people who are in that business on a larger scale than you. (Caveat: today's small office computers are quite capable of efficiently maintaining smaller prospect lists for newsletter publishers, but you do need someone on staff to work with them who both understands and likes working with computers.)

2. Make the whole list operation the responsibility of one person.

3. Set aside 10% of your total direct mail budget for list maintenance and development.

SUMMARY

Basically, searching for mailing lists combines (1) your absolute knowledge of your editorial product and where it fits into the universe and (2) your willingness to hunt for names and shop around for the best lists of them. The match-up of your publication with its audience should be one of the most profitable and interesting things you do. The name's the game, and without it, the world's best writing goes for naught.

Esquire Publishes List Rental Notice Within Magazine

Esquire magazine is handling the problem of possible objections to renting their subscriber lists by running a notice in the magazine itself under the heading "An Important Message to Esquire Subscribers."

"From time to time, we have made the Esquire subscriber list available to carefully screened organizations whose products and services may be of special interest to you. We supply these firms with your name and address. No other information is divulged to outside firms. Before our subscriber list is released, experienced staff members review and approve all promotional materials to be mailed to your attention."

"Most of our subscribers do not object to receiving promotional material in their mailbox. They find the material informative and useful. However, some people do object to having their name released to other companies. If you wish to have your name deleted from lists we make available to other firms, simply write to Esquire (address). Please be sure to spell your name exactly as it appears on your magazine label and allow approximately six weeks for your request to take effect."

The notice was in a reasonably prominent position (page 9). Such a program would eliminate the expense of a mailing of response cards to all subscribers, and might even marginally improve the marketability of your lists as you could indicate they were "cleaned" of any subscribers who don't wish to receive promotional mail.

Key Decisions in List Testing

In direct mail, you only do four mailings, (1) test, (2) retest, (3) roll-out and (4) repeat.

- test—in enough quantity to get 50 orders.
- retest—probably two to three times your initial quantity.
- roll-out—the rest of the list (but not more than 10 times a test amount).
- repeat—as soon as possible. The general guideline for your package—*If it worked the first time, don't change a comma.*

If you are in a hurry, send a repeat mailing ASAP, as soon as your half-life analysis shows the mailing is paying off. On consumer mailings you'll get 65% of the initial response the second time, and if you do an immediate third mailing, another 50% of initial response. With business audiences the response pattern can be very different, the second mailing can outpull the first.

How To Test On A Limited Budget

Test the items in your mailing in this order if you only have a few shekels.

1. test lists;

2. test lists and offers;

3. test copy and art/graphics as a package;

4. test format, (6 x 9 envelope vs. #10 self-mailer)

The economics here are obvious. You can test two lists by mailing 5,000 from each if you need a 1% response. On the other hand, to test 3 lists, two offers, two packages and two formats would require 90,000 pieces to cover the permutations.

Getting Government Mailing Lists

"You have to learn to think like a bureaucrat," marketing consultant Phil Dismukes explains as the secret of gaining access to government lists. "Never ask for a mailing list, because, first, they don't think of them in those terms. You might talk about the 'data base' and, second, many civil servants, in my experience, have 'archaic attitudes' about direct mail."

No one really knows how many lists the government maintains, but there are "at least thousands." Some types of government list information are not available to the public.

● Lists of taxpayers at IRS, Social Security recipients, postal patrons.

● Any lists which include people at their home address. (Dismukes notes, however, a wide variance among agencies in stringency of enforcement of this restriction.)

● Lists maintained by GPO for the Congress (which is exempt from FOIA requirements). It is evidently arguable that a list of an executive department agency is not exempt from FOIA only because it is physically maintained by GPO.

Some Sources for Finding Available Government Lists

● Government Directories and Publications. The government produces a myriad of publications which contain valuable list information. Often you can get not only a printout in label form of the list information in the directory, but also tapes which your computer house can convert for you (cheaper in the long run).

● Your Editorial Staff. A lot of these publications are announced in press releases. You may have the information already in your office.

● The Basic Government Form. Much of the information you may be seeking is generated from required government reports of various agencies. If you can get a copy of the basic form, it will tell you a lot about the information which will be contained and where to find it.

● The Official Responsible. Sometimes you find his name on the title page of the report. He/she is the best source of information on what is available from the government in that area.

How to Find the "Responsible Official"

Three places never to go are: (1) the agency public affairs office, (2) the agency publication office (who will give you a list of the publications they think of as intended for public distribution). (3) the Agency Freedom of Information Officer (who will automatically start the FOIA process running).

The person you want is usually a sub-agency mid-level executive (often with a title like "program, project or planning manager, data processing director, etc."). These people, when located, are usually happy to discuss their specialty (subject to the opening caveat about 'mailing lists'). From them you can get the exact name of the file used by the agency and the name, address and phone number of the specific freedom of information officer. Then you can start the process of initiating a request to get the information you want. It usually takes 'several months' even after confirmation for them to provide the date. "Creative persistance is the secret."

Finding New Lists to Test & Mail

"It seems too elementary, but the first things you have to know in order to get the best lists for your newsletter are your product and its market." according to Kay DiGiorgi, Marketing Director for Kephart Communications.

(a) Learn your product. Talk to the editors. Read what they write and try to read everything they read.

(b) Learn your market. Know who is buying your newsletter. Conventional newsletter wisdom says demographic information is not of real value but, DeGiorgi says, "Once I have information about our profile and I find a list which appears to fit, I'll certainly try it. One type of list which hasn't worked is other publications your subs read. We've gotten information on 'what are your three other favorite publications' and gone to those lists but that hasn't worked."

Six Ways to Find Lists

1, The SRDS Directory. It's hard to read, but it has a wealth of information about avilable lists. It's updated twice a year and change bulletins come out weekly.

2. List Cards. Kephart gets in about 100 list cards a week. "I never let one go by without looking at it."

3. Incoming Mail. "I try to see every piece of mail, especially direct response mail. Someone who has a product he wants to sell me may have lists I'd like to know about."

4. Incoming Publications. Especially the ads and the ads with coupons or other response devices—again, possible sources for related lists.

5. Your In-House List. Kephart manages about 300,000 names on 29 lists. "I want to know everyone who rents a list from us. We'll rent our active names, but only to people who reciprocate."

6. Conference Attendees. Better yet, exhibitors. People who take booths at trade shows also have lists of prospects.

Once you've located a potentially interesting list—eight things you want to know about the list before you touch it:

1. Universe (how many).
2. Cost.
3. Source (direct mail, compiled, etc.)
4. List updated (how often).
5. List cleaned (how often).
6. Recency (when was most recent for 4 and 5).
7. Selects (zip, SCF, income level, recent or multiple buyers—what's available?).
8. Usage (who uses it and who comes back for roll-outs—if they won't give you publication or company names, and they don't have to, ask what kind of people, financial newsletter publishers? Real estate books?, etc.).

Kay Mancini DeGiorgi, Kephart Communications, 1300 N. 17th St., Arlington, VA 22314 (703) 271-7600.

Quality Names for the Small Circulation NL

"The key to successful list acquisition for the high-price small circulation newsletter is quality of names, not quantity," says John Thompson of Capital Reports in DC. "Too often, lists are the last thing we think about in marketing. You plan a new publication or, at least, an all new package...you write the dynamite response copy. You incorporate the conventional wisdom on guarantee and order card design and there you are...all dressed up with no place to go."

Nine Potential Sources for Quality Names

1. *Associations.* There is one for every conceivable business or interest. Sometimes you can get the membership list, sometimes the directory. Sometimes the...

2. *Conference lists.* (Scan this kind of list when you get one—if your publication is $595 a year, and the list appears to have hundreds of high school teachers on it...)

3. *The Press. (New York Times, Washington Post, Business Week, Wall Street Journal.)* At least every week they have articles about people being appointed or promoted to something. "This is a time when they are really 'up' about themselves. We hit them with a 'congratulations and now you need the information only our newsletter can deliver letter' and a four-issue trial.

4. *Your Own Newsletter.* Make sure every name mentioned gets essentially the same treatment as #3.

5. *The Government.* "In better, pre-Reaganomics days, the government was an excellent market for many specialized newsletters. Despite anti-bureaucrat rhetoric, there are a lot of intelligent, dedicated people in government who need information. On our latest launch, *Federal Reserve Week,* we find we've sold initial subscriptions to almost every Federal Reserve District Bank. They need information that they can get from us and not 'official Washington'."

6. *FOIA.* "Freedom of Information Act proceedings can be a great friend to newsletter marketing. With a FOIA request, we got the Federal Reserve Bank press release list and it appears to be pulling about 6% for us."

7. *Capture Inquiries.* Develop a system which insures everyone who writes your office (or calls) for information not only gets a promotion package but also goes on your in-house list.

8. *Expires.* Get them on the prospect list again. You know who they are and where they are. If what you may not know, why they aren't subscribing anymore, is 'budget was short last fall'... you can get them back on board.

9. *Commercial Lists.* Last on my list, but good to give broad exposure, especially to new publications.

Two Drawbacks for the Small Publisher

1. Scutwork. When the person who has to 'go through this attendance list and add the names to our in-house file—check for duplications' is you, it's not rewarding work, but seeing that $595 check come in from a couple of them makes up for it.

2. Figures Don't Lie, but they don't reflect "quality names." All the work necessary to find 479 names from a conference list doesn't look worthwhile if your normal promotion response rate for an expensive newsletter is .5%—but again, these two new orders at $595 a year are more than worth the trouble.

Capitol Reports, Inc., 1750 Pennsylvania Ave., N.W., Washington, D.C. 20006

Dummy/Decoy Names Yield Vital Information

If you are becoming increasingly involved in the list business, both as a renter and a list provider, you may find you need to expand your use of "dummy" and/or "decoy" names.

Don't just use one or two names—scatter your dummies around the county. There are a couple of reasons for this. When someone rents your list, you need to be able to confirm three things: (1) Was the package mailed the one which you approved? (2) Was it mailed during the time specified? (3) Was there any unauthorized use of your list?

If your list becomes large enough that you might rent only sections of the country—and your dummy names are all in your local area, you've lost the capacity to gather any of this information. If anyone should intend to misuse your list, the first thing they would probably do is look it over to remove obvious dummies like the publisher's home address and General Robert E. Lee. Secondly, they would probably decide to omit your entire metro area from the names they remail. How can I locate dummy names in remote areas of the country?

There are mail receipt firms who you can use. Also, consultant Ed McLean recommends, "use your relatives—friends won't take the trouble. I use relatives and sweeten the pot with an over-generous Christmas gift. I send them a rubber stamp so they can date everything they receive before returning to me."

Use a unique group of "decoys" each time the list is mailed. If you become involved enough that you are renting several lists and fairly frequently, talk with your list manager about inserting specific decoy names into each rental. Otherwise, should you receive something which appears to be an unauthorized use of your list, all you know is one of all the different people who have rented it has reused. With this system you can determine who. Larger list houses can produce unique combinations of letters and number which can't be reformatted out.

Put your own dummy names into an outside list you rent. You aren't concerned about misuse but you still want information on when your package is received—and what it contained. Mistakes at the mailinghouse can happen and, if 25% of your mailing went out without the sales letter, that would certainly affect your response. Checking the packages your dummy names receive is one way to learn this.

CHAPTER XVI
Useful Articles about Aspects of Management of Successful Newsletter Publishing Businesses Which Didn't Appear to Fit in Easily Anywhere Else.

Structure Products to Maximize Profits

From my own experience, says Glen K. Parker, publisher at the Institute for Econometric Research, "I've drawn four fundamental conclusions about the newsletter business:

1. Most publishers don't promote enough.

2. Most publishers don't attempt to renew strongly enough. "In both cases I attribute this to a reluctance to mail down to the break-even point. If one more renewal piece in the series will bring in even one additional percent return—and that is profitable, do it."

3. Newsletter prices in general are too low.

4. Most publishers offer too few products.

"I generalize these from our own experience. My partner, Norm Fosback, and I set out to publish the world's finest financial advisory newsletter. We studied all of what we felt were the desirable features. We spent a good deal more than most on preliminary research ("a low-six figure amount") to design what we then described as "the only financial advisory service you will need." When we were ready to publish, we took the average price of what we regarded as our strongest competitors and went into the mail at half that ($35). Not only did we offer subs for $35 but we offered extended subs—including a four-year deal for $79 which included a free binder. We were very successful. In just a couple years our *Market Logic* grew to be a dominant force in the market. Then a series of events taught us some things which caused institution of some policy changes which helped us change a business which was interesting and exciting to one which is interesting, exciting and profitable.

We decided a boom in 'new issues' was coming and, further, the nature of the news and reporting required was such that we simply could not cover it adequately in *Market Logic*. We decided to launch *New Issues* and tested the water with an insert flyer to our current subscribers. The cost was under $500 and the immediate return was $75,000. However, when we offered the product to our prospect universe we failed. In fact, it was two years before prospects were willing to believe us in this particular subject area.

From this experience we learned:

(a) We had developed sufficient credibility with our readers that they were willing to trust our judgments, and,

(b) Our subscribers had additional dollars to spend on acquiring information and they were willing to spend it with us.

With this realization, we completely altered our basic structure. Our goal is now to develop as many products as we can (aiming at one new newsletter a year) and both market and price them aggressively. In four years we have taken the price of *Market Logic* from $35 to $49, $68 and $95. (All of those are 'true prices' discounted 30% from list—everyone is a 'charter subscriber' and will be forever.)

For the future we are looking very strongly at computer-based information services. These are very expensive to develop which may make them hard to compete with and, once in place, they are relatively inexpensive to produce. Each year the price of computers goes down as the cost of editorial talent goes up.

• "What has happened to our renewals? Frankly, I don't worry too much about our renewal rates. We keep ours low by pricing so aggressively. We still have readers coming off the end of 4-year $79 subscriptions (with free binder) and when they are billed for $95 we lose quite a few."

"My present thinking is that, in one sense, what each subscriber is paying us for is the privilege of receiving advertising matter for a year. We never send an issue without materials describing other products and services they can get from the Institute.

• We've gotten out of the seminar business. You can bring in $100,000 on a successful conference but your direct costs might be $50,000. If you can generate $100,000 in new subscription business your "true cost" might be $0.00—because you can sell enough additional products over the course of the term to fully amortize fulfillment costs.

• We give occasional bonuses. Special reports, back issues, etc. This can be useful to muddy the waters and distract the reader from our constant efforts to sell. The things we give away would not be profitable. We did a detailed analysis of the new tax law. Instead of selling it for $5, we're giving it away. There won't be a comparable change for ten years. Should I be selling this one now and planning to sell another one then? It isn't worth the trouble.

Glen K. Parker, The Institute for Econometric Research, 3471 N. Federal Highway, Ft. Lauderdale, FL (305) 561-5105.

Find Profits in "Marginal Orders"

"We try to maintain good records for source codes, but, nevertheless, you receive a certain number which are untraceable," comments Glen K. Parker, publisher of *Market Logic,* "and we discovered when we totaled them that, over the entire history of our company, the gross revenues from untraceable orders exceeds the profits which the company has made. From this surprisng fact, I conclude the entire source of profit in newsletter publishing is the 'marginal order.'"

Four suggestions from Parker for maximizing revenues and/or controlling marketing costs.

• Cross-promote to subscribers. They know you and have demonstrated willingness to pay for information. (The Institute now tries to send a promotion for some additional product with every issue.)

- Look into Select Information Exchange (and other coop deals) to see if you can appropriately pick up any additional names.
- To attempt to reduce promotional cost Parker is going to:

(a) test a self-mailer

(b) test converting to bulk from first class

- Give away free samples. A prospect who can be induced to write you for the free special report or sample issue is an excellent name—even better if he included a Self-Addressed Stamped Envelope (SASE).

Financing Your NL Growth With Free Money

"Learn to finance the growth of your newsletter business with "Free Money," says Bill Donoghue of P & S Publishing (author of "Donoghue's Complete Money Market Guide").

Four Sources of "Free Money"

1. *The IRS.* Use the accrual accounting system and minimize tax liability. *You have to get permission from IRS to do this.* You get this by filing an IRS form during your first year of operation. (If you haven't done it, get your accountant to help you straighten it out and make the proper conversion.)

2. *Your Subscribers.* (a) do an advance renewal campaign every year, (b) get into ancillary services. You can sell seminar workbook/materials to non-delegates. This will usually bring in enough $$$ to cover costs of promotions.

3. *Your Prospects.* Working harder to sell new subs is a longer-term source of cash but aggressively renting your mailing lists can bring in money much more quickly.

4. *Your Suppliers.* Take advantage of trade credits. You can get terms from every supplier but USPS. (A caveat, "If you abuse it, you lose it.") You can work with printers and negotiate a longer-term payment schedule timed to meet your cash flow. You can pre-pay a portion in return for a discount or 60-90 day payment. As long as you're up-front with them, there can be a lot of options.

How to Handle it While You Have it

1. Don't let it rot in your checking account. If you're considering a loan application, try to hammer out of the bank what they really think about "compensating balances" and then "leave 75% of the minimum in the account and haggle..."

2. Use a money fund. If your bookkeeper can't understand how to write checks from two accounts, fire him and hire one who can.

3. Put your cash to work faster. Make daily deposits, not weekly. As soon as you accumulate $7000 in checks, *wire transfer* it to your money fund.

4. Investigate the cash flow level at which it would pay to establish a bank lockbox and have them open your mail and immediately deposit.

Bill Donoghue, P & S Publications, Box 542, 770 Washington Street, Holliston, MA 01746

Tips on Managing a Successful Newsletter

"At the hazard of being obvious, the single best way to publish a profitable newsletter is to produce a high-quality product," says Consultant Stan Mayes. "Despite the fact that direct marketing was my specialty and was my chief responsibility for over 20 years with the *Kiplinger Letter,* the strength of the product is what leads to renewals and profits. Be willing to spend up front for that quality. Hire the best writers and pay them scale plus."

● Have a marketing budget and plan. Analysis of your renewal track record and your own assumptions for growth will tell you you need to sell 5,000 new orders in the coming year to reach your target—if your historic response rate is 1%, you also know that means you need to mail 500,000 pieces. From these numbers you can develop a work plan which schedules the dates you'll mail, the lists you'll use, etc. Results from this type of planning are usually far superior to haphazard promotional efforts and, if the number of promotional pieces you need to mail to meet this goal seems forbiddingly high, remember the sure-fire method to raise your renewal rate is to stop promoting. As you slide into the red, your hard core of loyal subscribers will be renewing at a gratifying high percentage.

● Determine your own seasonality. There are pretty well established patterns of response in direct mail which may have nothing to do with your publications.

● "I have no particular reason to think the "boom and inflation" letter which has worked for Kiplinger for over 20 years would work for you...there are no absolutes. Consider going to a consultant who will take a more objective look at your package, your price and your product than you can."

● Think about establishing an exclusive arrangement with a list broker, perhaps on an annual fee basis rather than the usual percentage of every rental. Yes, you might miss a list or two which he can't get for you, but you'll more than make up the difference in improved service.

● Appreciate the value of renewals. One of the mysteries of the newsletter business is why publishers are willing to mail tens-of-thousands of promotional packages and be perfectly happy with response rates of one percent or less but aren't willing to continue mailing renewal efforts which bring in at least the same return. How much does it cost to buy 100 new subscriptions? With today's typical package and a one percent response rate, probably about $3,500. Another renewal effort, bulk mail, will cost about half that per piece so, if it pulls in even one more check for each 200 pieces, it is as cost-effective as seeking new orders.

● The very best renewal techniques are the ones which bring you a certain amount of nasty mail about being hectored by endless renewal notices. I usually recommend a series which includes at least 4-5 efforts post-expire. At Kiplinger we found that our most efficient trial order conversion series included 14 pieces.

Stan Mayes, Consultant, 1101 New Hampshire Avenue, N.W., Suite #701, Washington, DC 20037 (202) 466-2578.

Publishing NL's as a Business

Newsletter publishing is a deceptive business. It's often said 'you can begin with very little money and become a millionaire' and half of that statement is true," comments Ken Kovaly of *Technical Insights* discussing operating a successful newsletter publishing business. "As far as I can see, one of the single, largest determining factors in the success of a newsletter venture is your decision on building a business, or running a newsletter as a hobby."

Here are five keystones in building a newsletter business operation.

1. *Keep Records.* Lots of them. Records of everything. How many pieces you've mailed. Year to date. Last year this date. To which lists. On what dates. Response. Bad debts. Cancels. Fufillment Costs. Cost Per Order. etc. Ours is deceptive business because we take cash up front, but you have to know what to do with it. In newsletter publishing you can go broke both by not promoting enough and also by promoting too much. If you can't answer all the questions above, you don't really know whether or not you're making money. *If you don't know whether you're making $$, you're not really in business.*

2. *Plan.* Seriously. On paper. For the longer term (3-5 years). A friend asked me years ago if I "had a business plan",

"of course," I said

"Show it to me," he asked

"Well, I mean I have it in my head," to which he responded

"You don't have a plan."

You can outline one just by listing the decisions you will need to make. Should we launch a new newsletter? Add a Washington correspondent? Use a professional marketing consultant? Put a marketing person on staff? Get into the conference business? Plan this way for your publication(s) as well. What should they look like—New features? New format? Frequency?, etc. This isn't set in concrete. Go back every 12-18 months, see how it's going and revise it. I hate to say it, but if you don't have goals, how do you know if you're getting there?

3. *Administer your business.* This is different than running it. I'm talking about the parts which aren't fun. When you are in business, you have to buy typewriter ribbons and office insurance. You have to manage people. Newsletter publishing is a people business. They are the only real asset we have. You certainly couldn't realize a great deal on your typewriters and desks. To be successful, we have to get the best people and small companies like mine have to realize they are competing with McGraw-Hill for those people. That means developing benefit programs, profit sharing and pensions. These are important. I know how good McGraw-Hill's programs are because I used to work there. At the NAA conference in Washington, I heard someone answer a question about what to pay correspondents by saying "As little as you can get away with." Seriously, in a business where our people determine the quality of our products, I can't imagine such an attitude.

Overpay. I didn't really begin to intentionally, but it seems to have happened.

Technical Insights pays well. More than I "have to." I find two benefits to this "policy."

(a) It lays a guilt trip on your employees who tend to work harder and produce more to justify to themselves what they are earning.

(b) If someone isn't producing, I find it easier, from my viewpoint, to justify letting them go when I can say 'he's being paid a first-class salary for this responsibility'.

Give Responsibility. This is one place our companies have the advantage of McGraw-Hill. We can give performers more responsibility and sooner. *Do it.* Yes, your people will make mistakes, but very probably not as many as you will make if you continue to try to be personally responsible for four-to-five different areas.

4. *Seek New Opportunities to Grow.* Build your business. Not necessarily in number of newsletters but in dollars. In my view, one newsletter grossing $400,000 is better than four grossing $100,000 each. Look for synergism. Opportunities for related products—special reports and books. Each of our new newsletters has grown out of subject areas we found being much in the news in *Inside R&D. Acquisitions are the most dangerous game for newsletter publishers.* I suspect most of the acquisitions which are made are for less than $250,000. I've never seen a newsletter available at that price which I wanted to buy. They look more like problems than opportunities to me.

5. *Work Yourself Out of a Job.* Once your newsletter business has been in operation for 5-7 years, if you, the publisher/editor are still the key person, the irreplaceable asset, you aren't doing your management job. When I launched *Inside R&D,* I kept my regular job and worked on the newsletter nights and weekends. What would I do, I was asked, if I got sick? "I don't get sick" was my policy. Fortunately, I didn't. As your business grows, however, without being morbid, you need a plan for what happens if you can't go to work tomorrow. Again, I mean a real plan. In my case it's a trust agreement with our bank in which I specify how the business is to be operated. *Technical Insights* has about reached the point where I am totally dispensable. With our editors, marketing and fulfillment people, the business could go on without me. Possibly not as well as it does with me, *but it would run* ... One of the major benefits of this is, on a day-to-day basis, I'm free to concentrate on what I believe is my strongest asset. Developing new products. When I first launched, people asked why I didn't call the newsletter '*The Kovaly Report.*' Two reasons. (1) My name was not a household word in the R&D community, and (2) From the beginning, I hoped to build a business, not a personal vehicle and should I decide to sell one day, I'm certain *Inside R&D* will be a lot more marketable.

Technical Insights, Inc., 2337 LeMoine Avenue, Fort Lee, NJ 07024 (201) 944-6204.

Kiplinger Calls Utility the Key to Success

The most significant test of editorial excellence in a newsletter publication is survivability according to Austin Kiplinger, publisher of the *Kiplinger*

Washington Letter. "The purpose of our kind of journalism is to service readers and no set of publications is closer to this objective than newsletters. I find renewal rates to be an excellent composite measure of success because they include a reading on your editorial policy, production quality, promotional effort and original selection of market."

How to Design Editorial Product—Kiplinger says the key is to think about readers and what they need. Development of editorial philosophy should precede development of the promotion effort. "I believe a newsletter editorial structure should be:

- utilitarian
- reader-minded
- forward-looking
- an aid to the decision-making capability of the subscriber."

This philosophy has aided the Kiplinger organization in producing an editorial product which, by the standards of renewal and survivability, has few peers in the specialized publishing industry. "Although my definition of editorial excellence is not what the critics would say and it isn't what young journalists appear to think it is..."

Kiplinger spoke at the NAA Journalism Awards presentation and concluding that, he stated: "Of course, it is always nice to receive awards if you can remember what Adlai Stevenson once said, 'flattery is all right if you don't inhale.' Our business contains its own corrective in that after you receive an award, you have to go back and sit down at the typewriter and begin work on the next issue."

BNA Chairman Offers Nine Guidelines for Success in Business Publishing

John Stewart, Chairman and Chief Executive Officer of the Bureau of National Affairs, Washington, D. C., was the featured speaker at the luncheon of the NAA Editorial Management Seminar. Stewart has been with BNA for 40 years, since he and four others purchased the operation from founder David Lawrence and the U.S. News organization. In that time, it has grown to a firm employing over 1,000 with gross revenues of over $70,000,000 (1979) from more than 50 information services, reference files and specialized business publications.

In his remarks to the NAA members, Stewart outlined nine rules which he believes have contributed to the success of BNA both editorially and operationally.

1. Rank Has its Obligations
2. Deadlines are Better than Timeclocks
3. Renewals are Everything
4. Promote from Within
5. Budget from the Bottom Up
6. Be Conservative in Your Accounting

7. The Only Market Survey Worth a Darn is One which Asks the Prospect to Commit Money.

8. Make All Your Pricing Mistakes on the High Side.

9. Give Your Employees a Chance to Have a Piece of the Action.

"Basically," Stewart concluded, "there are only two sins in our kind of journalism. (1) Writing something that isn't true, and (2) writing something that is true, but is so dull no one wants to read it."

Are Subscription Agency Services Worth Giving a Discount?

"Should I be giving discounts to subscription agencies on my publication or am I giving away money?" Consensus of publishers is that giving a small discount to subscription agencies is worthwhile for two basic reasons.

1. Agency orders come with checks. ("It's worth 5% to us anytime to get the check with the order.")

2. Agency-placed orders tend to have excellent renewal records and don't require extensive renewal series programs.

The following points about subscription agencies are also heard:

● Agencies will take orders for publications which don't give discounts (as a convenience to their customers), but we can't imagine they work very hard to get business for those publishers. The contrary opinion, however, is that agencies don't work very hard to sell orders for anyone, but function more as an administrative convenience for libraries and other oganizations which prefer a centralized purchasing service. (So why pay them for what they're doing anyway?)

● Some agencies offer their clients and publishers an "automatic renewal" service where subscriptions are continued indefinitely.

● Some publishers believe that agencies pick up a few extra orders for them from sources to which they don't generally promote. This may mean, however, that the agencies are simply serving as order points for customers you do have on your prospect lists. Capitol Publications once decided they were getting so many orders on education newsletters from libraries through agencies, that they should promote directly to the librarians. "It bombed totally, zip, zero."

GLOSSARY

While not intended to be comprehensive (especially in such areas as printing terminology), the following list of terms common to newsletter publishing may be of assistance to newcomers to the business. Each term is further defined within the text of the book.

AAP, Association of American Publishers—book publishers' association.

ABP, American Business Press—trade association of publishers of trade magazines.

ACR, Address Correction Requested—when placed on carrier envelope, USPS will return with new address. Current fee is 25¢ apiece. No permit is required. Used on third-class mail which is not forwardable.

Advance Renewal—a special offer to renew prior to normal date. Usually done at once for the entire subscriber list, often as an inflation fighter offer.

Ancillary—collateral or service revenue. Related business income newsletter publishers may derive from special reports, books, conferences, list rentals, etc.

Bill-Me Orders—offers which accept unpaid orders which are to be invoiced later.

Blue Line—proof delivered by printer to check before final production.

Bleed—colors running to the edge of paper in a printing job.

BRC, Business Reply Card—same as envelope. Both require USPS permit.

BRE, Business Reply Envelope—usually provided with promotional packages. Normally postage-paid for convenience of the prospect.

Bulk Mail—third-class mail. Never synonymous with 'junkmail' in the newsletter business.

Business Newsletters—a newsletter aimed at a business audience which is normally purchased by company check as a deductible expense.

Carrier Envelope—outer envelope in promotional package.

Cash-With—opposite of bill-me, offers which require prepayment.

CCC, Copyright Clearance Center—agency through which publishers can establish a vehicle for making copies of copyrighted material and receive a fee.

Charter Offer—(also introductory offer), promotional technique offering a discount to new subscribers, some publishers use them forever.

Cheshire Label—common format for paper mailing labels, produced on a cheshire machine. Usually delivered either one or four across (one-up or four-up).

"Clean the List"—do an ACR or first-class mailing to update the accuracy of the addresses on your mailing list.

Compiled List—a mailing list which has been assembled from one or more sources, such as association membership lists and industry directories.

Consumer Newsletter—newsletter aimed at individuals which is normally paid for out of the personal checkbook.

Continuation—a second or third larger test of an extremely large mailing list.

Contract Editor—a non-staff employee who produces editorial copy, usually on a per-subscription-sold compensation contract.

Copyright Deposit—achieved by spending two copies of each issue to the Library of Congress.

Copyright Registration—also requires a Library of Congress TX form and fee with each issue. Gives greater statutory protection to the holder.

Corner Card—return address on carrier envelope.

Decoy Names—usually synonymous with "dummy names." Sometimes used more specifically to indicate names that are inserted for one particular mailing, as opposed to dummy names which are left seeded on the list permanently.

DMMA, Direct Mail Marketing Association—trade association of direct mail companies, major members are very large mailers like L.L. Bean, Franklin Mint, etc.

Dummy Names—names inserted on a mailing list to check what is actually mailed and when delivered.

Early Bird Renewal—used to mean either renewal-at-birth or advance renewal.

800 Number—toll free number offered in promotions to accept telephone orders.

Endorsement—testimonial.

Fair Use—Section 107 of the 1978 Copyright Act setting up standards to determine what may be legally copied from a copyrighted publication.

FIM Marks, Facing Identification Marks—required by USPS on upper right of business reply mail and cards. Regulations cover size, color and placement.

FOG Index—a calculation to determine the level of education required to read editorial materials, *Paradise Lost* is 26, the Gettysburg Address is 10.

FOIA, Freedom of Information Act—permits publishers to seek information and lists of names maintained by government agencies.

Frequency—schedule of publication for a newsletter—daily, weekly, etc.

Fulfillment—process of sending a subscriber regular newsletter issues.

Grace Issue(s)—extra issues sent after expiration of a paid subscription as a part of a continuing renewal effort.

Hand Delivery—services offered in Manhattan and Washington, D.C. for for delivery of subscriber copies of your newsletter (as opposed to regular mail).

IABC, International Association of Business Communicators—trade association of people who produce in-house corporate newsletters and other publications.

Illustrated Letter—another name for a brochure, includes pictures or drawings of the product in use or special features, etc.

Indicia—printing of postage on an envelope. Can be metered or preprinted.

Inflation Fighter—an advance renewal offer normally made to give subscribers an opportunity to extend at the current rate in advance of a coming price increase.

Inverted Pyramid Style—"classic newspaper journalism." Lead and all important material at the top of the story.

Involvement Device—a token or sticker used on some order cards, "Place this sticker on the spot to order the special bonus premium."

ISSN, International Standard Serial Number—issued by the Library of Congress to periodical publications. Not required for newsletters but recommended.

Justified Column—right-hand column that is even down the page—produced in typeset or word-processor-generated newsletters.

List Broker or Manager—firm which manages a number of mailing lists for various owners and offers them for rental.

Loose Deck Mailings—a series of postcards on various related products and services mailed for a number of companies at once—usually comes shrink-packaged.

Mail-Cross—additional renewal invoices reaching the subscriber before payment has been recorded by the publisher.

Masthead or Flag—the masthead normally appears at the bottom of page one or inside of a newsletter and gives information on publisher, copyright, editor, price, frequency, etc. Sometimes used interchangably with 'flag' which means specifically the title and graphics appearing at the top of the first page.

Merge-Purge—technique of matching mailing lists by computer to eliminate duplicate names which appear on more than one list.

#9 Envelope—usual size for return mail envelopes, fits into a #10.

#10 Envelope—normal business letter size envelope.

Offer—the combination of price, term, premium, etc., which is being made available to the prospect—defined in gradations from "soft" (no-risk, free trial) to "hard" (requires full prepayment with order).

Package—normal direct mail effort, usually contains carrier envelope, BRE, sales letter, brochure, and response device.

PMS—color chart used by most printers to specify color gradations.

Premium—an enticement or gift offered with a promotional mailing, most commonly a book or special report.

Publishers Letter—also known as *Lift Letter*. A second, smaller letter included in a promotional package usually inscribed on the outside, "Do Not Read This Letter Unless You've Decided Not to Accept Our Free Trial Offer."

Ragged Right—typical typewriter copy newsletter with uneven right hand margins.

Recency—time since a mailing list was last cleaned.

Renewal at Birth—technique of offering new subscribers an immediate opportunity to extend their subscription. Also called *Upgrading*.

Renewal Notice—accompanies renewal sales letter. Not an invoice (this is prohibited, you can not bill people for material they have not ordered.)

Response Device—the portion of a direct mail package which the prospect returns to enter his order. Also called *Order Card*.

Response (Direct Response)—synonymous with direct mail . . . advertising.

Response List—a mailing list of prospects who have responded, preferably by direct mail, to other offers.

Response Rate—percentage of return on a promotional mailing.

Roll-Out—additional mailing to remainder of prospects on mailing list after successful test.

Section 455—the section of the IRS code which authorizes accrual accounting and development of liability for unfulfilled subscription income.

Seed the List—add some dummy and/or decoy names to allow list owner to check results.

Semi-Monthly—also called bi-monthly or biweekly, used to mean 24 to 26 times annually.

Serifs—little squiggly things on letters, as here, are serifs. Most recommend using a serif typeface, as opposed to sans serif, for newsletter editorial copy.

Service Bureau—a computer fulfillment company which prepared mailing labels, renewal invoices and financial statements for publishers.

Spin-Off—a new newsletter developed from material carried in another newsletter from the same publisher.

SRDS, Standard Rate and Data Service—publishes a directory of mailing lists available for rent.

Sub-S Corporation—Section of IRS code which permits incorporation but retains some of the benefits of unincorporated operations.

Subscription Agency—places orders with publishers for clients, usually expects a discount on price.

Teaser Copy—material printed on the carrier envelope to entice the reader to open and see what is inside . . .

Testimonial—an endorsement of the newsletter by an individual or company.

Trade Mark—granted by U.S. Patent & Trademark Office for the title of a newsletter (not the company name), not required for newsletters.

Typewriter Copy—classic newsletter style, printed from copy prepared on typewriter.

Window Envelope—envelope with a hole through which address appears, usually affixed to the order form.

BIBLIOGRAPHY

The following bibliography is not complete but includes a number of books which will be of interest to those planning a commercial newsletter launch.

We believe "Success in Newsletter Publishing, A Practical Guide" is *the only book specifically targeted at the business of publishing a commercial for-profit newsletter,* but the following books are all good on various aspects of newsletter publishing. Those marked with an asterisk are considered "standards" in the direct marketing field, but are not specifically aimed at newsletter publishing.

Publishing Newsletters
  published by Charles Scribner

Howard Penn Hudson
The Newsletter Clearinghouse
44 West Market Street
Rhinebeck, NY 12572
205pp

How to Put Out a Newsletter

Newsletter Services
1545 New York Avenue, N.E.
Washington, DC 20002
16pp—Free

Editing Your Newsletter

Mark Beach
Coast to Coast Books
2934 N.E. 16th Street
Portland, OR 97212
128pp

Newsletter Editor's Deskbook

Arth/Ashmore
Parkway Press
Box 8158
Shawnee Mission, KS 66208
136pp

The Best of Impact

Robert L. Baker
Impact Publications
203 N. Wabash Avenue
Chicago, IL 60601
172pp

*Direct Mail & Mail Order Handbook

Richard S. Hodgson
Dartnell
4660 N. Ravenswood Avenue
Chicago, IL 60640
1534pp

*Successful Direct Marketing Methods

Robert Stone
Crain Books
740 Rush Street
Chicago, IL 60611
370pp

*The Handbook of Circulation Management	Folio Magazine Edited by Barbara Love 125 Elm Street New Canaan, CT 06840 311pp
*Direct Marketing Strategy/ Planning/Execution	Edward L. Nash McGraw-Hill Publishing Company 190 East 72nd Street New York, NY 10020 422pp
The Basics of Copy	Ed McLean Ryan Gilmore Publishing Company 1280 Saw Mill River Road Yonkers, NY 100710 131pp

And could we not at least suggest a number of newsletters which should be of interest to persons considering a publishing venture. These newsletters, all published by members of NAA, are ones we find ourselves reading thoroughly as soon as each issue comes.

Copley Mail Order Advisor	Robert Jay Copley Communications Box 405 Prudential Center Boston, MA 02199
Newsletter on Newsletters	Howard Penn Hudson The Newsletter Clearinghouse 44 West Market Street Rhinebeck, NY 12572
Direct Response	Infomat 708 Silver Spur Road Rolling Hills Estates, CA 90274
The Editorial Eye	Editorial Experts, Inc. 5905 Pratt Street Alexandria, VA 22310
Business Mailers Review	Van Seagraves 1813 Shepard Street, N.W. Washington, DC 20011
The List Research Letter	Agora Publishing 2201 Saint Paul Street Baltimore, MD 21218

Postal World   United Publishing
                                          1406 Fenwick Lane
                                          Silver Spring, MD